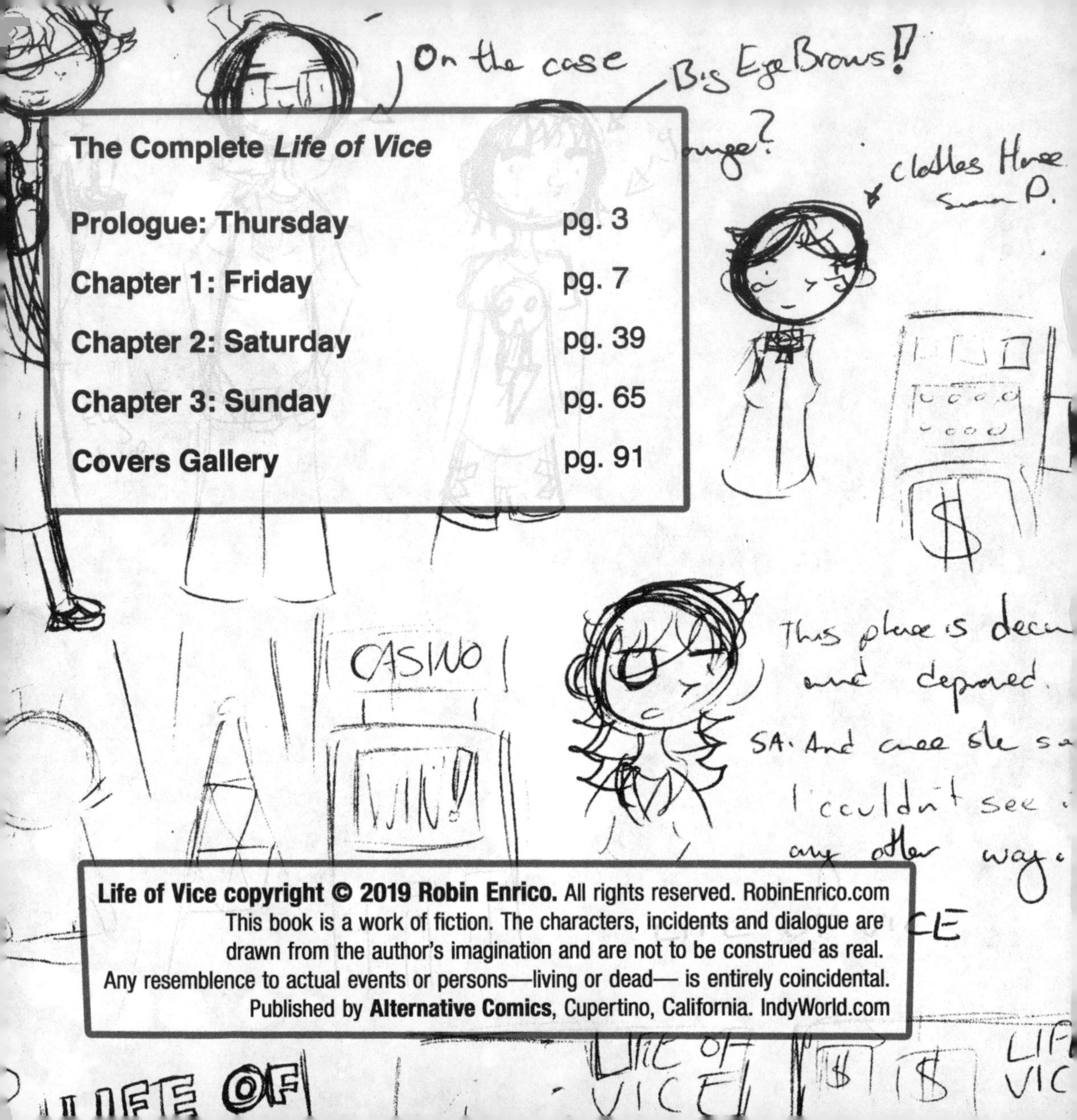
On the case
Big Eye Brows!
Younger?
CASINO
WIN!
any other way.
LIFE OF
LIFE OF VICE

The Complete *Life of Vice*

Published by **Alternative Comics**, Cupertino, California. IndyWorld.com

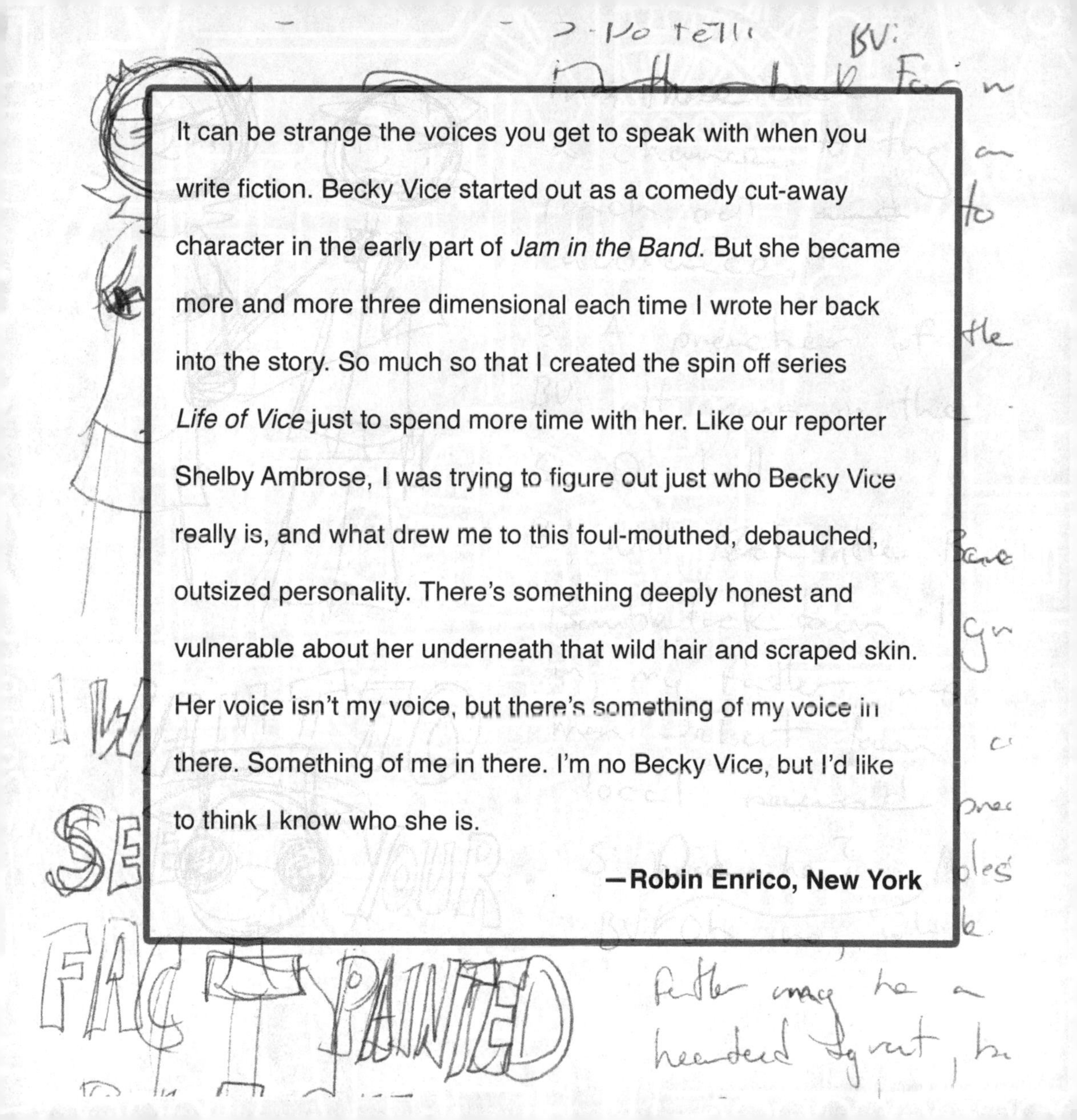

It can be strange the voices you get to speak with when you write fiction. Becky Vice started out as a comedy cut-away character in the early part of *Jam in the Band*. But she became more and more three dimensional each time I wrote her back into the story. So much so that I created the spin off series *Life of Vice* just to spend more time with her. Like our reporter Shelby Ambrose, I was trying to figure out just who Becky Vice really is, and what drew me to this foul-mouthed, debauched, outsized personality. There's something deeply honest and vulnerable about her underneath that wild hair and scraped skin. Her voice isn't my voice, but there's something of my voice in there. Something of me in there. I'm no Becky Vice, but I'd like to think I know who she is.

—Robin Enrico, New York

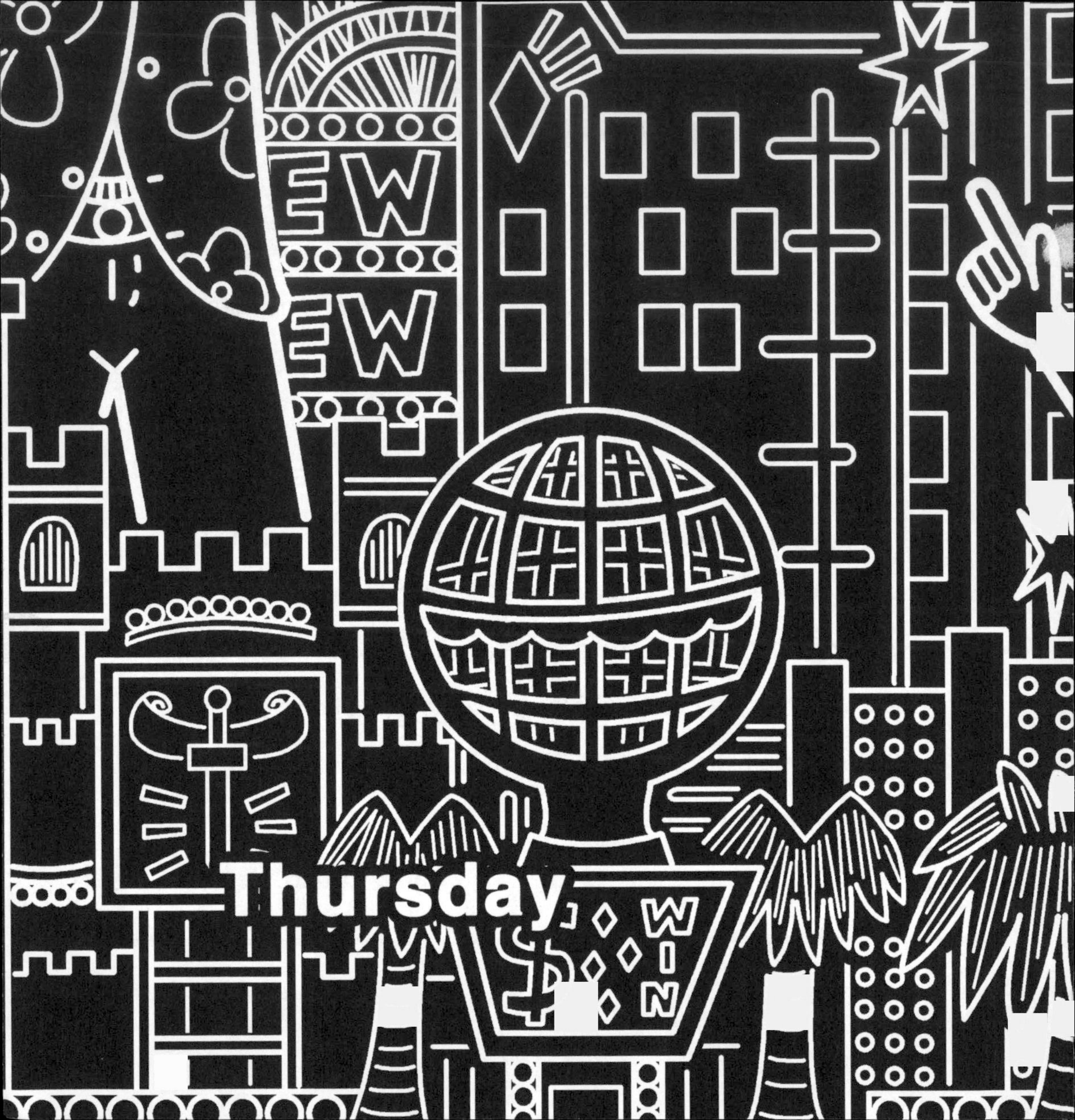
EW
EW
WIN

Thursday

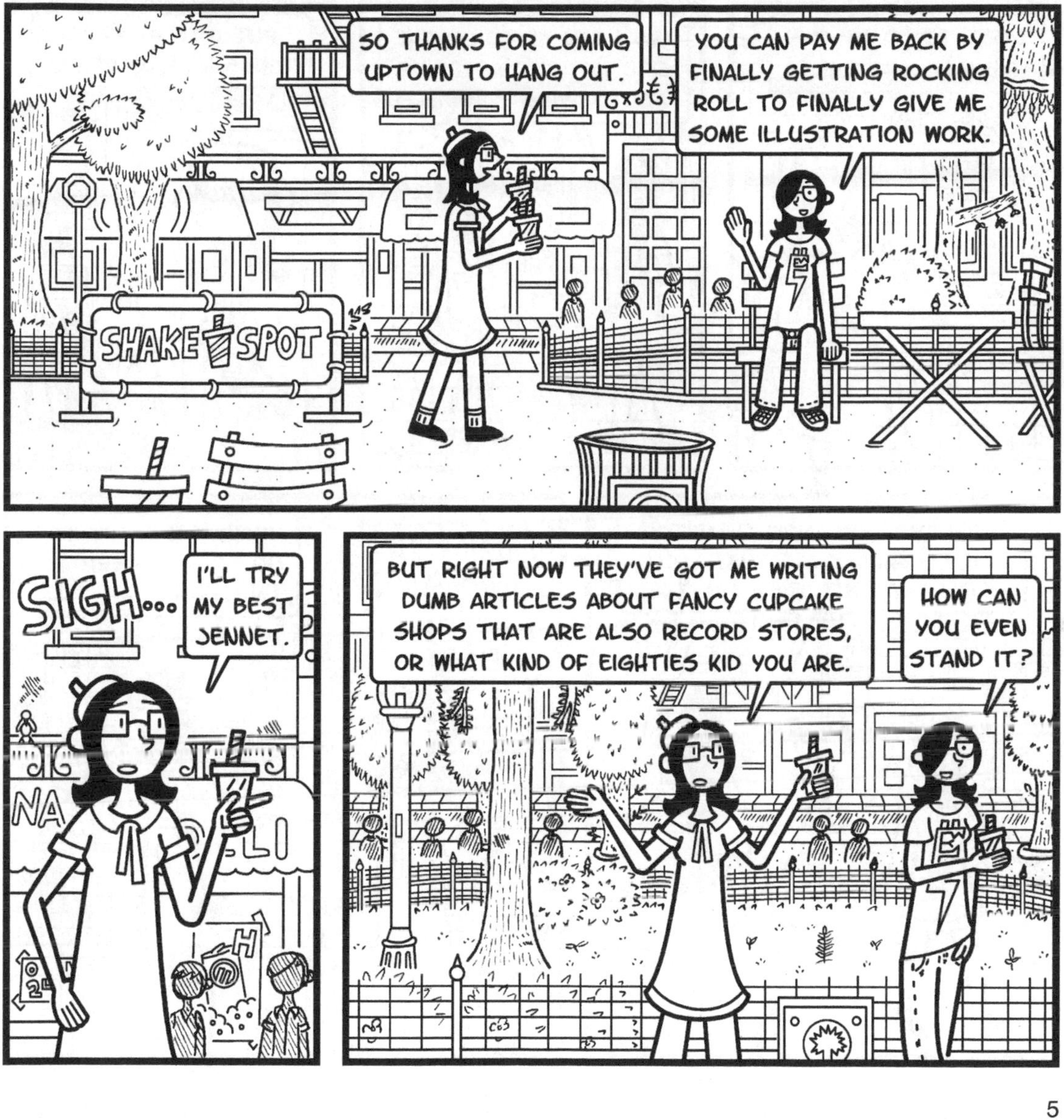
SO THANKS FOR COMING UPTOWN TO HANG OUT.
YOU CAN PAY ME BACK BY FINALLY GETTING ROCKING ROLL TO FINALLY GIVE ME SOME ILLUSTRATION WORK.
SHAKE SPOT
SIGH...
I'LL TRY MY BEST JENNET.
BUT RIGHT NOW THEY'VE GOT ME WRITING DUMB ARTICLES ABOUT FANCY CUPCAKE SHOPS THAT ARE ALSO RECORD STORES, OR WHAT KIND OF EIGHTIES KID YOU ARE.
HOW CAN YOU EVEN STAND IT?

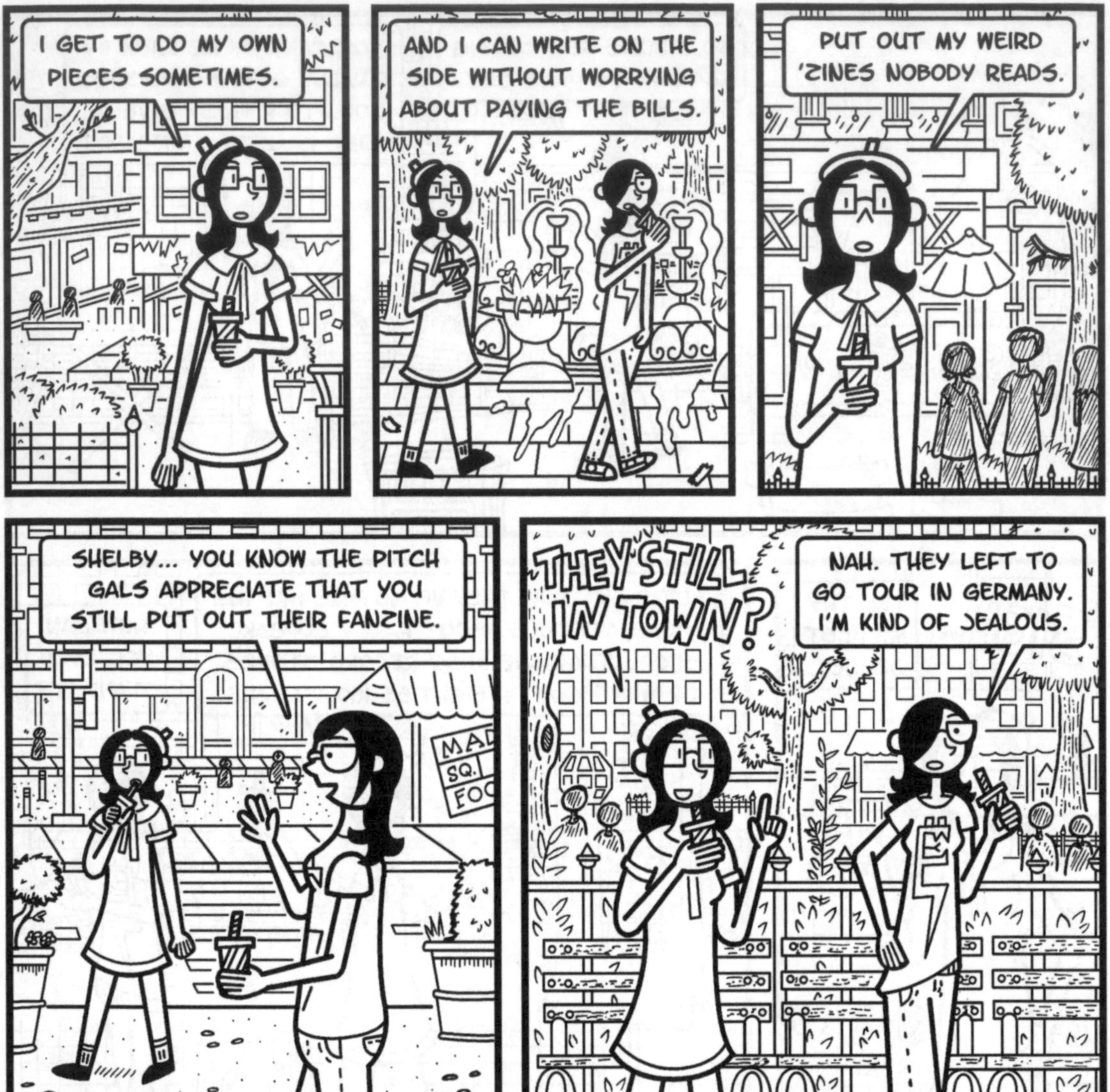
I GET TO DO MY OWN PIECES SOMETIMES.
AND I CAN WRITE ON THE SIDE WITHOUT WORRYING ABOUT PAYING THE BILLS.
PUT OUT MY WEIRD 'ZINES NOBODY READS.
SHELBY... YOU KNOW THE PITCH GALS APPRECIATE THAT YOU STILL PUT OUT THEIR FANZINE.
MAD SQ. FOO
THEY STILL IN TOWN?
NAH. THEY LEFT TO GO TOUR IN GERMANY. I'M KIND OF JEALOUS.

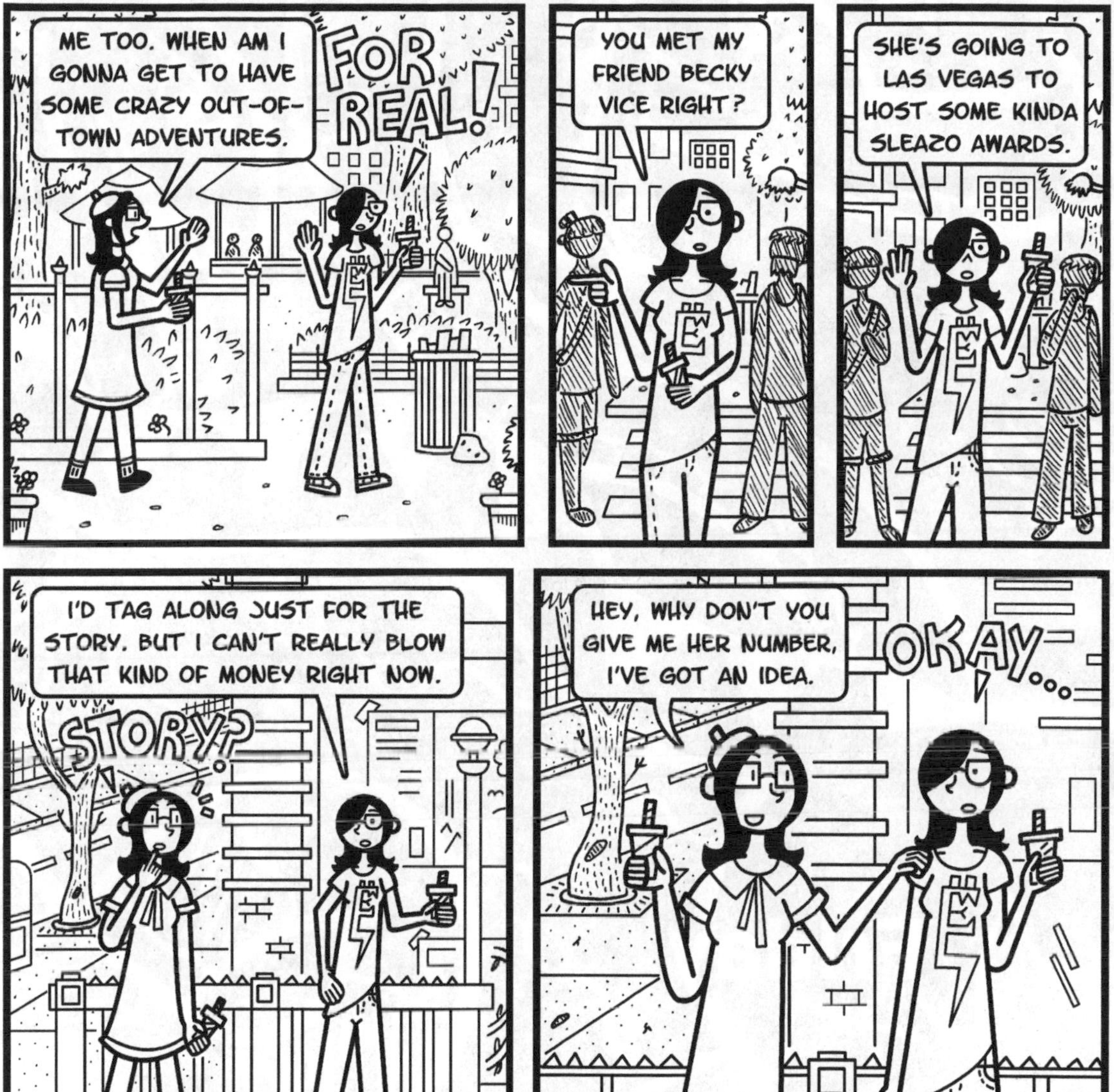

ME TOO. WHEN AM I GONNA GET TO HAVE SOME CRAZY OUT-OF-TOWN ADVENTURES.
FOR REAL!
YOU MET MY FRIEND BECKY VICE RIGHT?
SHE'S GOING TO LAS VEGAS TO HOST SOME KINDA SLEAZO AWARDS.
I'D TAG ALONG JUST FOR THE STORY. BUT I CAN'T REALLY BLOW THAT KIND OF MONEY RIGHT NOW.
STORY?
HEY, WHY DON'T YOU GIVE ME HER NUMBER, I'VE GOT AN IDEA.
OKAY...

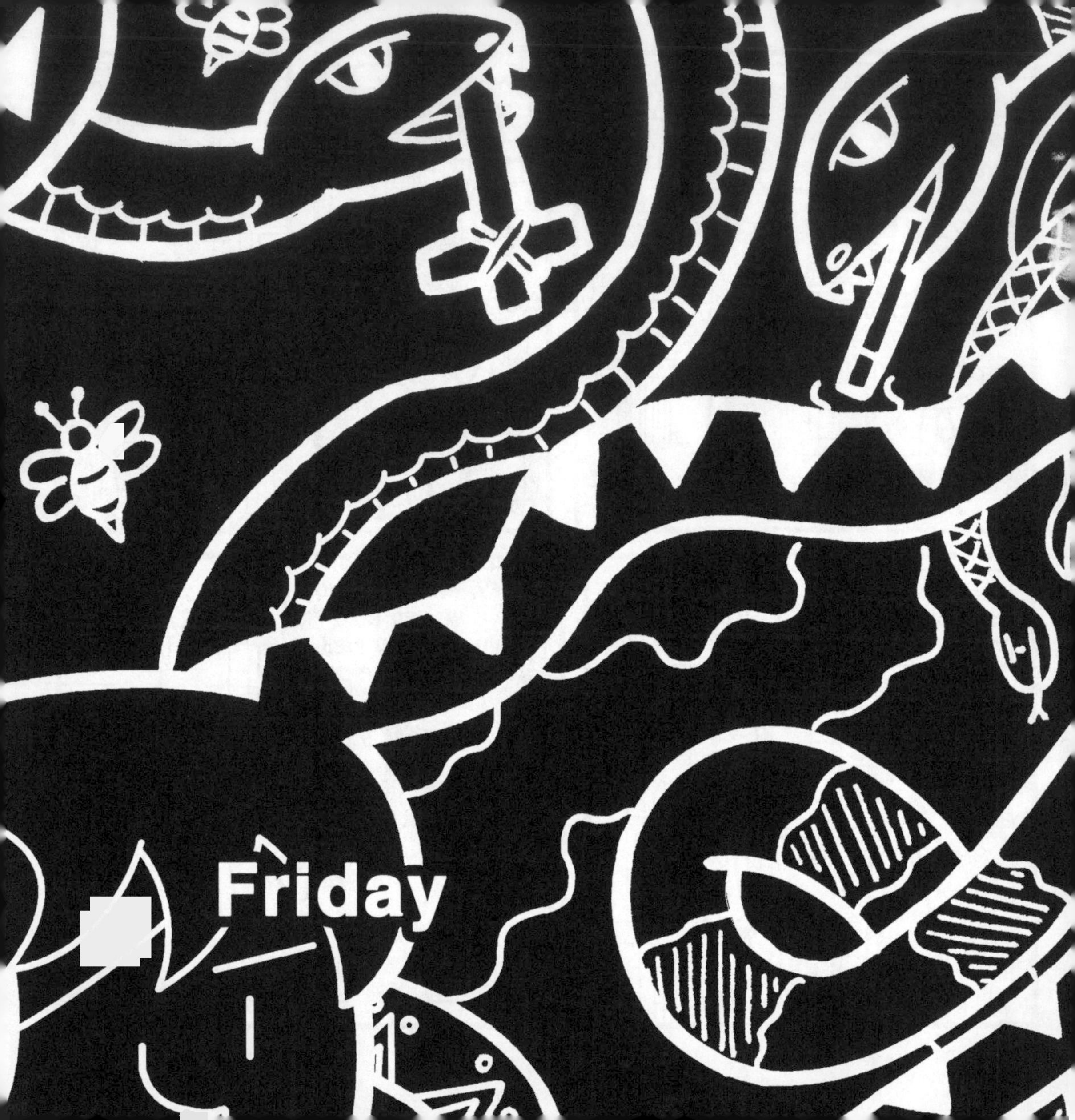
Friday

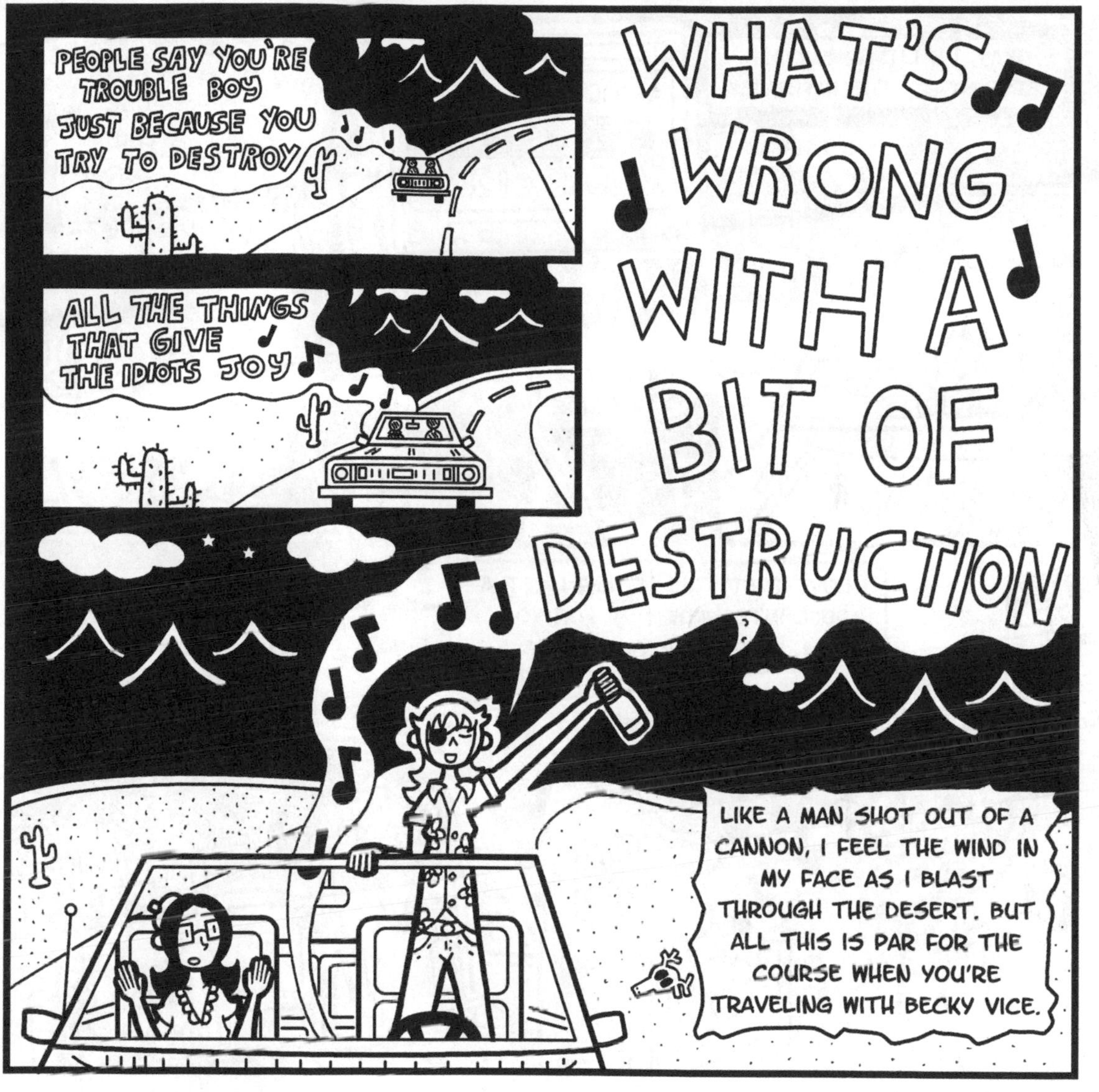
PEOPLE SAY YOU'RE TROUBLE BOY
JUST BECAUSE YOU TRY TO DESTROY
ALL THE THINGS THAT GIVE THE IDIOTS JOY
WHAT'S WRONG WITH A BIT OF DESTRUCTION
LIKE A MAN SHOT OUT OF A CANNON, I FEEL THE WIND IN MY FACE AS I BLAST THROUGH THE DESERT. BUT ALL THIS IS PAR FOR THE COURSE WHEN YOU'RE TRAVELING WITH BECKY VICE.

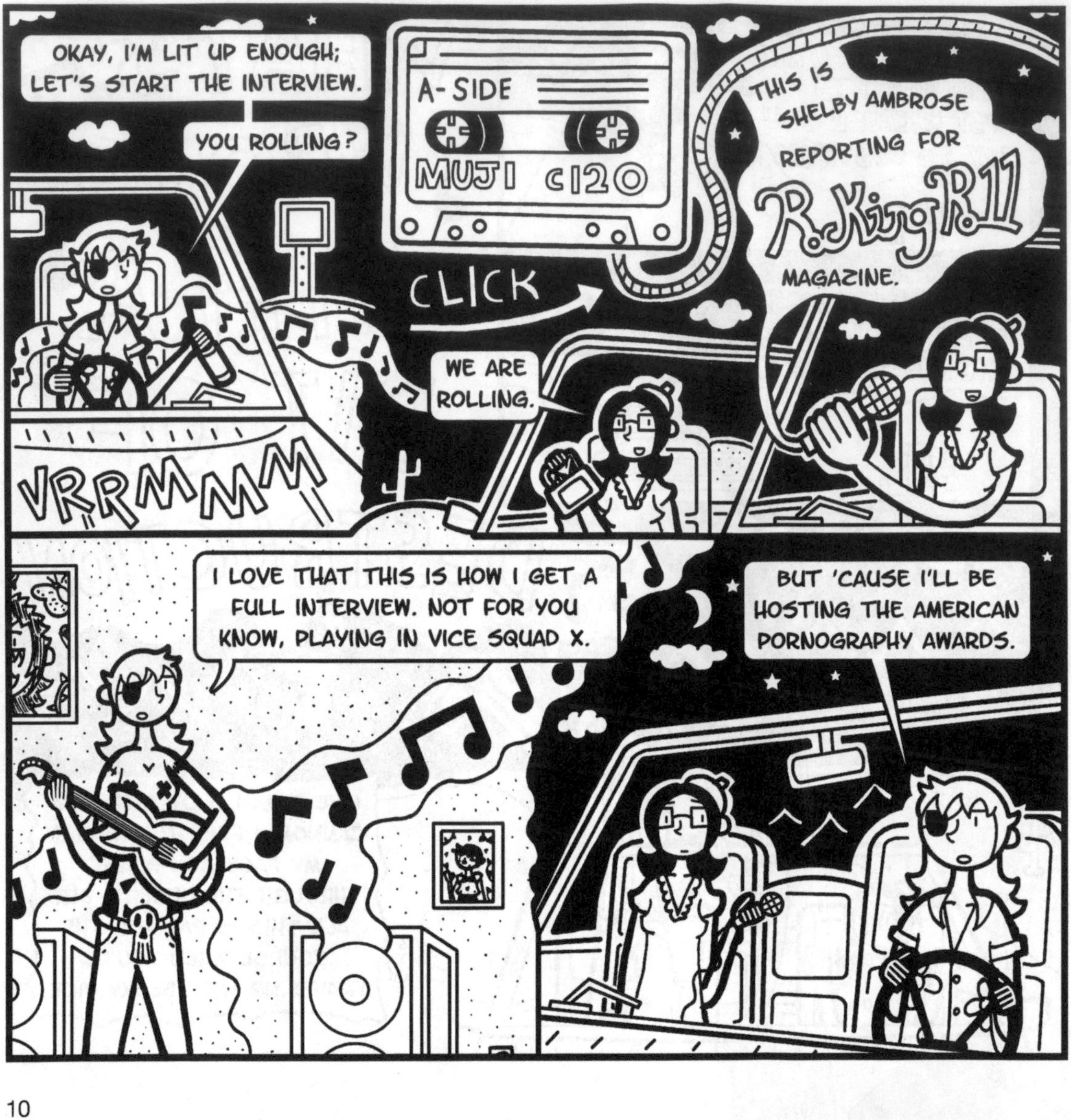
OKAY, I'M LIT UP ENOUGH; LET'S START THE INTERVIEW.
YOU ROLLING?
A-SIDE
MUJI c120
CLICK
VRRMMMM
WE ARE ROLLING.
THIS IS SHELBY AMBROSE REPORTING FOR
R.King R.11
MAGAZINE.
I LOVE THAT THIS IS HOW I GET A FULL INTERVIEW. NOT FOR YOU KNOW, PLAYING IN VICE SQUAD X.
BUT 'CAUSE I'LL BE HOSTING THE AMERICAN PORNOGRAPHY AWARDS.

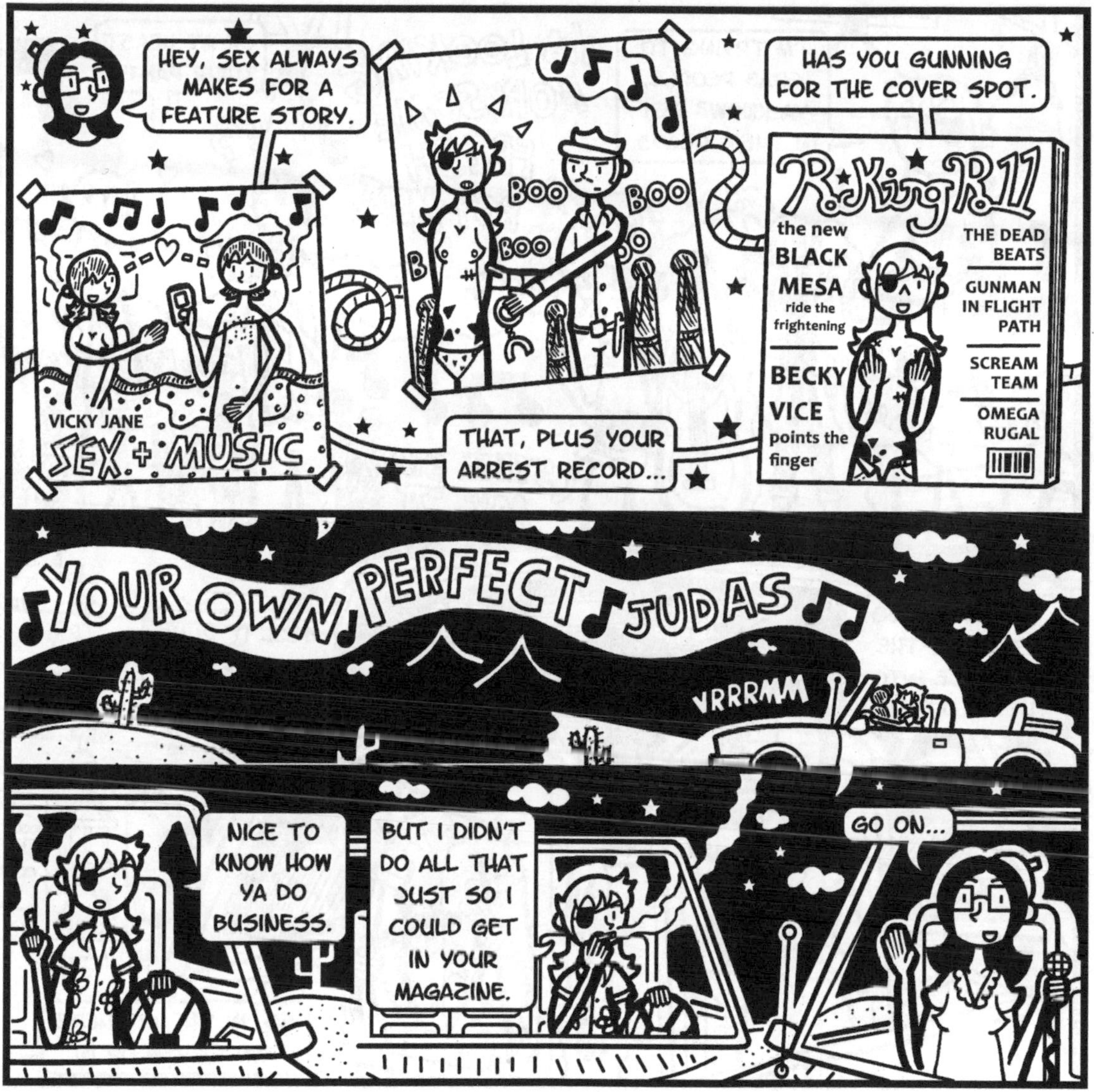
HEY, SEX ALWAYS MAKES FOR A FEATURE STORY.
VICKY JANE
SEX + MUSIC
BOO
BOO
BOO
HAS YOU GUNNING FOR THE COVER SPOT.
RockingR11
the new BLACK MESA ride the frightening
BECKY VICE points the finger
THE DEAD BEATS
GUNMAN IN FLIGHT PATH
SCREAM TEAM
OMEGA RUGAL
THAT, PLUS YOUR ARREST RECORD...
YOUR OWN PERFECT JUDAS
VRRRMM
NICE TO KNOW HOW YA DO BUSINESS.
BUT I DIDN'T DO ALL THAT JUST SO I COULD GET IN YOUR MAGAZINE.
GO ON...

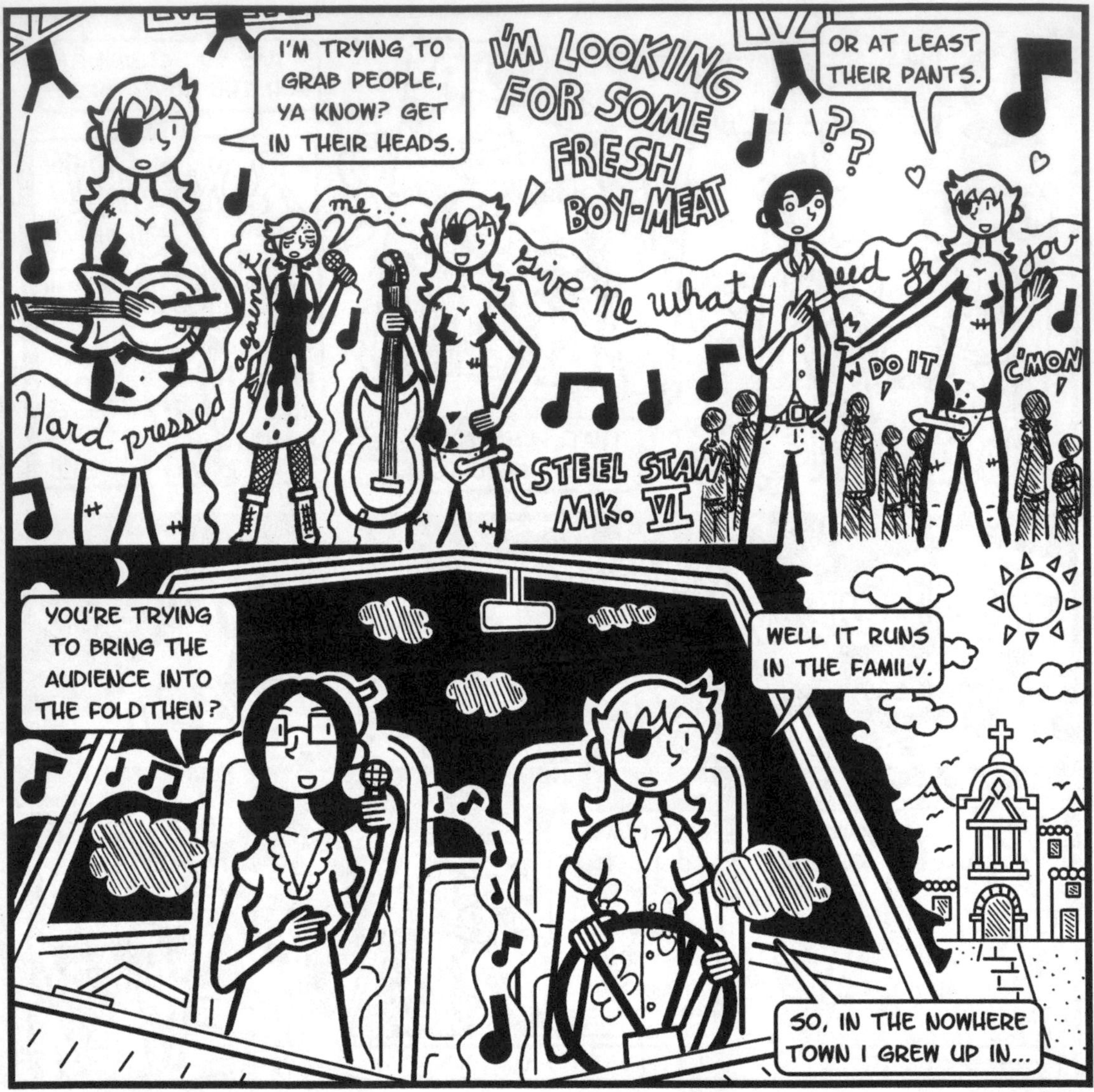
I'M TRYING TO GRAB PEOPLE, YA KNOW? GET IN THEIR HEADS.
I'M LOOKING FOR SOME FRESH BOY-MEAT
OR AT LEAST THEIR PANTS.
Hard pressed against me
give me what
STEEL STAN MK. VI
DO IT
C'MON
YOU'RE TRYING TO BRING THE AUDIENCE INTO THE FOLD THEN?
WELL IT RUNS IN THE FAMILY.
SO, IN THE NOWHERE TOWN I GREW UP IN...

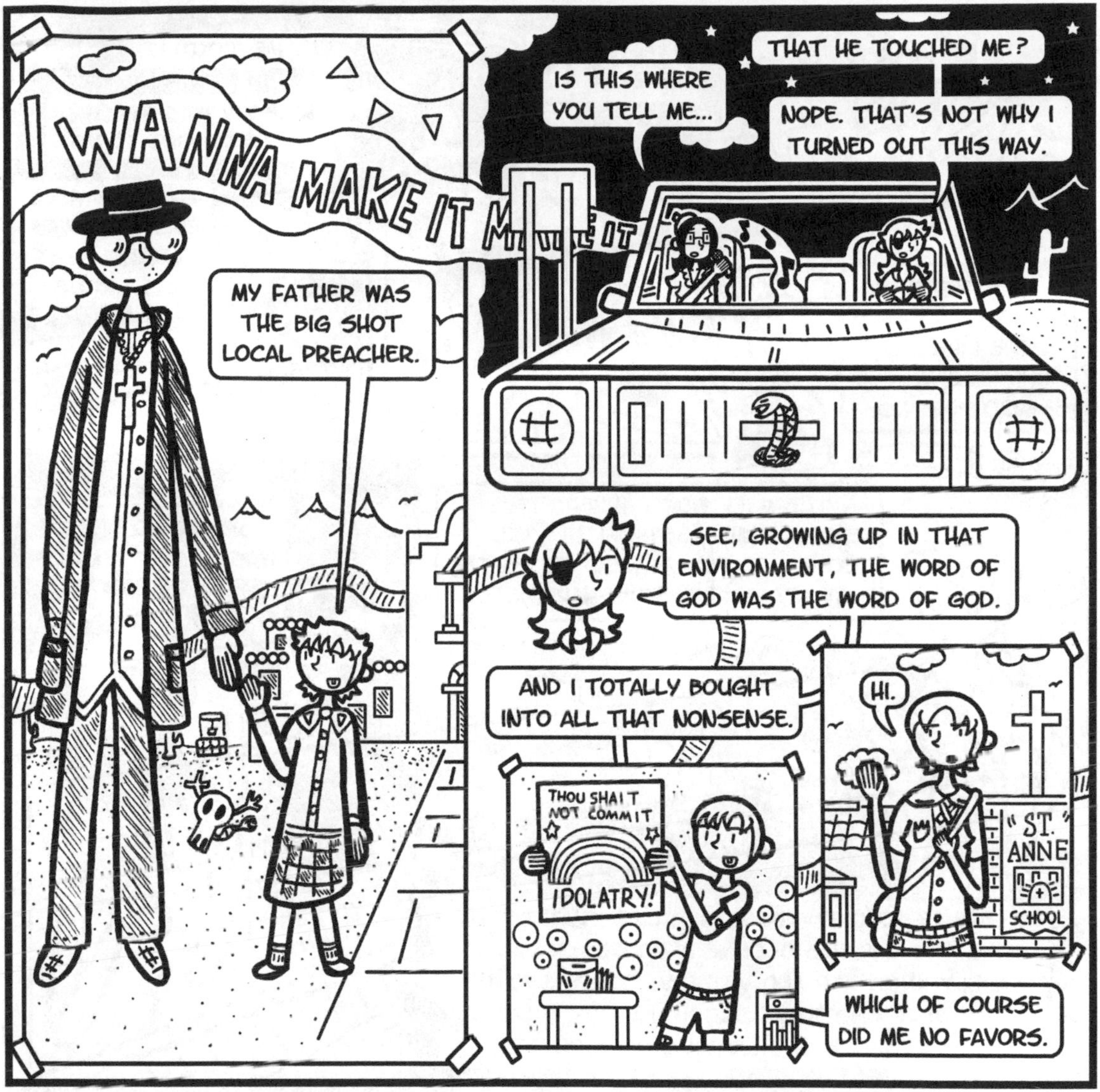
I WANNA MAKE IT
MY FATHER WAS THE BIG SHOT LOCAL PREACHER.
IS THIS WHERE YOU TELL ME...
THAT HE TOUCHED ME?
NOPE. THAT'S NOT WHY I TURNED OUT THIS WAY.
SEE, GROWING UP IN THAT ENVIRONMENT, THE WORD OF GOD WAS THE WORD OF GOD.
AND I TOTALLY BOUGHT INTO ALL THAT NONSENSE.
THOU SHALT NOT COMMIT IDOLATRY!
HI.
"ST. ANNE" SCHOOL
WHICH OF COURSE DID ME NO FAVORS.

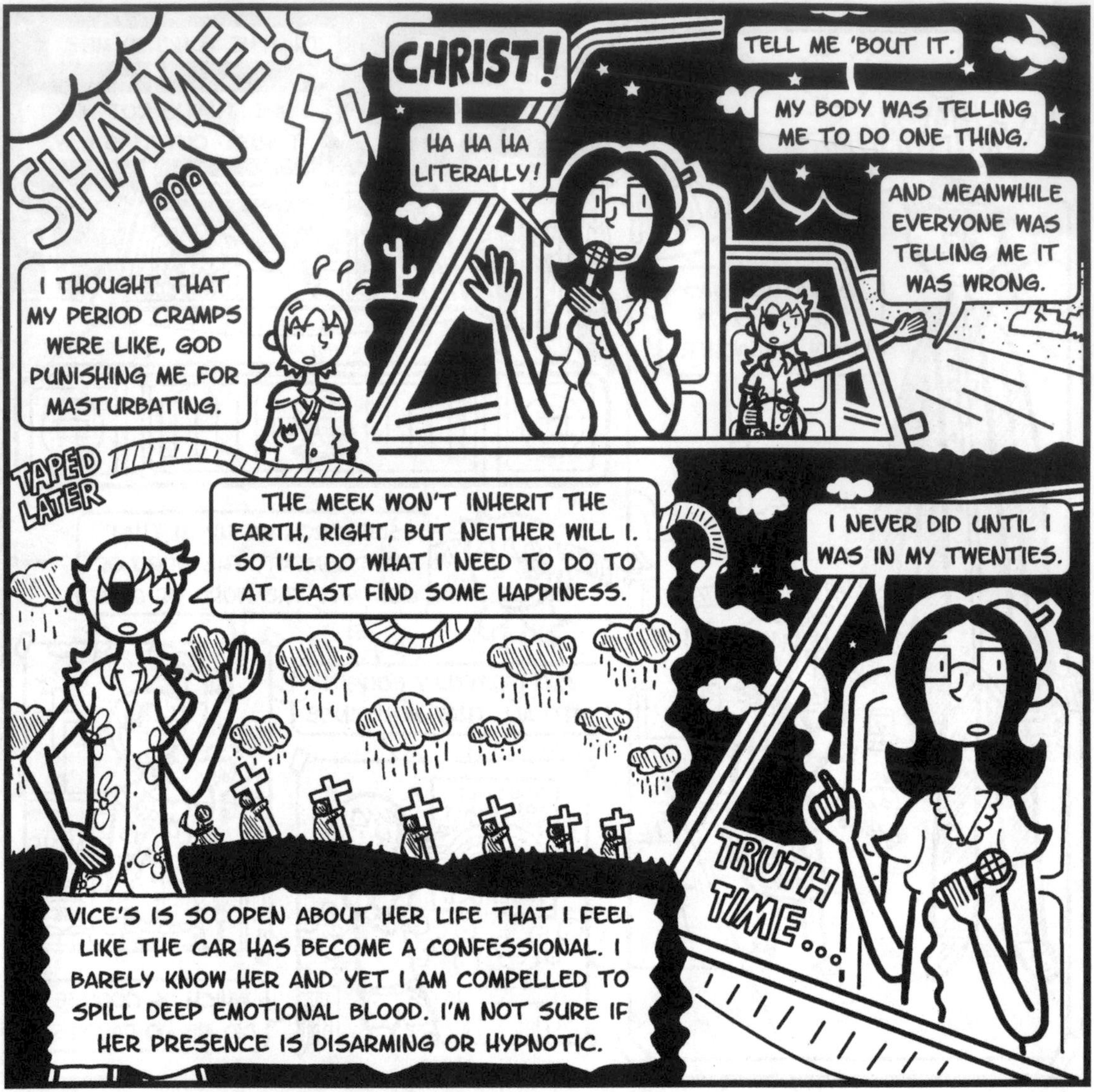
SHAME!
CHRIST!
HA HA HA LITERALLY!
TELL ME 'BOUT IT.
MY BODY WAS TELLING ME TO DO ONE THING.
AND MEANWHILE EVERYONE WAS TELLING ME IT WAS WRONG.
I THOUGHT THAT MY PERIOD CRAMPS WERE LIKE, GOD PUNISHING ME FOR MASTURBATING.
TAPED LATER
THE MEEK WON'T INHERIT THE EARTH, RIGHT, BUT NEITHER WILL I. SO I'LL DO WHAT I NEED TO DO TO AT LEAST FIND SOME HAPPINESS.
I NEVER DID UNTIL I WAS IN MY TWENTIES.
TRUTH TIME...
VICE'S IS SO OPEN ABOUT HER LIFE THAT I FEEL LIKE THE CAR HAS BECOME A CONFESSIONAL. I BARELY KNOW HER AND YET I AM COMPELLED TO SPILL DEEP EMOTIONAL BLOOD. I'M NOT SURE IF HER PRESENCE IS DISARMING OR HYPNOTIC.

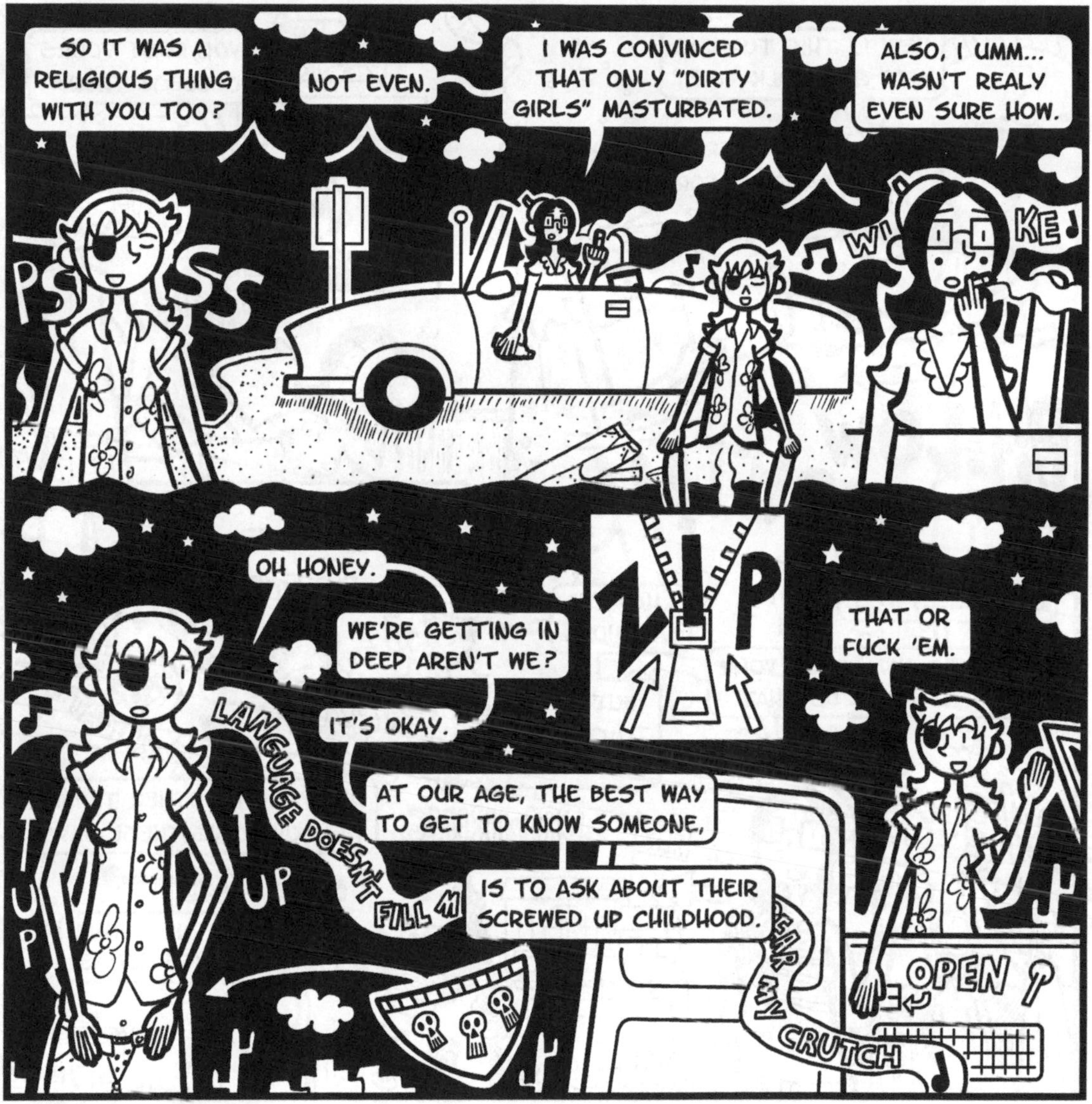

SO IT WAS A RELIGIOUS THING WITH YOU TOO?
NOT EVEN.
I WAS CONVINCED THAT ONLY "DIRTY GIRLS" MASTURBATED.
ALSO, I UMM... WASN'T REALY EVEN SURE HOW.
PSSSS
WI KE
OH HONEY.
WE'RE GETTING IN DEEP AREN'T WE?
IT'S OKAY.
AT OUR AGE, THE BEST WAY TO GET TO KNOW SOMEONE,
IS TO ASK ABOUT THEIR SCREWED UP CHILDHOOD.
ZIP
THAT OR FUCK 'EM.
LANGUAGE DOESN'T FILL M
UP
UP
UP
OPEN
MY CRUTCH

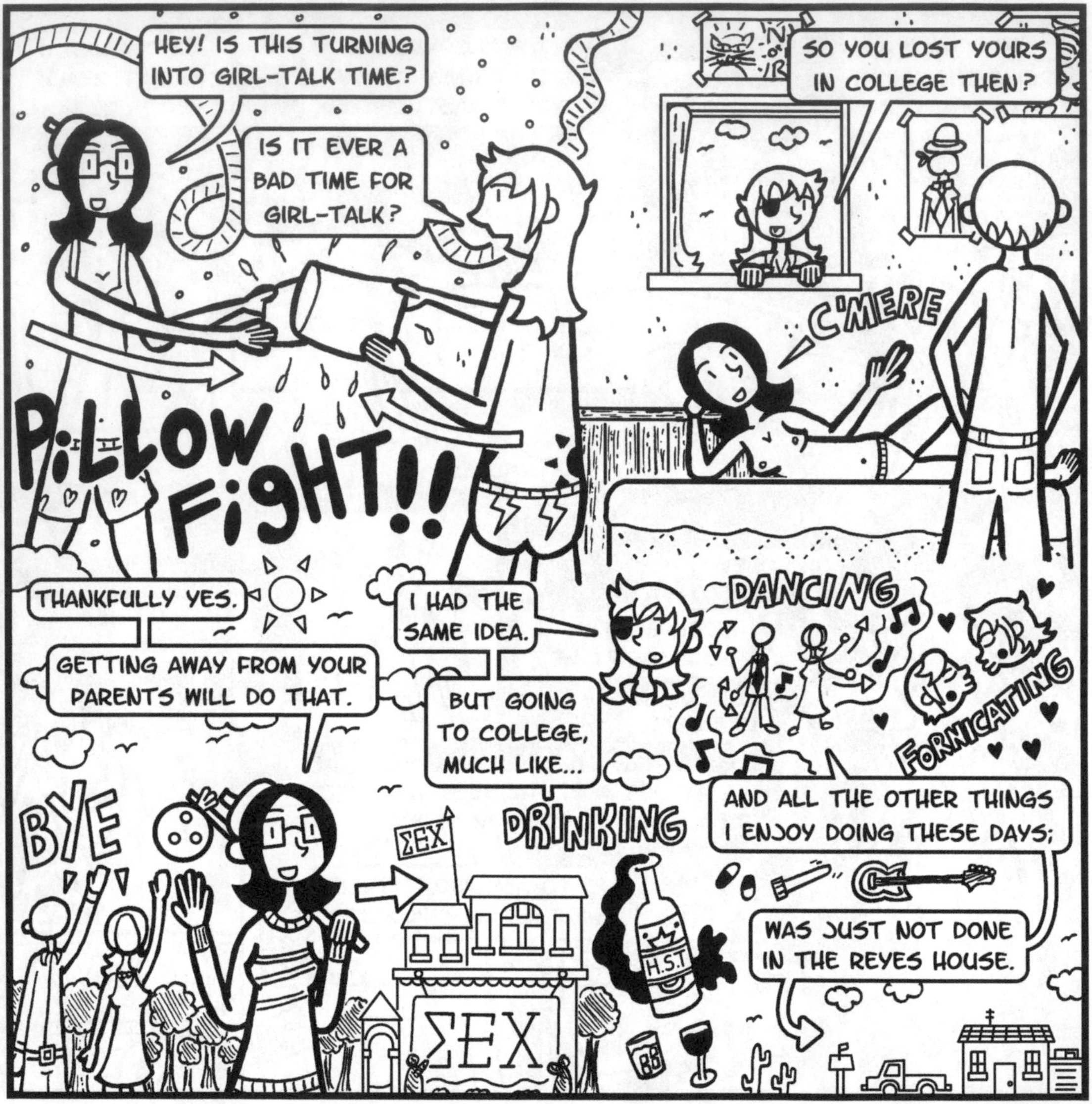
HEY! IS THIS TURNING INTO GIRL-TALK TIME?
IS IT EVER A BAD TIME FOR GIRL-TALK?
PILLOW FIGHT!!
SO YOU LOST YOURS IN COLLEGE THEN?
C'MERE
THANKFULLY YES.
GETTING AWAY FROM YOUR PARENTS WILL DO THAT.
I HAD THE SAME IDEA.
BUT GOING TO COLLEGE, MUCH LIKE...
DANCING
FORNICATING
DRINKING
AND ALL THE OTHER THINGS I ENJOY DOING THESE DAYS;
WAS JUST NOT DONE IN THE REYES HOUSE.
BYE
ΣΕΧ
ΣΕΧ
H.S.T.

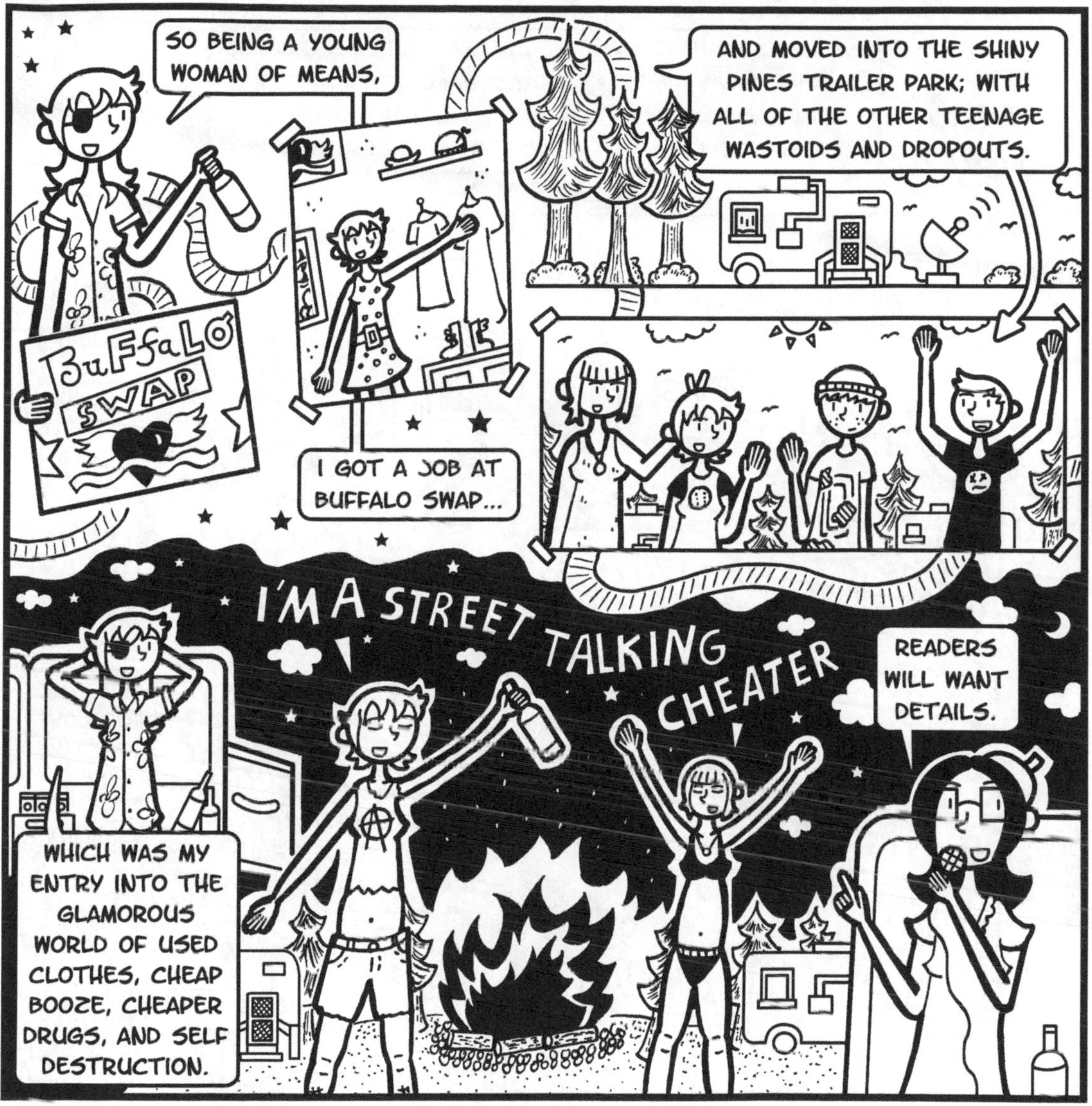
SO BEING A YOUNG WOMAN OF MEANS,
BUFFALO SWAP
I GOT A JOB AT BUFFALO SWAP...
AND MOVED INTO THE SHINY PINES TRAILER PARK; WITH ALL OF THE OTHER TEENAGE WASTOIDS AND DROPOUTS.
I'M A STREET TALKING CHEATER
WHICH WAS MY ENTRY INTO THE GLAMOROUS WORLD OF USED CLOTHES, CHEAP BOOZE, CHEAPER DRUGS, AND SELF DESTRUCTION.
READERS WILL WANT DETAILS.

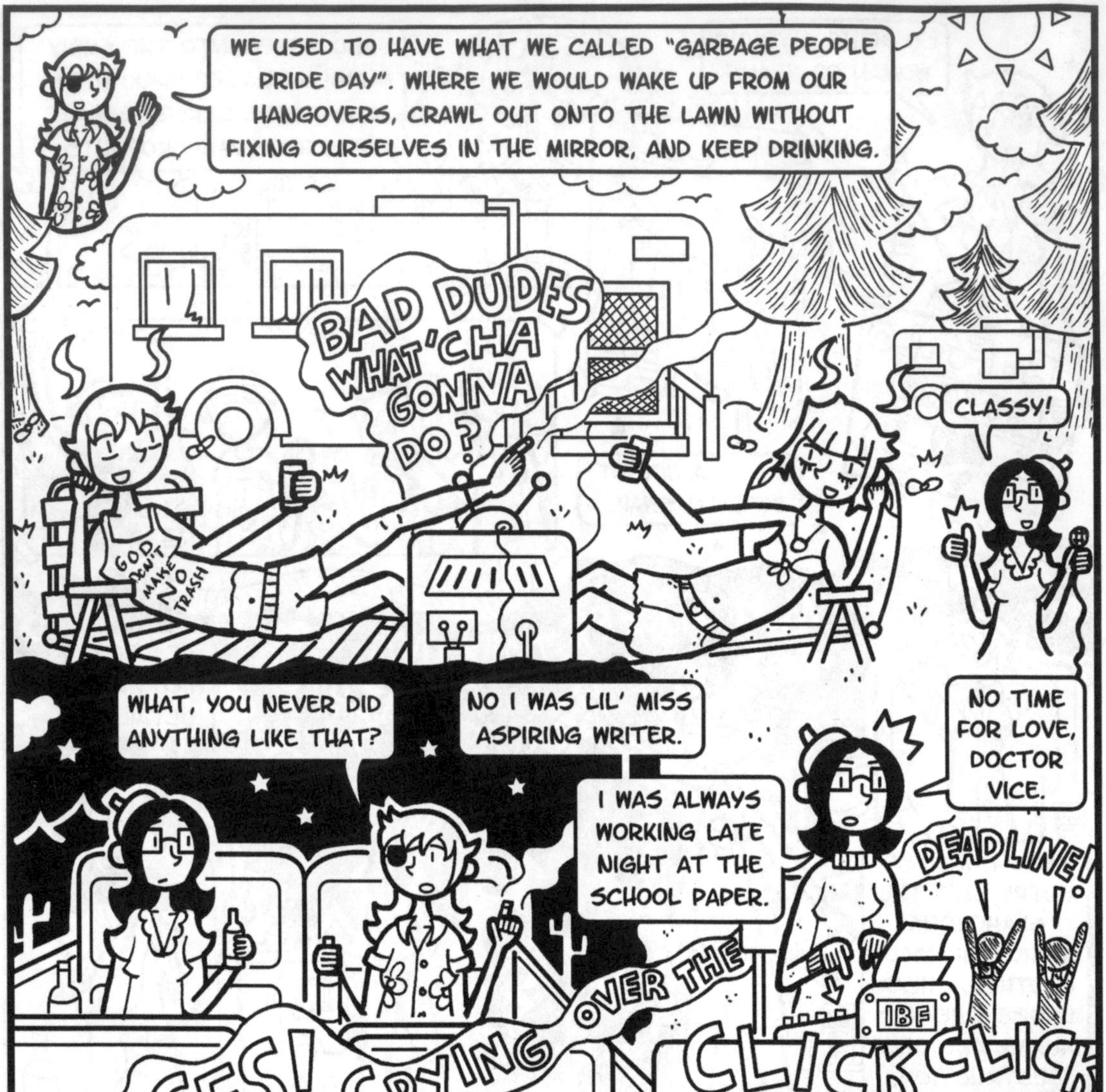
WE USED TO HAVE WHAT WE CALLED "GARBAGE PEOPLE PRIDE DAY". WHERE WE WOULD WAKE UP FROM OUR HANGOVERS, CRAWL OUT ONTO THE LAWN WITHOUT FIXING OURSELVES IN THE MIRROR, AND KEEP DRINKING.
BAD DUDES WHAT'CHA GONNA DO?
GOD DON'T MAKE NO TRASH
CLASSY!
WHAT, YOU NEVER DID ANYTHING LIKE THAT?
NO I WAS LIL' MISS ASPIRING WRITER.
I WAS ALWAYS WORKING LATE NIGHT AT THE SCHOOL PAPER.
NO TIME FOR LOVE, DOCTOR VICE.
DEADLINE!
CRYING OVER THE
CLICKCLICK
IBF

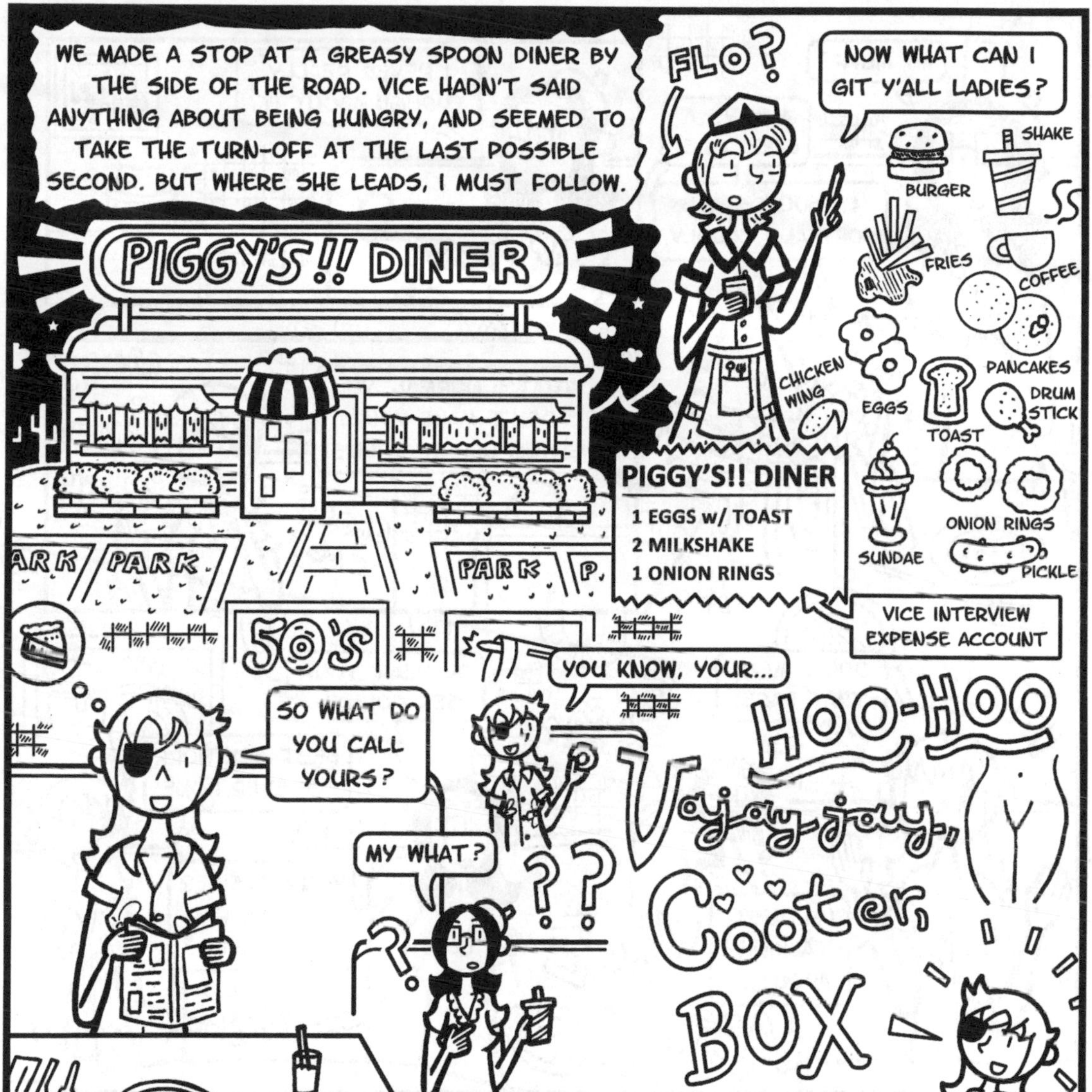
WE MADE A STOP AT A GREASY SPOON DINER BY THE SIDE OF THE ROAD. VICE HADN'T SAID ANYTHING ABOUT BEING HUNGRY, AND SEEMED TO TAKE THE TURN-OFF AT THE LAST POSSIBLE SECOND. BUT WHERE SHE LEADS, I MUST FOLLOW.
PIGGY'S!! DINER
PARK
PARK
PARK
P.
50'S
FLO?
NOW WHAT CAN I GIT Y'ALL LADIES?
BURGER
SHAKE
FRIES
COFFEE
PANCAKES
CHICKEN WING
EGGS
TOAST
DRUM STICK
PIGGY'S!! DINER
1 EGGS w/ TOAST
2 MILKSHAKE
1 ONION RINGS
SUNDAE
ONION RINGS
PICKLE
VICE INTERVIEW EXPENSE ACCOUNT
SO WHAT DO YOU CALL YOURS?
YOU KNOW, YOUR...
MY WHAT?
HOO-HOO
Vajayjay,
Cooter,
BOX

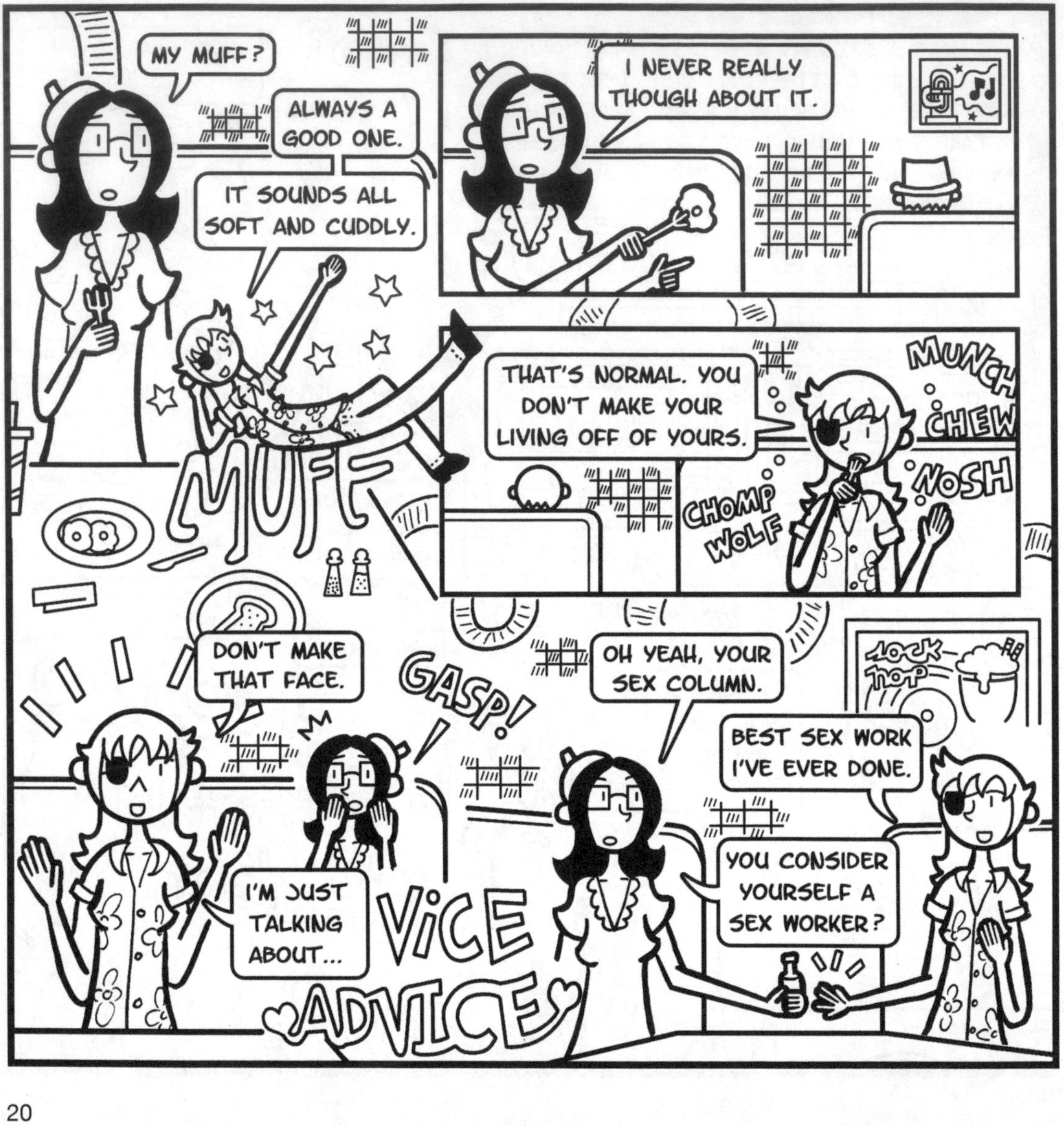
MY MUFF?
ALWAYS A GOOD ONE.
IT SOUNDS ALL SOFT AND CUDDLY.
MUFF
I NEVER REALLY THOUGH ABOUT IT.
THAT'S NORMAL. YOU DON'T MAKE YOUR LIVING OFF OF YOURS.
MUNCH
CHEW
NOSH
CHOMP
WOLF
DON'T MAKE THAT FACE.
GASP!
I'M JUST TALKING ABOUT...
VICE ADVICE
OH YEAH, YOUR SEX COLUMN.
YOU CONSIDER YOURSELF A SEX WORKER?
BEST SEX WORK I'VE EVER DONE.

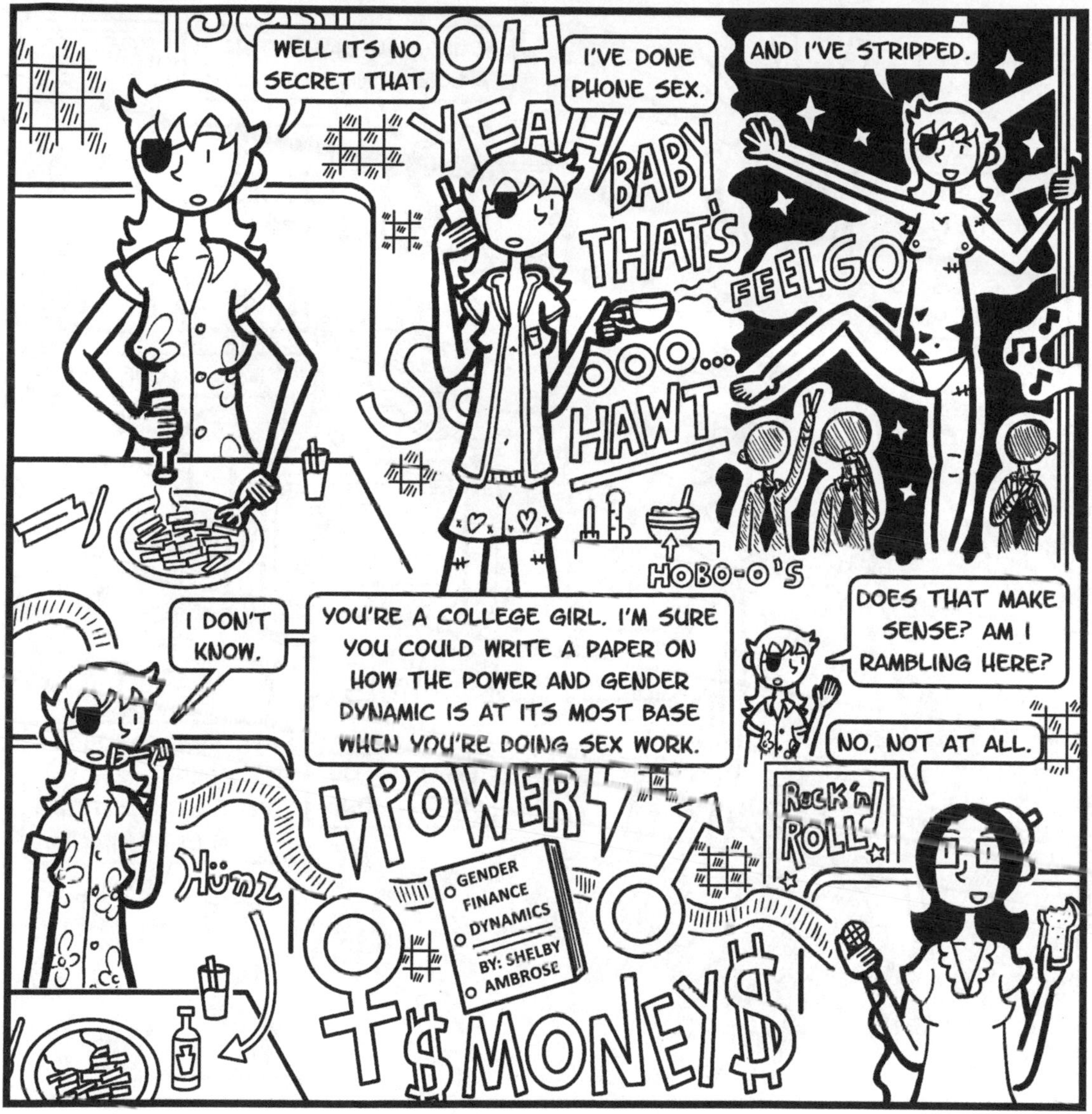

WELL ITS NO SECRET THAT,
OH YEAH BABY THAT'S SOOO... HAWT
I'VE DONE PHONE SEX.
AND I'VE STRIPPED.
FEELGO
HOBO-O'S
I DON'T KNOW.
YOU'RE A COLLEGE GIRL. I'M SURE YOU COULD WRITE A PAPER ON HOW THE POWER AND GENDER DYNAMIC IS AT ITS MOST BASE WHEN YOU'RE DOING SEX WORK.
DOES THAT MAKE SENSE? AM I RAMBLING HERE?
NO, NOT AT ALL.
Rock'n ROLL
POWER
Hünz
GENDER FINANCE DYNAMICS BY: SHELBY AMBROSE
$MONEY$

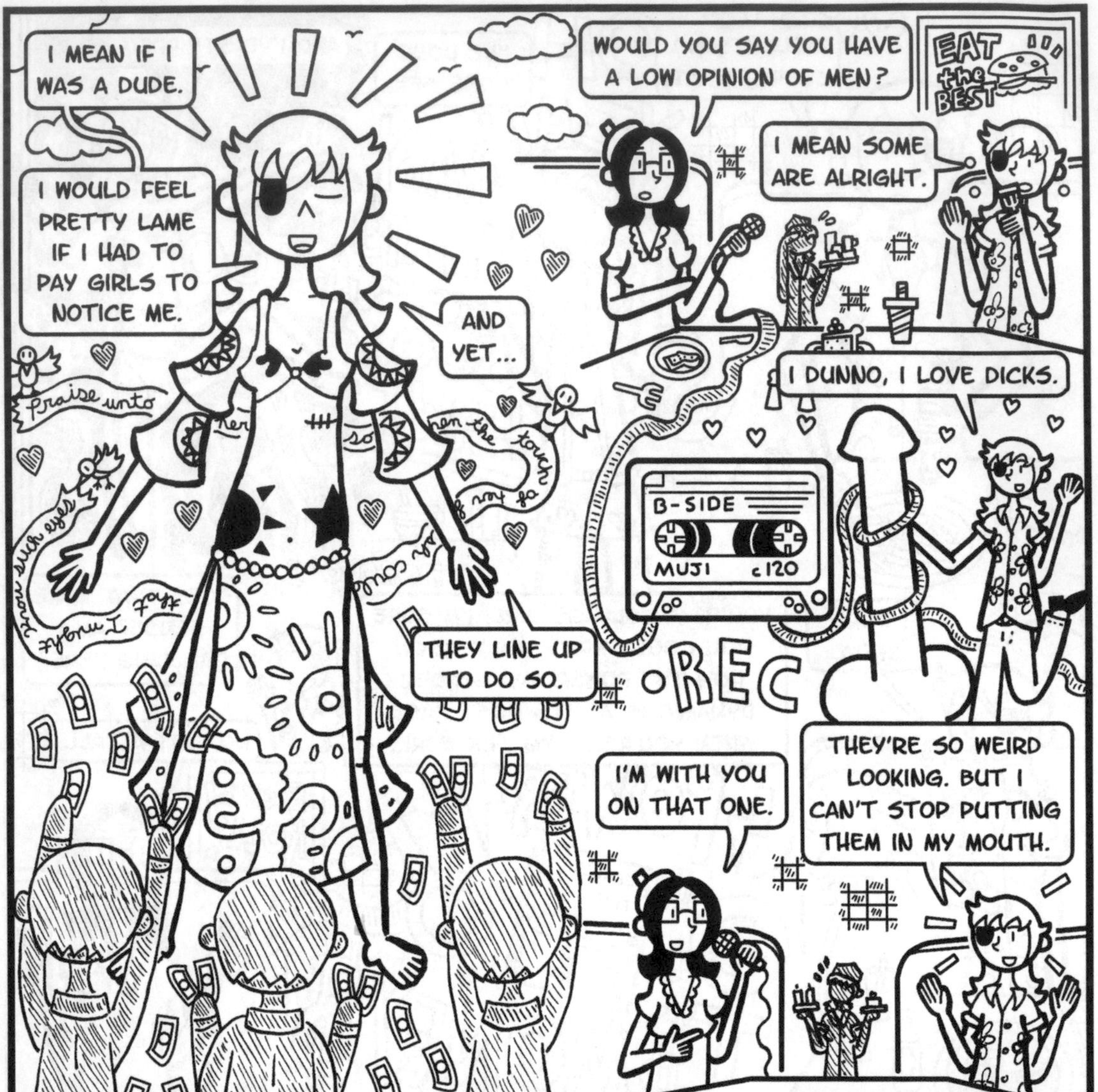

I MEAN IF I WAS A DUDE.
I WOULD FEEL PRETTY LAME IF I HAD TO PAY GIRLS TO NOTICE ME.
AND YET...
THEY LINE UP TO DO SO.
praise unto
WOULD YOU SAY YOU HAVE A LOW OPINION OF MEN?
EAT the BEST
I MEAN SOME ARE ALRIGHT.
I DUNNO, I LOVE DICKS.
B-SIDE
MUJI
c120
REC
I'M WITH YOU ON THAT ONE.
THEY'RE SO WEIRD LOOKING. BUT I CAN'T STOP PUTTING THEM IN MY MOUTH.

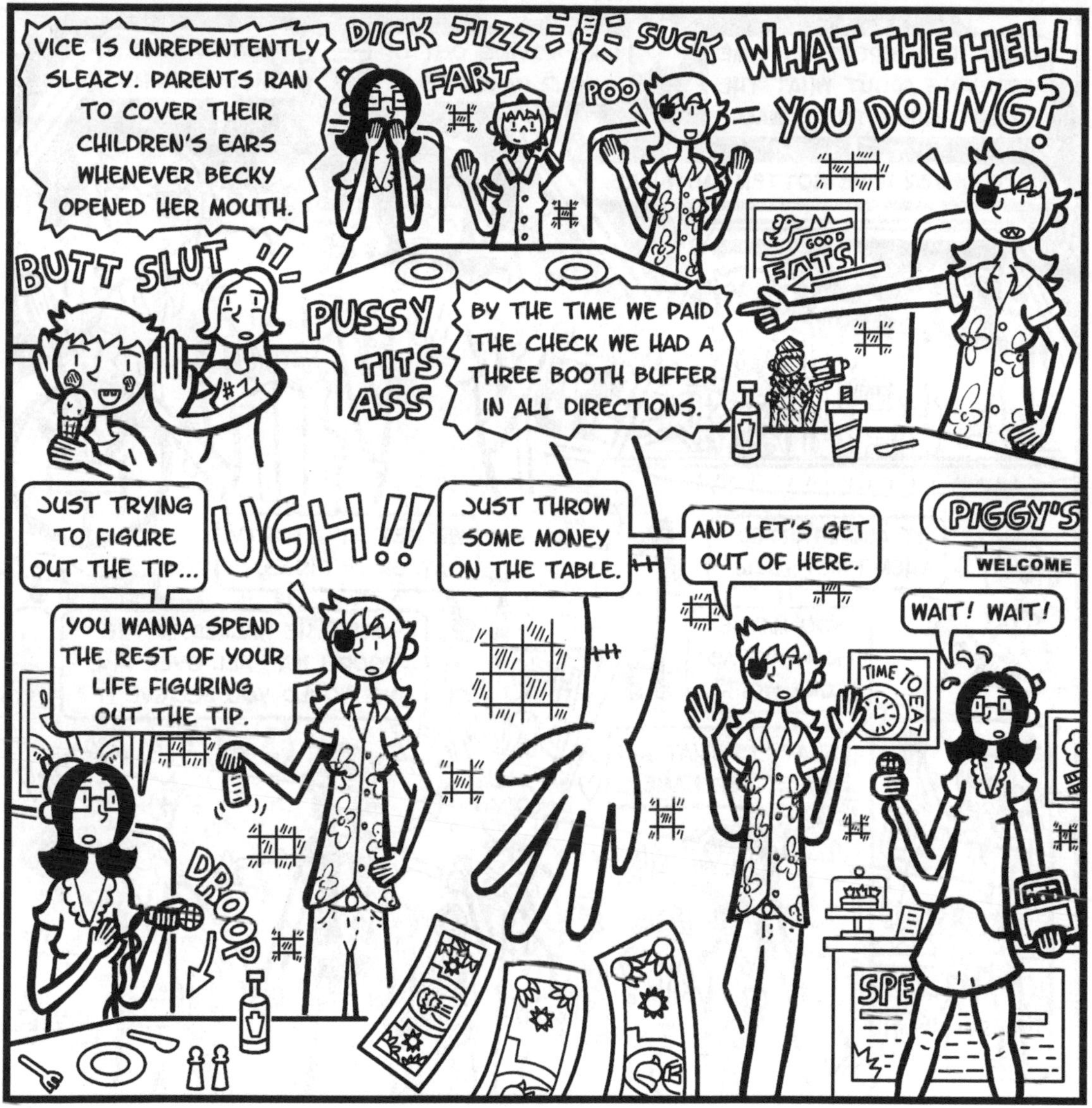

VICE IS UNREPENTENTLY SLEAZY. PARENTS RAN TO COVER THEIR CHILDREN'S EARS WHENEVER BECKY OPENED HER MOUTH.
DICK
JIZZ
FART
SUCK
POO
WHAT THE HELL YOU DOING?
BUTT SLUT
PUSSY
TITS
ASS
BY THE TIME WE PAID THE CHECK WE HAD A THREE BOOTH BUFFER IN ALL DIRECTIONS.
GOOD EATS
JUST TRYING TO FIGURE OUT THE TIP...
UGH!!
YOU WANNA SPEND THE REST OF YOUR LIFE FIGURING OUT THE TIP.
JUST THROW SOME MONEY ON THE TABLE.
AND LET'S GET OUT OF HERE.
PIGGY'S
WELCOME
WAIT! WAIT!
TIME TO EAT
DROOP
SPE

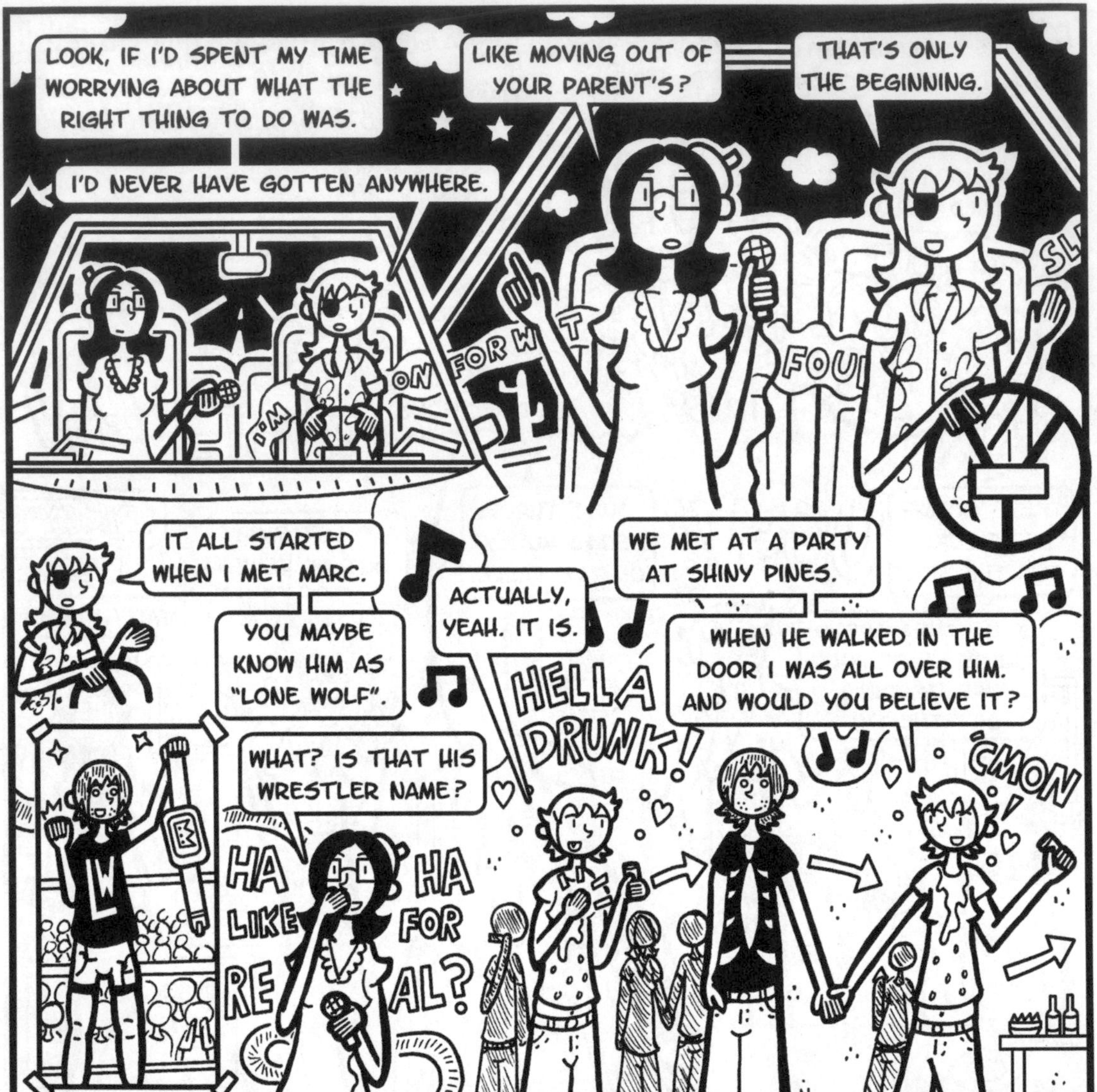

LOOK, IF I'D SPENT MY TIME WORRYING ABOUT WHAT THE RIGHT THING TO DO WAS.
I'D NEVER HAVE GOTTEN ANYWHERE.
LIKE MOVING OUT OF YOUR PARENT'S?
THAT'S ONLY THE BEGINNING.
IT ALL STARTED WHEN I MET MARC.
YOU MAYBE KNOW HIM AS "LONE WOLF".
WHAT? IS THAT HIS WRESTLER NAME?
HA HA LIKE FOR REAL?
ACTUALLY, YEAH. IT IS.
WE MET AT A PARTY AT SHINY PINES.
WHEN HE WALKED IN THE DOOR I WAS ALL OVER HIM. AND WOULD YOU BELIEVE IT?
HELLA DRUNK!
'CMON!

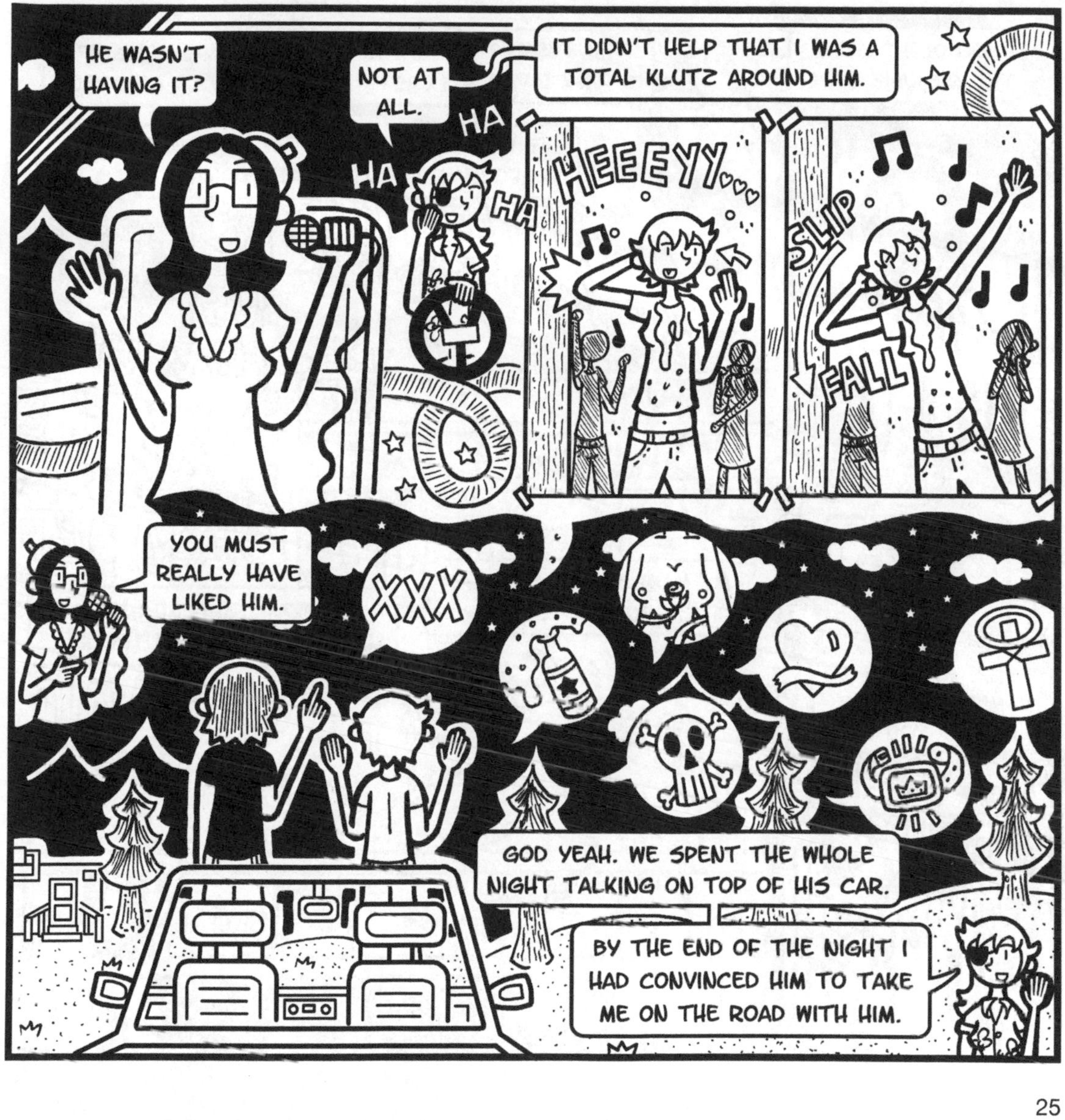
HE WASN'T HAVING IT?
NOT AT ALL.
HA
HA
HA
IT DIDN'T HELP THAT I WAS A TOTAL KLUTZ AROUND HIM.
HEEEYY
SLIP
FALL
YOU MUST REALLY HAVE LIKED HIM.
XXX
GOD YEAH. WE SPENT THE WHOLE NIGHT TALKING ON TOP OF HIS CAR.
BY THE END OF THE NIGHT I HAD CONVINCED HIM TO TAKE ME ON THE ROAD WITH HIM.

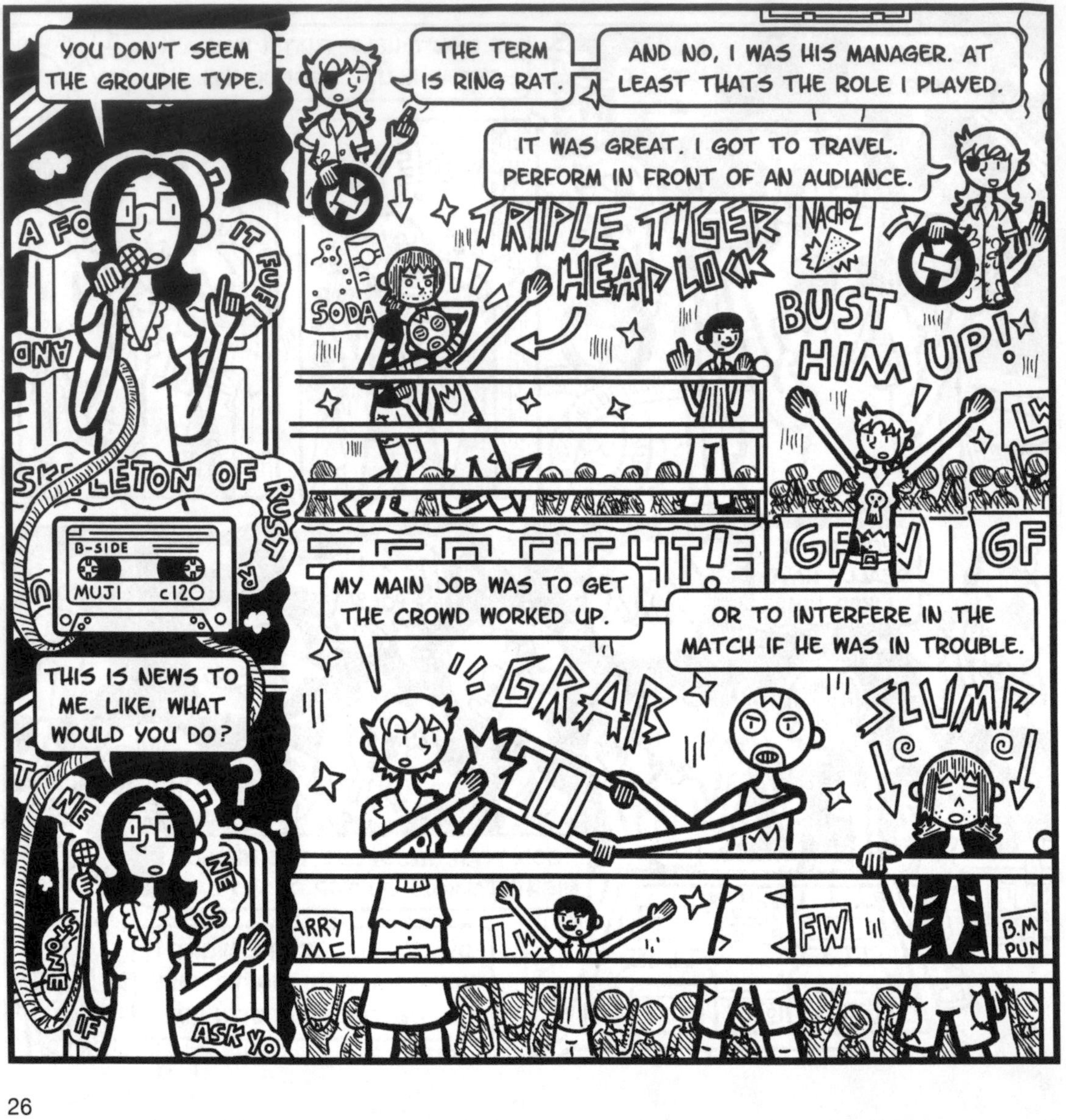
YOU DON'T SEEM THE GROUPIE TYPE.
THE TERM IS RING RAT.
AND NO, I WAS HIS MANAGER. AT LEAST THATS THE ROLE I PLAYED.
IT WAS GREAT. I GOT TO TRAVEL. PERFORM IN FRONT OF AN AUDIANCE.
SODA
NACHOZ
TRIPLE TIGER HEADLOCK
BUST HIM UP!
B-SIDE
MUJI c120
MY MAIN JOB WAS TO GET THE CROWD WORKED UP.
OR TO INTERFERE IN THE MATCH IF HE WAS IN TROUBLE.
GRAB
SLUMP
THIS IS NEWS TO ME. LIKE, WHAT WOULD YOU DO?
FW

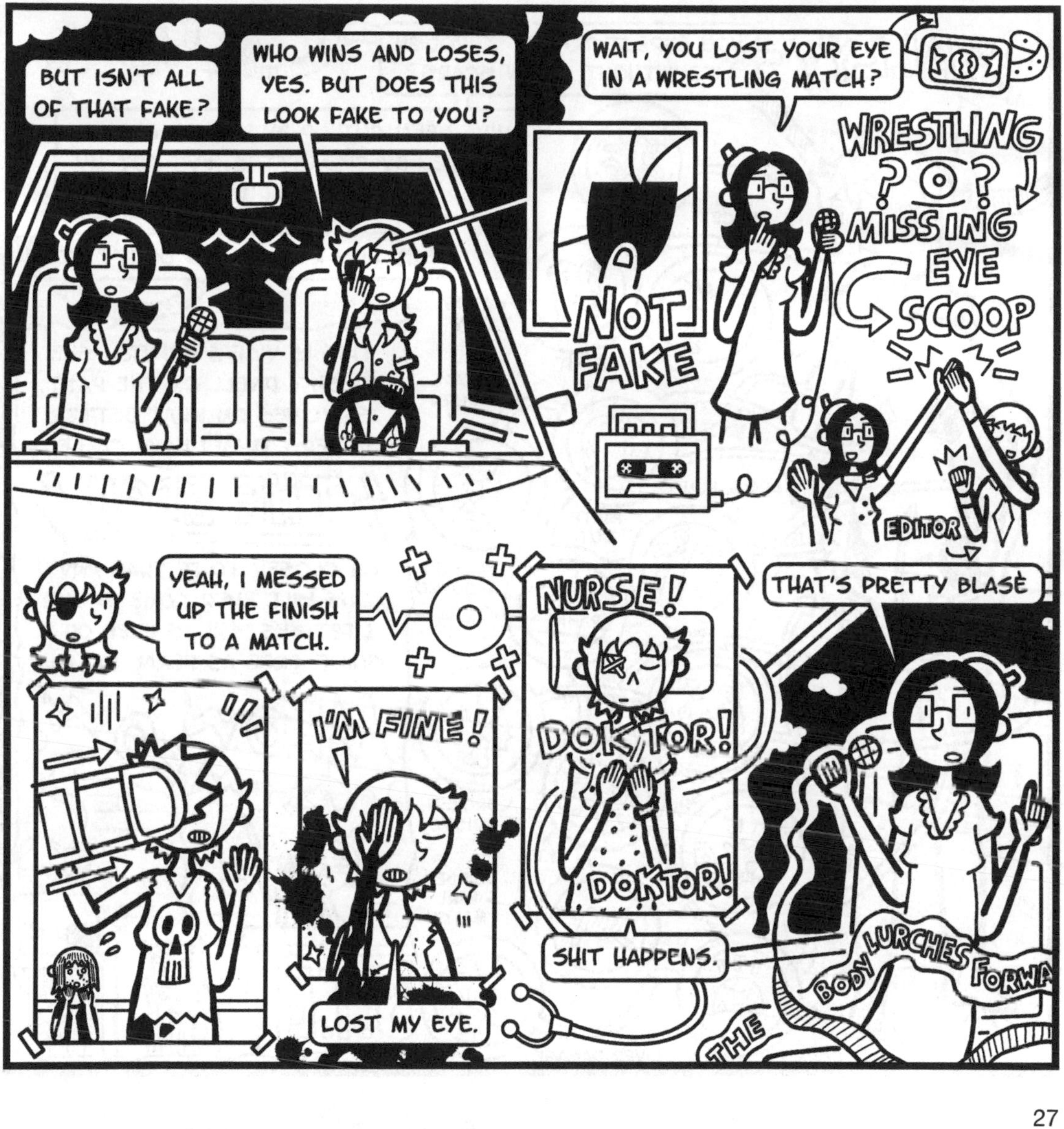
BUT ISN'T ALL OF THAT FAKE?
WHO WINS AND LOSES, YES. BUT DOES THIS LOOK FAKE TO YOU?
NOT FAKE
WAIT, YOU LOST YOUR EYE IN A WRESTLING MATCH?
WRESTLING
MISSING EYE
SCOOP
EDITOR
YEAH, I MESSED UP THE FINISH TO A MATCH.
I'M FINE!
LOST MY EYE.
NURSE!
DOKTOR!
DOKTOR!
SHIT HAPPENS.
THAT'S PRETTY BLASÉ
THE BODY LURCHES FORWA

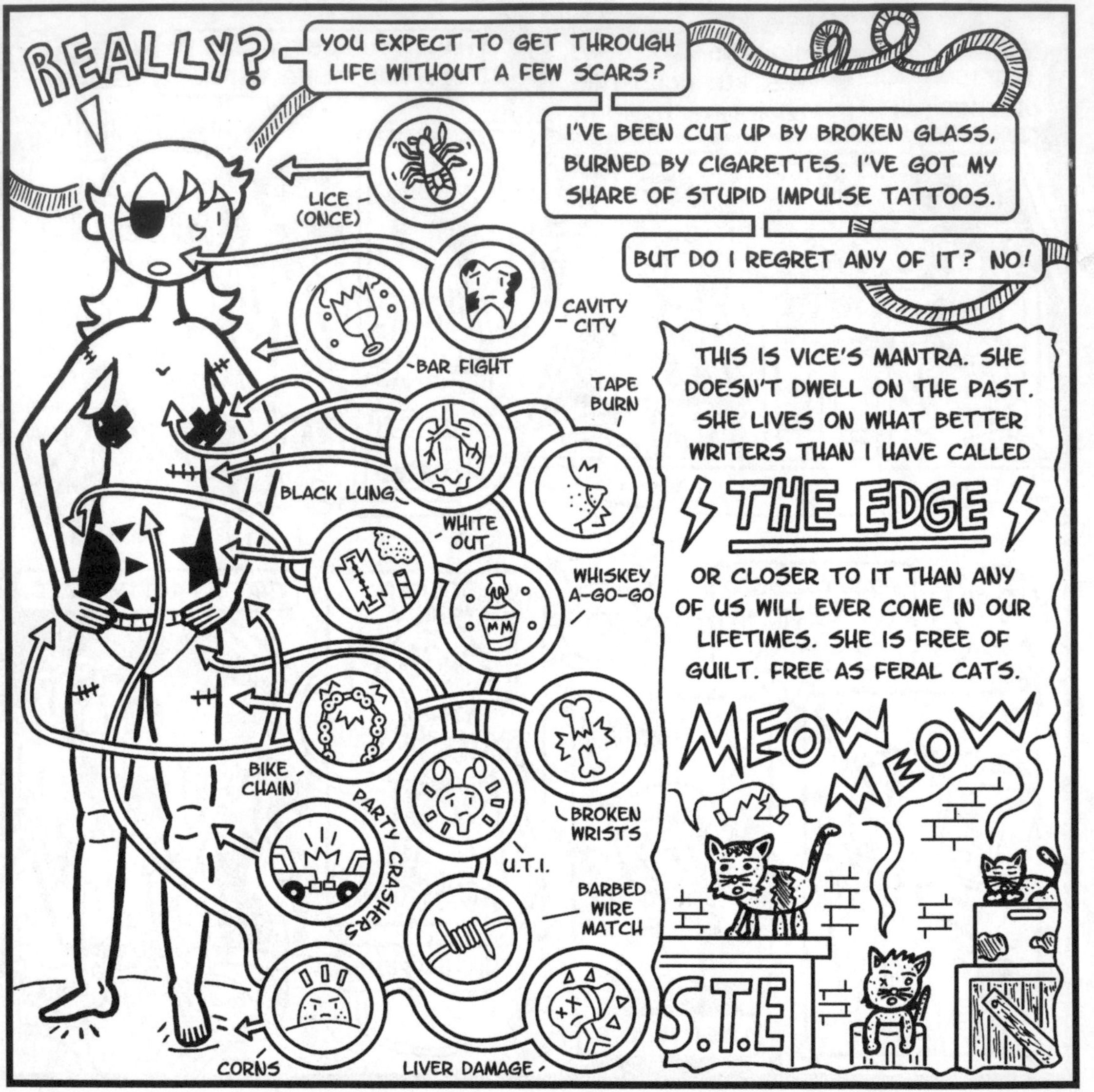
REALLY?
YOU EXPECT TO GET THROUGH LIFE WITHOUT A FEW SCARS?
I'VE BEEN CUT UP BY BROKEN GLASS, BURNED BY CIGARETTES. I'VE GOT MY SHARE OF STUPID IMPULSE TATTOOS.
BUT DO I REGRET ANY OF IT? NO!
LICE (ONCE)
CAVITY CITY
BAR FIGHT
TAPE BURN
BLACK LUNG
WHITE OUT
WHISKEY A-GO-GO
BIKE CHAIN
PARTY CRASHERS
BROKEN WRISTS
U.T.I.
BARBED WIRE MATCH
CORNS
LIVER DAMAGE
THIS IS VICE'S MANTRA. SHE DOESN'T DWELL ON THE PAST. SHE LIVES ON WHAT BETTER WRITERS THAN I HAVE CALLED
THE EDGE
OR CLOSER TO IT THAN ANY OF US WILL EVER COME IN OUR LIFETIMES. SHE IS FREE OF GUILT. FREE AS FERAL CATS.
MEOW MEOW MEOW
S.T.E

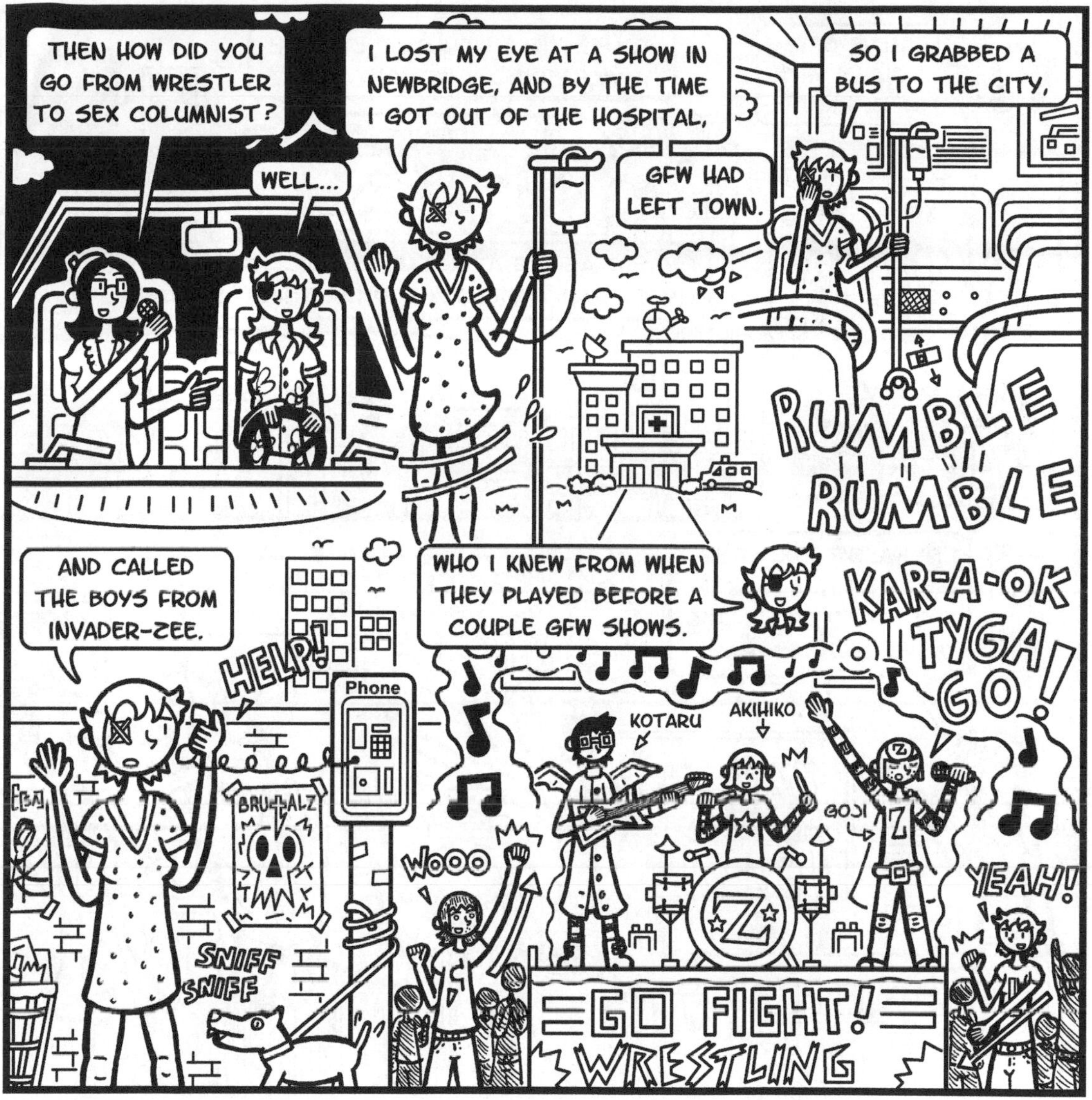

THEN HOW DID YOU GO FROM WRESTLER TO SEX COLUMNIST?
WELL...
I LOST MY EYE AT A SHOW IN NEWBRIDGE, AND BY THE TIME I GOT OUT OF THE HOSPITAL,
GFW HAD LEFT TOWN.
SO I GRABBED A BUS TO THE CITY,
RUMBLE RUMBLE
AND CALLED THE BOYS FROM INVADER-ZEE.
HELP!
Phone
BRUTALZ
SNIFF SNIFF
WHO I KNEW FROM WHEN THEY PLAYED BEFORE A COUPLE GFW SHOWS.
KAR-A-OK TYGA GO!
KOTARU
AKIHIKO
GOJI
WOOO
YEAH!
GO FIGHT! WRESTLING

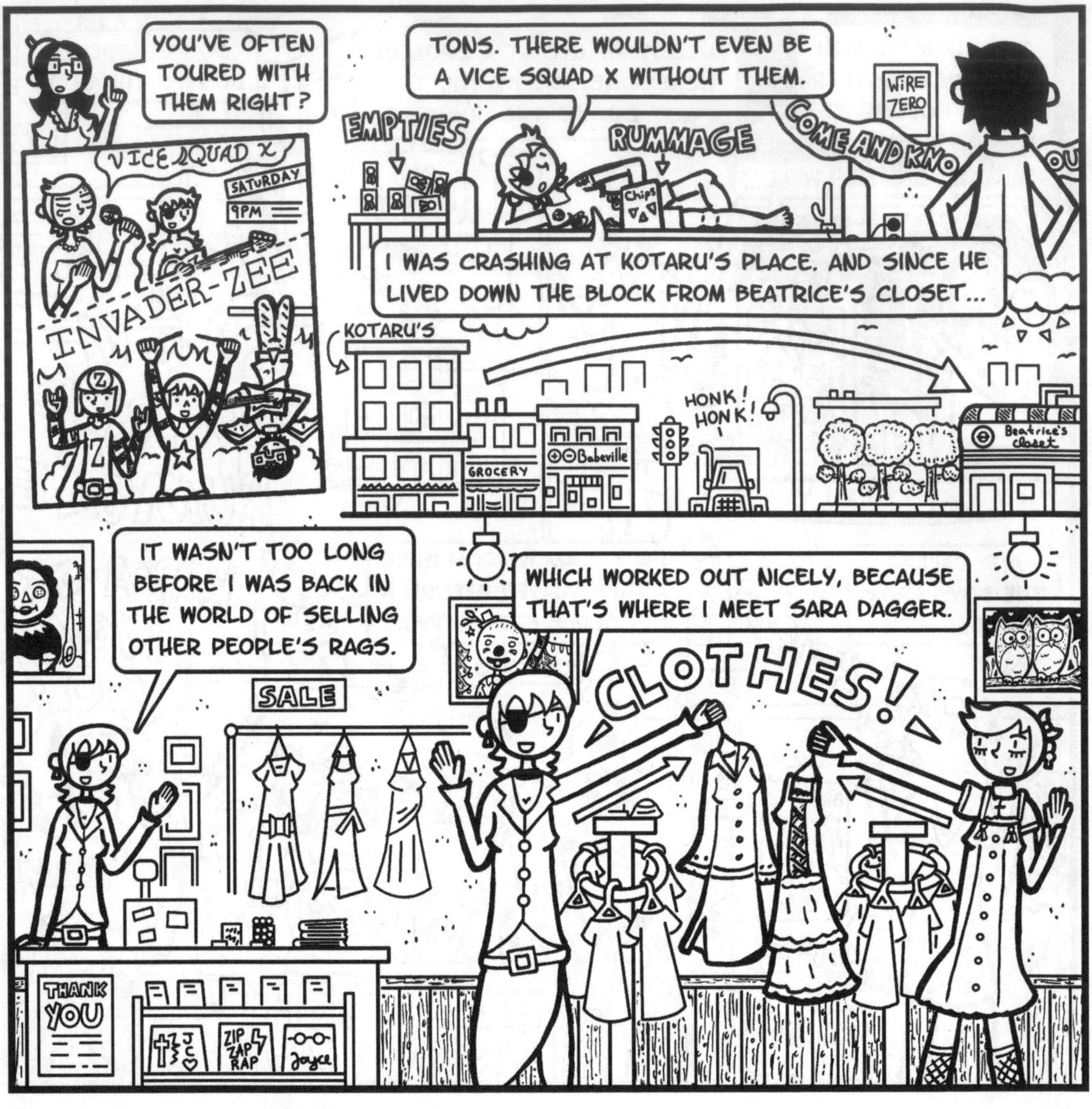
YOU'VE OFTEN TOURED WITH THEM RIGHT?
TONS. THERE WOULDN'T EVEN BE A VICE SQUAD X WITHOUT THEM.
VICE SQUAD X
SATURDAY
9PM
INVADER-ZEE
EMPTIES
RUMMAGE
Chips
WIRE ZERO
COME AND KNO
I WAS CRASHING AT KOTARU'S PLACE. AND SINCE HE LIVED DOWN THE BLOCK FROM BEATRICE'S CLOSET...
KOTARU'S
HONK! HONK!
GROCERY
Babeville
Beatrice's Closet
IT WASN'T TOO LONG BEFORE I WAS BACK IN THE WORLD OF SELLING OTHER PEOPLE'S RAGS.
WHICH WORKED OUT NICELY, BECAUSE THAT'S WHERE I MEET SARA DAGGER.
SALE
CLOTHES!
THANK YOU
ZIP ZAP RAP
Joyce

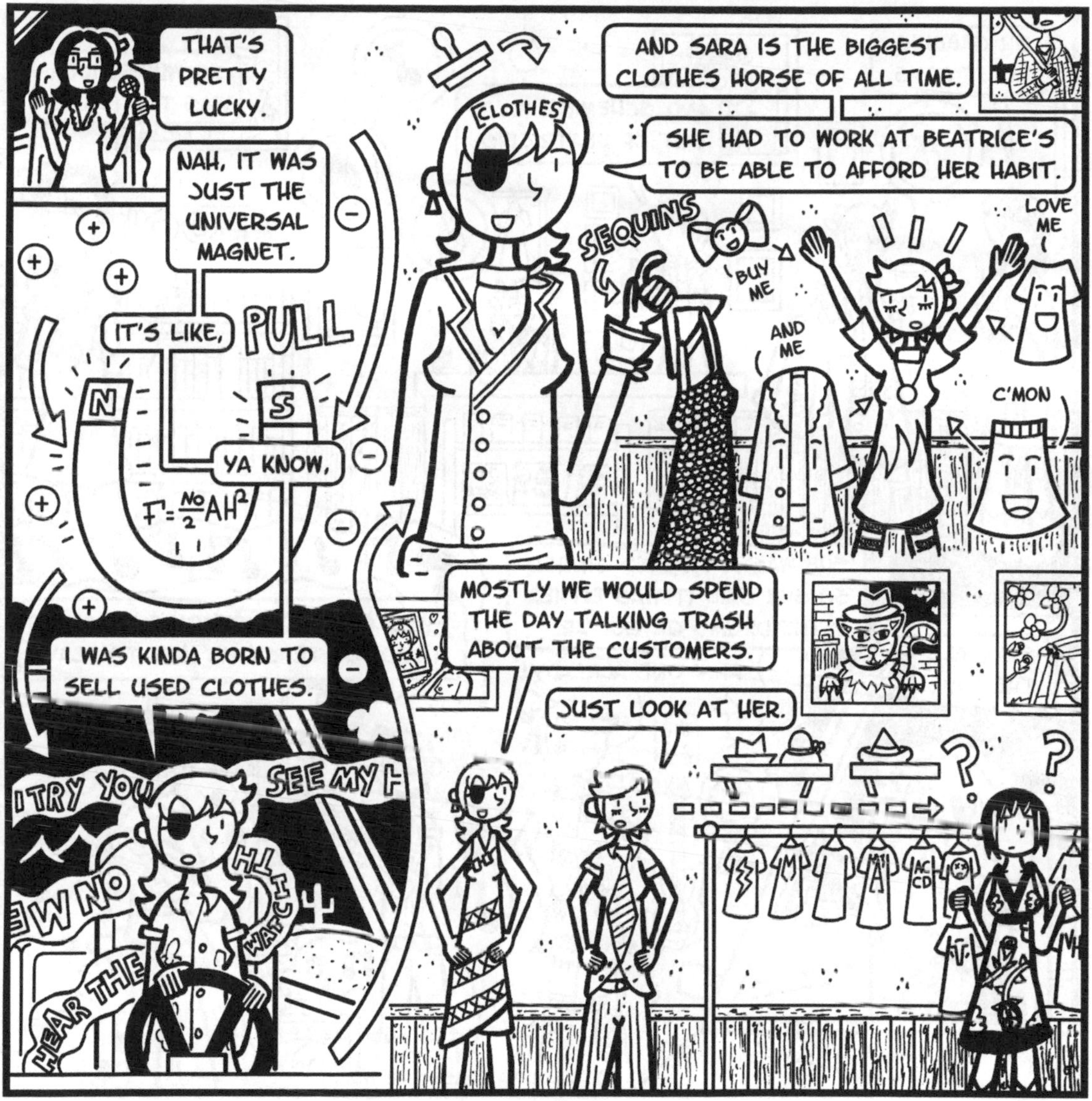

THAT'S PRETTY LUCKY.
NAH, IT WAS JUST THE UNIVERSAL MAGNET.
IT'S LIKE,
PULL
N
S
YA KNOW,
I WAS KINDA BORN TO SELL USED CLOTHES.
CLOTHES
AND SARA IS THE BIGGEST CLOTHES HORSE OF ALL TIME.
SHE HAD TO WORK AT BEATRICE'S TO BE ABLE TO AFFORD HER HABIT.
SEQUINS
BUY ME
AND ME
LOVE ME
C'MON
MOSTLY WE WOULD SPEND THE DAY TALKING TRASH ABOUT THE CUSTOMERS.
JUST LOOK AT HER.
I TRY YOU
SEE MY
HEAR THE

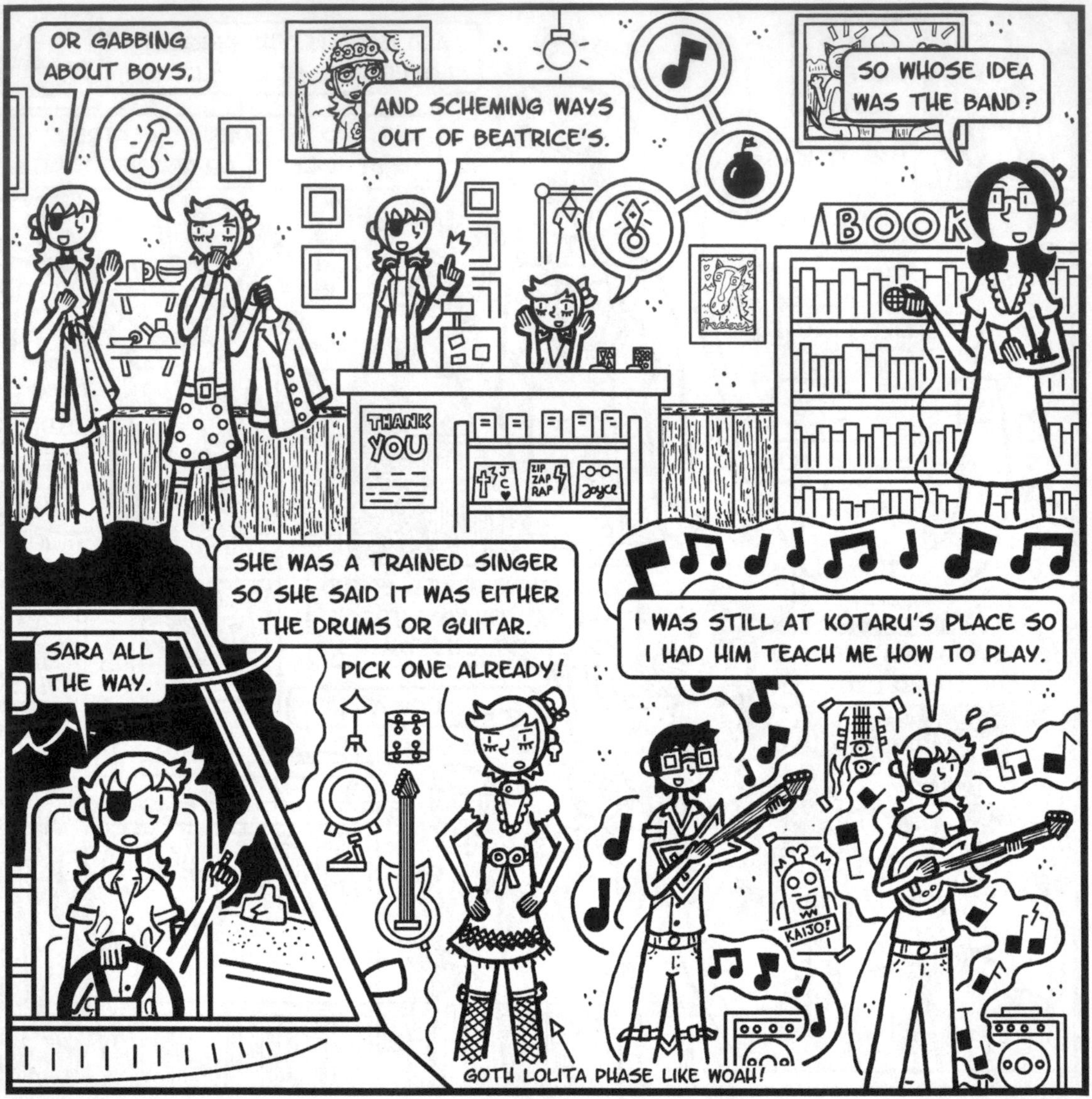
OR GABBING ABOUT BOYS,
AND SCHEMING WAYS OUT OF BEATRICE'S.
SO WHOSE IDEA WAS THE BAND?
BOOK
THANK YOU
JC
ZIP ZAP RAP
Joyce
Precious
SHE WAS A TRAINED SINGER SO SHE SAID IT WAS EITHER THE DRUMS OR GUITAR.
SARA ALL THE WAY.
PICK ONE ALREADY!
I WAS STILL AT KOTARU'S PLACE SO I HAD HIM TEACH ME HOW TO PLAY.
KAIJO!
GOTH LOLITA PHASE LIKE WOAH!

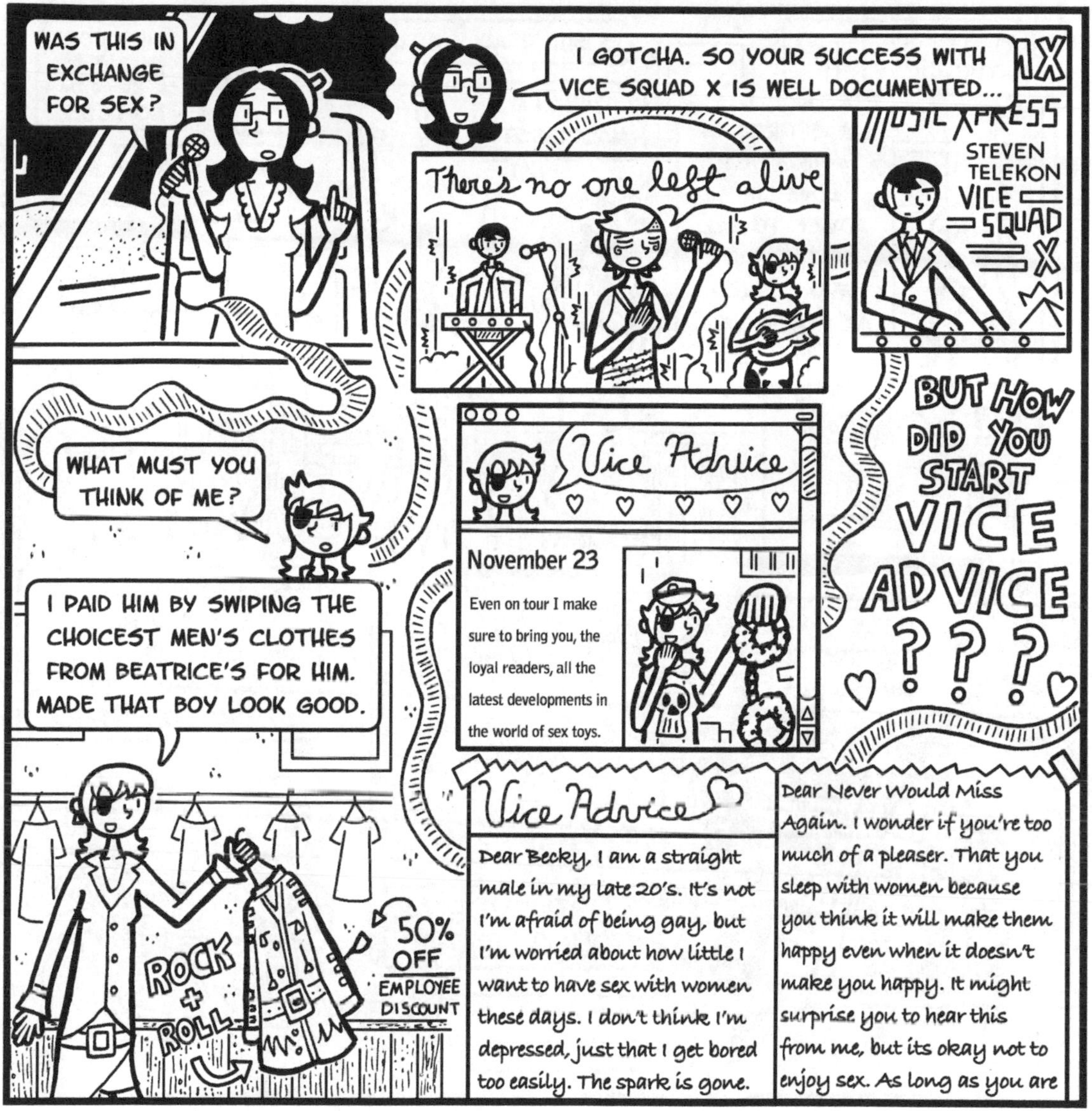
WAS THIS IN EXCHANGE FOR SEX?
I GOTCHA. SO YOUR SUCCESS WITH VICE SQUAD X IS WELL DOCUMENTED...
There's no one left alive
STEVEN TELEKON
VICE SQUAD X
WHAT MUST YOU THINK OF ME?
Vice Advice
November 23
Even on tour I make sure to bring you, the loyal readers, all the latest developments in the world of sex toys.
BUT HOW DID YOU START VICE ADVICE???
I PAID HIM BY SWIPING THE CHOICEST MEN'S CLOTHES FROM BEATRICE'S FOR HIM. MADE THAT BOY LOOK GOOD.
ROCK + ROLL
50% OFF
EMPLOYEE DISCOUNT
Vice Advice
Dear Becky, I am a straight male in my late 20's. It's not I'm afraid of being gay, but I'm worried about how little I want to have sex with women these days. I don't think I'm depressed, just that I get bored too easily. The spark is gone.
Dear Never Would Miss Again. I wonder if you're too much of a pleaser. That you sleep with women because you think it will make them happy even when it doesn't make you happy. It might surprise you to hear this from me, but its okay not to enjoy sex. As long as you are

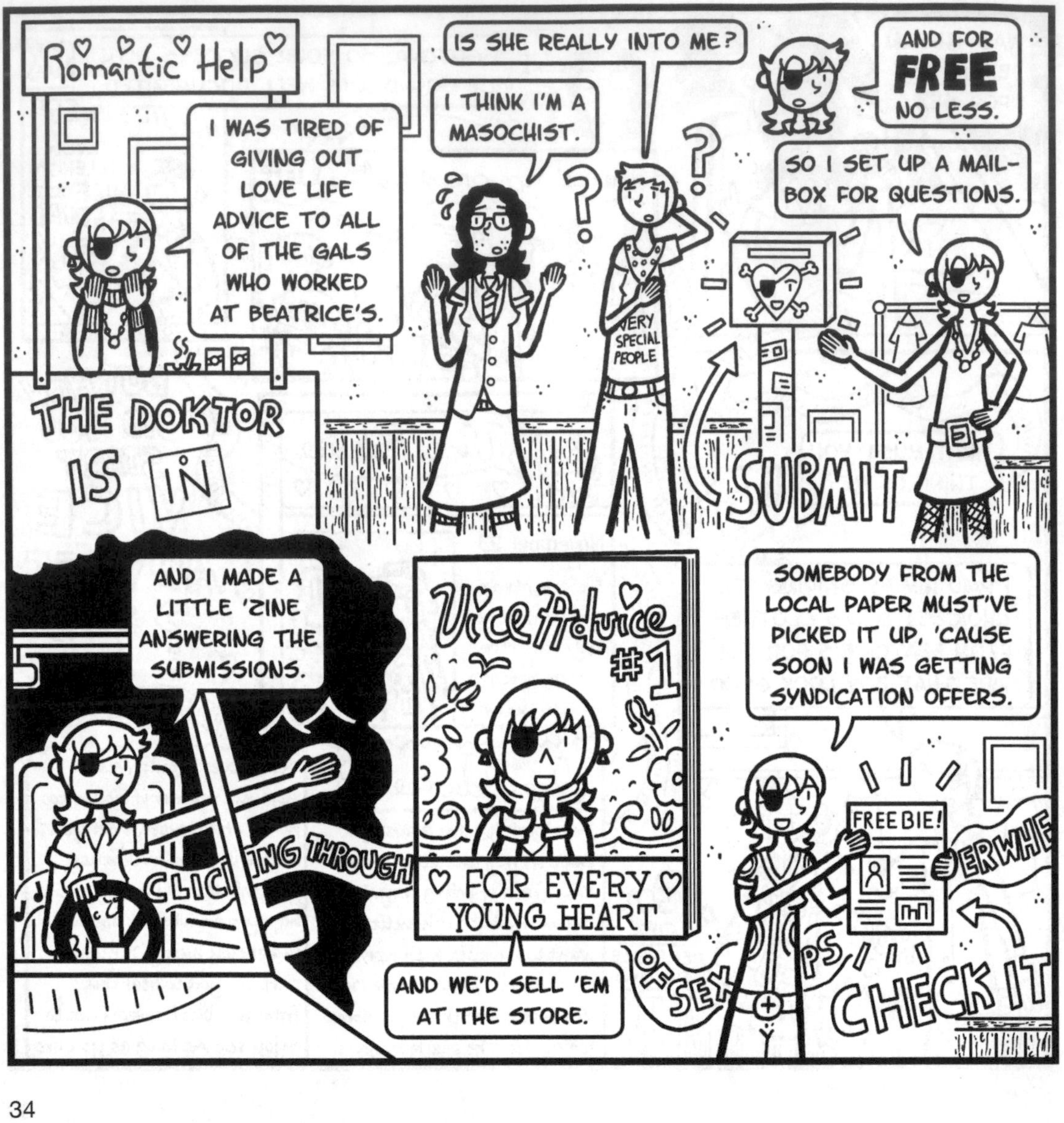
Romantic Help
I WAS TIRED OF GIVING OUT LOVE LIFE ADVICE TO ALL OF THE GALS WHO WORKED AT BEATRICE'S.
THE DOKTOR IS IN
I THINK I'M A MASOCHIST.
IS SHE REALLY INTO ME?
VERY SPECIAL PEOPLE
AND FOR FREE NO LESS.
SO I SET UP A MAIL-BOX FOR QUESTIONS.
SUBMIT
AND I MADE A LITTLE 'ZINE ANSWERING THE SUBMISSIONS.
CLICKING THROUGH
Vice Advice #1
FOR EVERY YOUNG HEART
AND WE'D SELL 'EM AT THE STORE.
SOMEBODY FROM THE LOCAL PAPER MUST'VE PICKED IT UP, 'CAUSE SOON I WAS GETTING SYNDICATION OFFERS.
FREEBIE!
CHECK IT

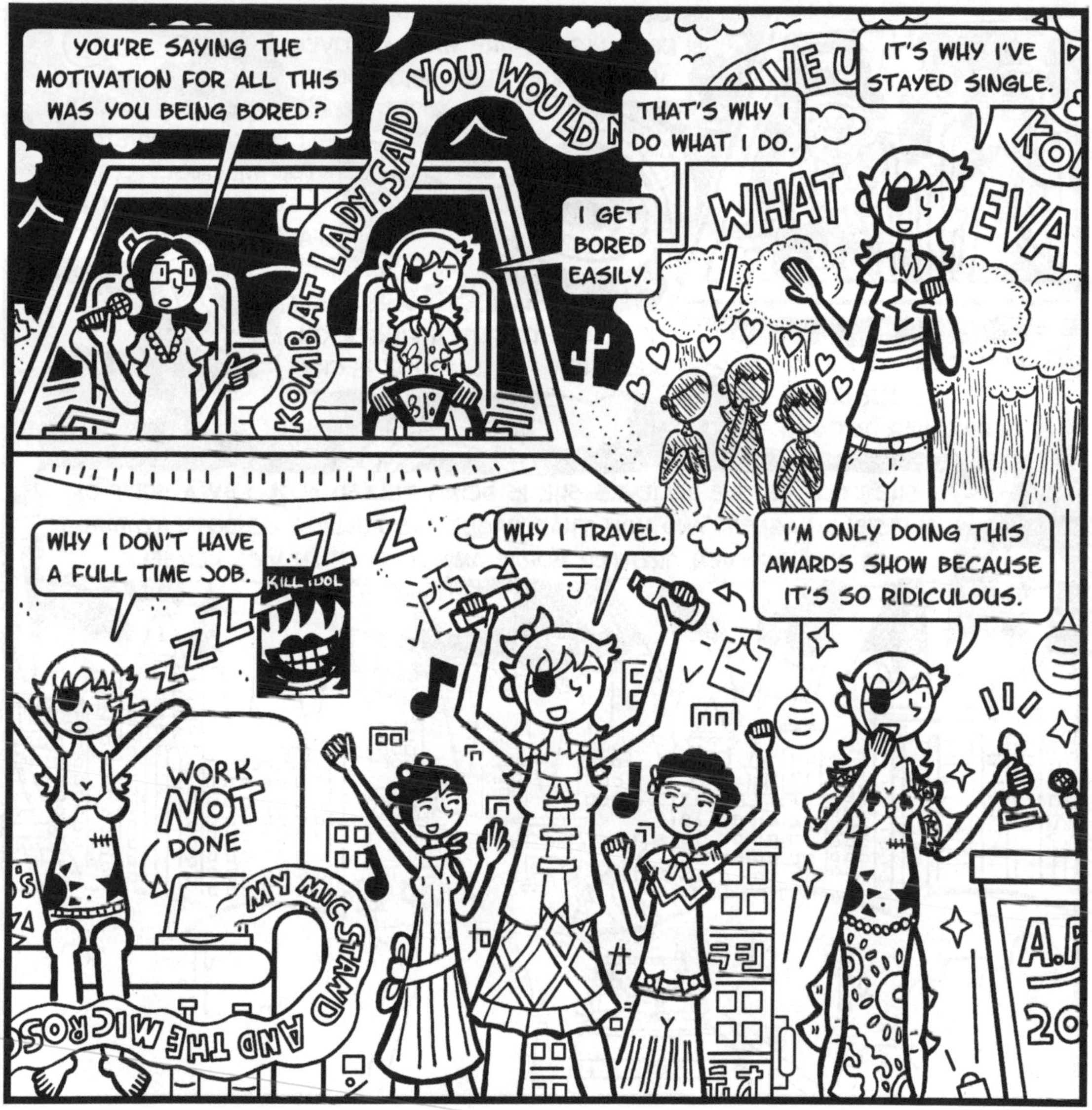
YOU'RE SAYING THE MOTIVATION FOR ALL THIS WAS YOU BEING BORED?
KOMBAT LADY SAID YOU WOULD
I GET BORED EASILY.
THAT'S WHY I DO WHAT I DO.
IT'S WHY I'VE STAYED SINGLE.
WHAT EVA
WHY I DON'T HAVE A FULL TIME JOB.
KILL IDOL
WORK NOT DONE
MY MIC STAND AND THE MICROS
WHY I TRAVEL.
I'M ONLY DOING THIS AWARDS SHOW BECAUSE IT'S SO RIDICULOUS.

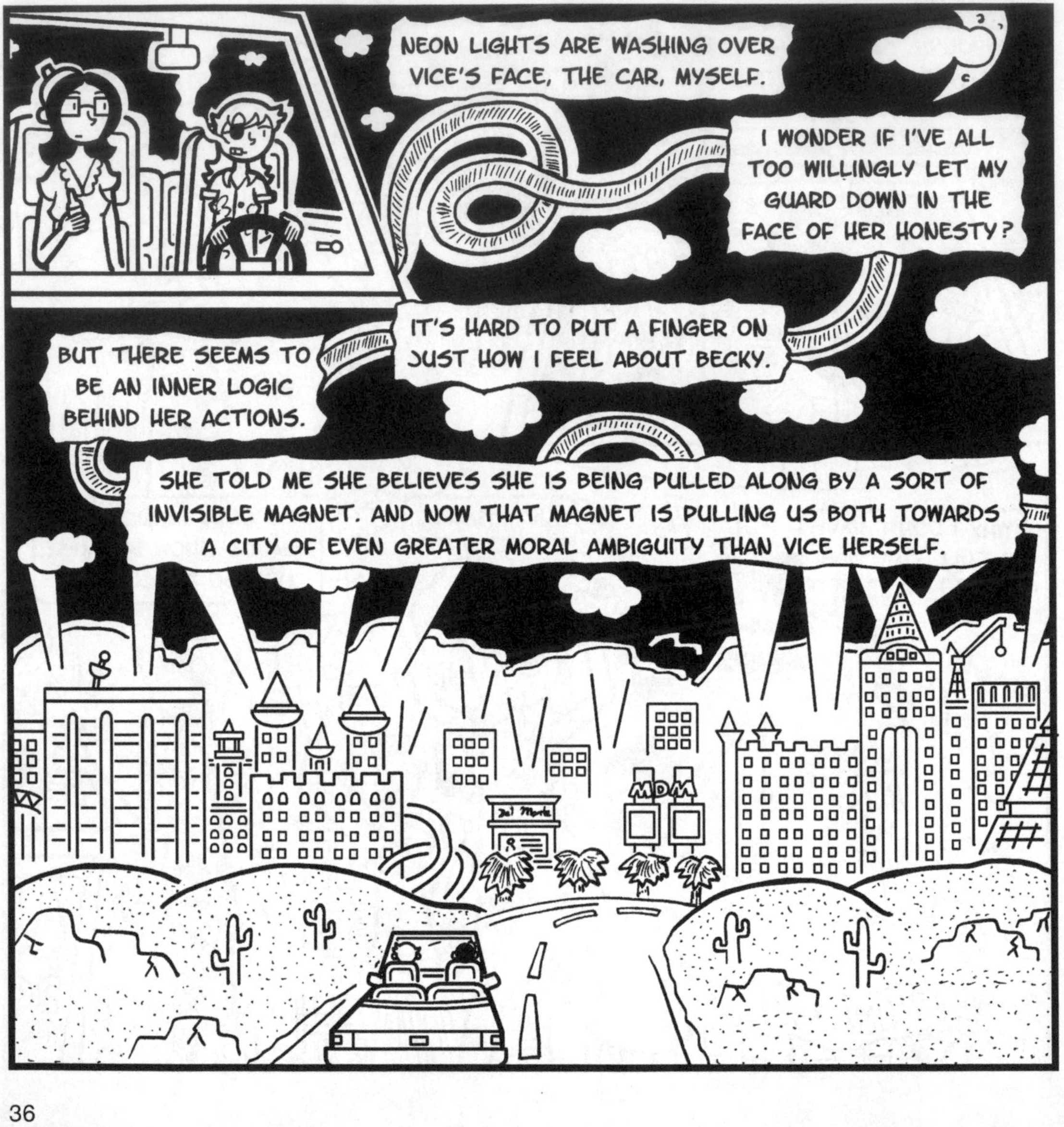
NEON LIGHTS ARE WASHING OVER VICE'S FACE, THE CAR, MYSELF.
I WONDER IF I'VE ALL TOO WILLINGLY LET MY GUARD DOWN IN THE FACE OF HER HONESTY?
IT'S HARD TO PUT A FINGER ON JUST HOW I FEEL ABOUT BECKY.
BUT THERE SEEMS TO BE AN INNER LOGIC BEHIND HER ACTIONS.
SHE TOLD ME SHE BELIEVES SHE IS BEING PULLED ALONG BY A SORT OF INVISIBLE MAGNET. AND NOW THAT MAGNET IS PULLING US BOTH TOWARDS A CITY OF EVEN GREATER MORAL AMBIGUITY THAN VICE HERSELF.
MDM

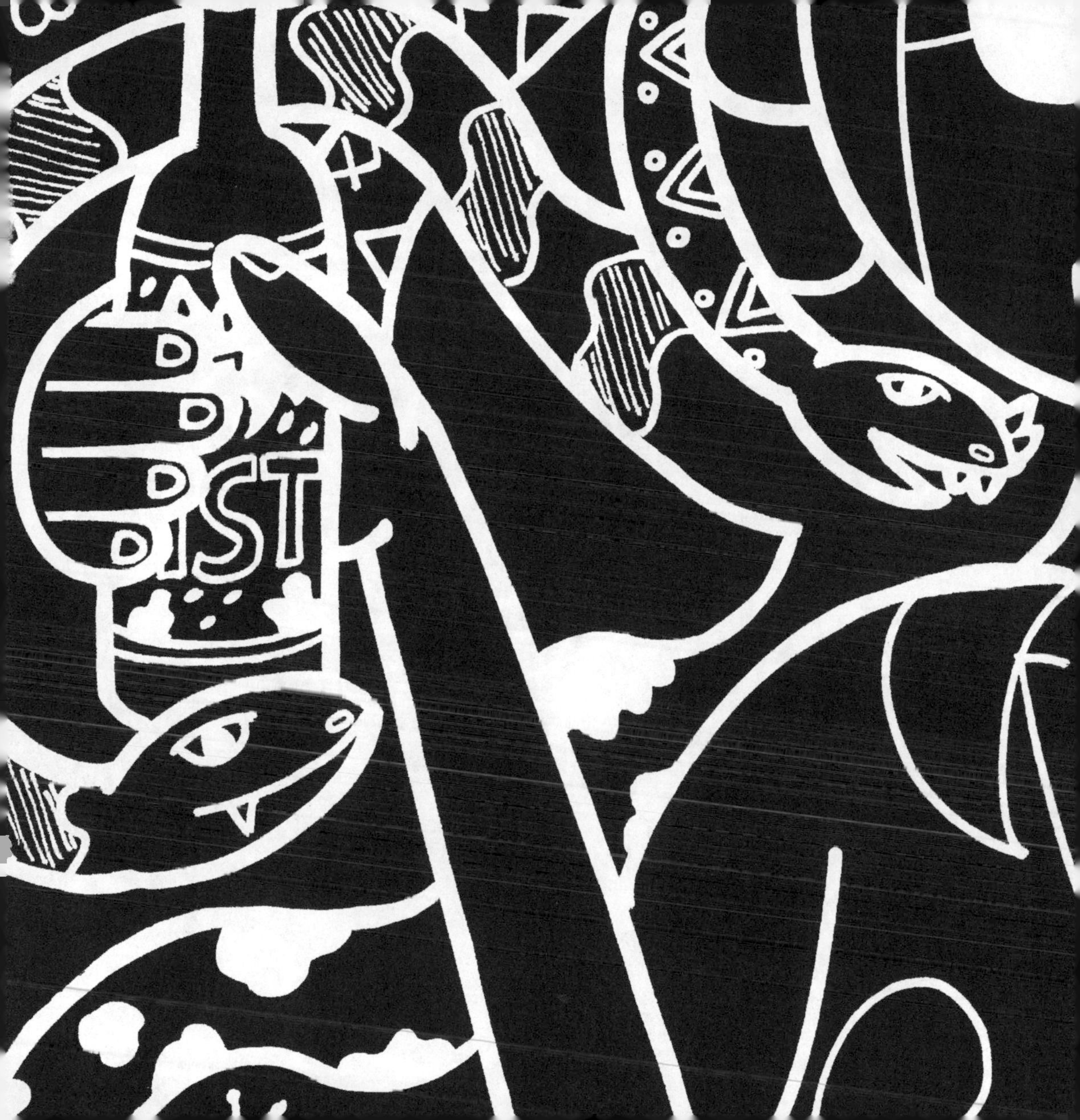
DIST

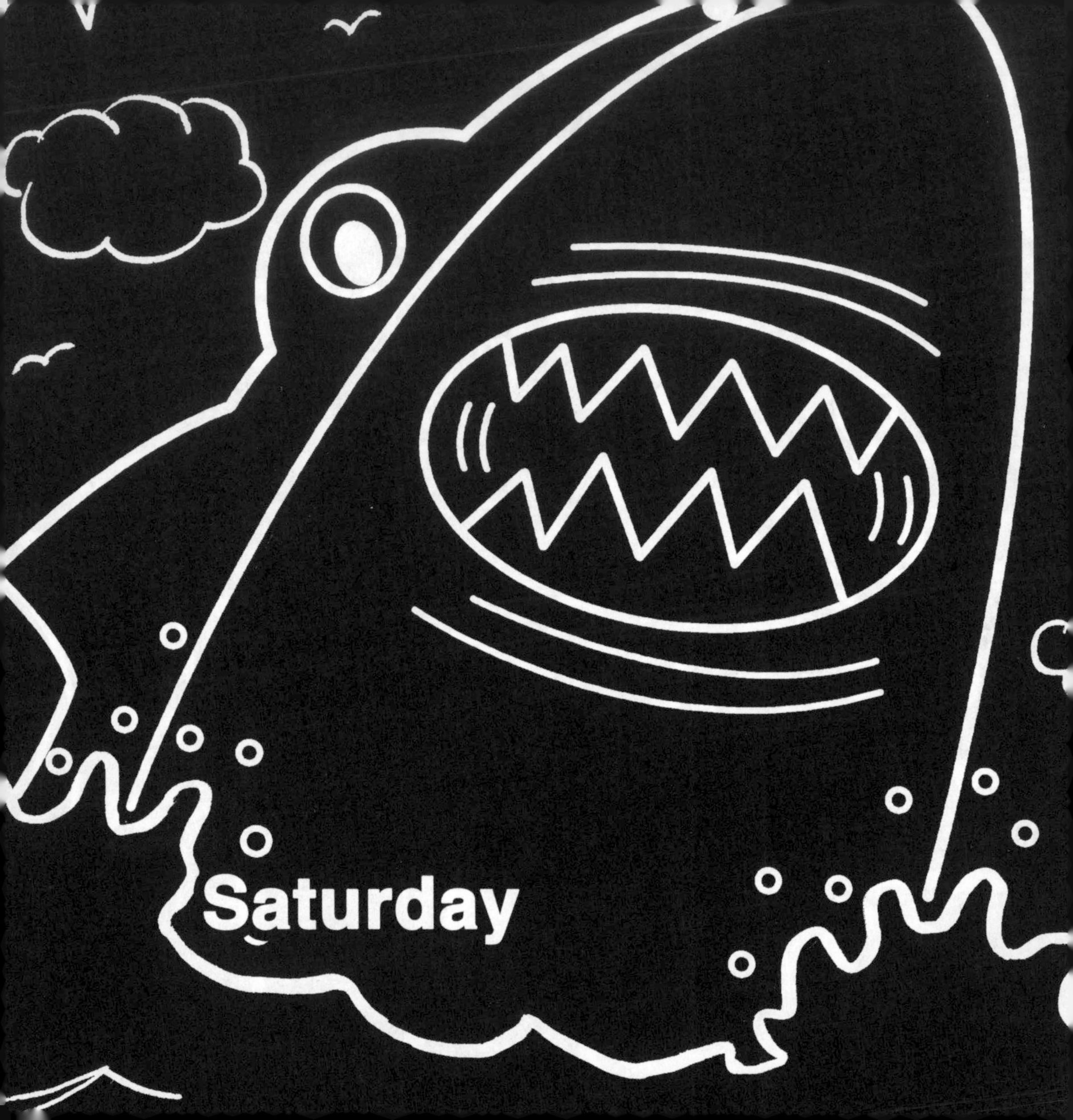
Saturday

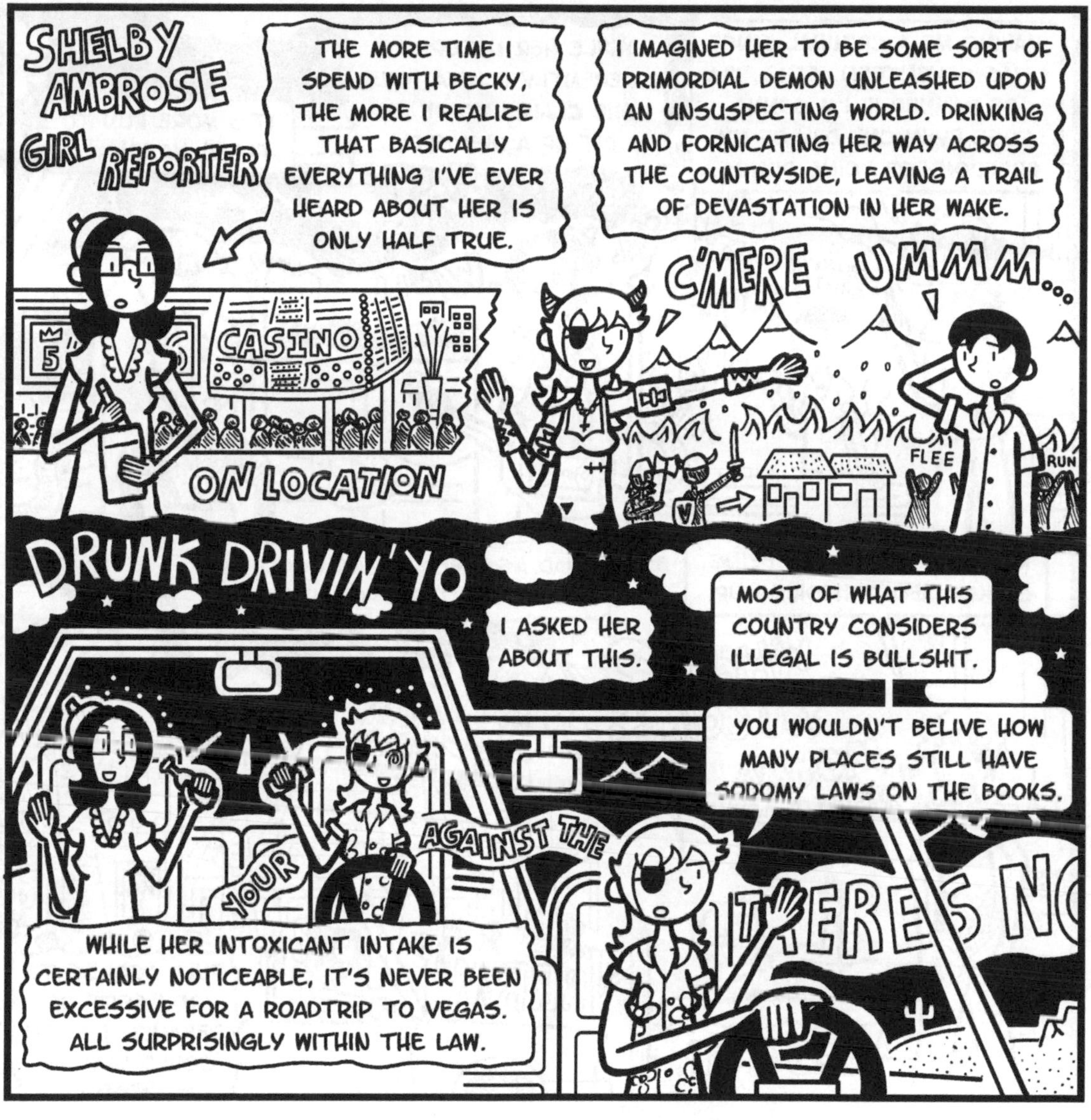
SHELBY AMBROSE GIRL REPORTER
THE MORE TIME I SPEND WITH BECKY, THE MORE I REALIZE THAT BASICALLY EVERYTHING I'VE EVER HEARD ABOUT HER IS ONLY HALF TRUE.
I IMAGINED HER TO BE SOME SORT OF PRIMORDIAL DEMON UNLEASHED UPON AN UNSUSPECTING WORLD. DRINKING AND FORNICATING HER WAY ACROSS THE COUNTRYSIDE, LEAVING A TRAIL OF DEVASTATION IN HER WAKE.
CASINO
C'MERE
UMMM...
FLEE
RUN
ON LOCATION
DRUNK DRIVIN' YO
I ASKED HER ABOUT THIS.
MOST OF WHAT THIS COUNTRY CONSIDERS ILLEGAL IS BULLSHIT.
YOU WOULDN'T BELIVE HOW MANY PLACES STILL HAVE SODOMY LAWS ON THE BOOKS.
YOUR AGAINST THE
THERE'S NO
WHILE HER INTOXICANT INTAKE IS CERTAINLY NOTICEABLE, IT'S NEVER BEEN EXCESSIVE FOR A ROADTRIP TO VEGAS. ALL SURPRISINGLY WITHIN THE LAW.

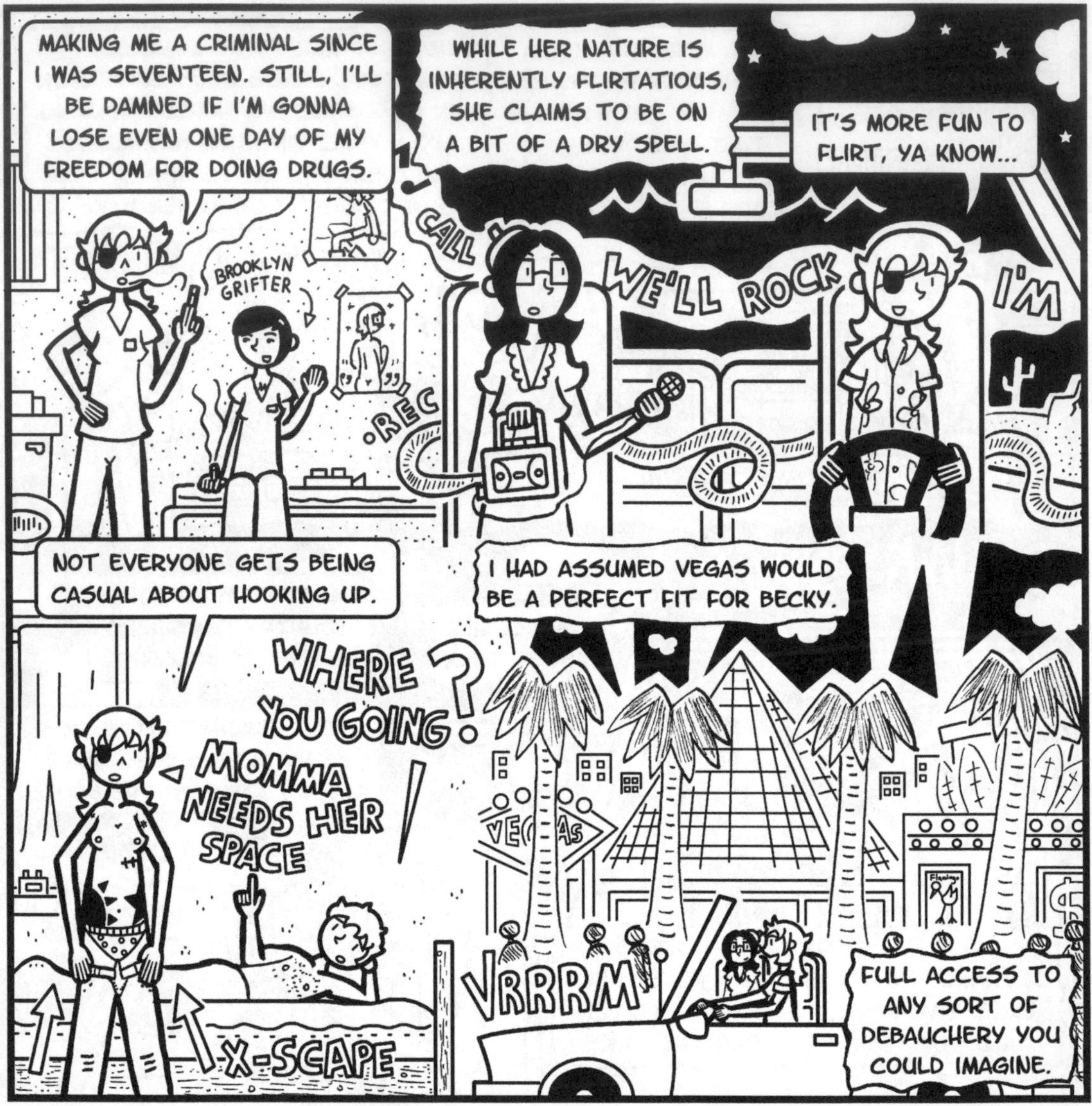
MAKING ME A CRIMINAL SINCE I WAS SEVENTEEN. STILL, I'LL BE DAMNED IF I'M GONNA LOSE EVEN ONE DAY OF MY FREEDOM FOR DOING DRUGS.
BROOKLYN GRIFTER
WHILE HER NATURE IS INHERENTLY FLIRTATIOUS, SHE CLAIMS TO BE ON A BIT OF A DRY SPELL.
CALL
REC
WE'LL ROCK
IT'S MORE FUN TO FLIRT, YA KNOW...
I'M
NOT EVERYONE GETS BEING CASUAL ABOUT HOOKING UP.
WHERE YOU GOING?
MOMMA NEEDS HER SPACE!
X-SCAPE
I HAD ASSUMED VEGAS WOULD BE A PERFECT FIT FOR BECKY.
VEGAS
VRRRM
FULL ACCESS TO ANY SORT OF DEBAUCHERY YOU COULD IMAGINE.

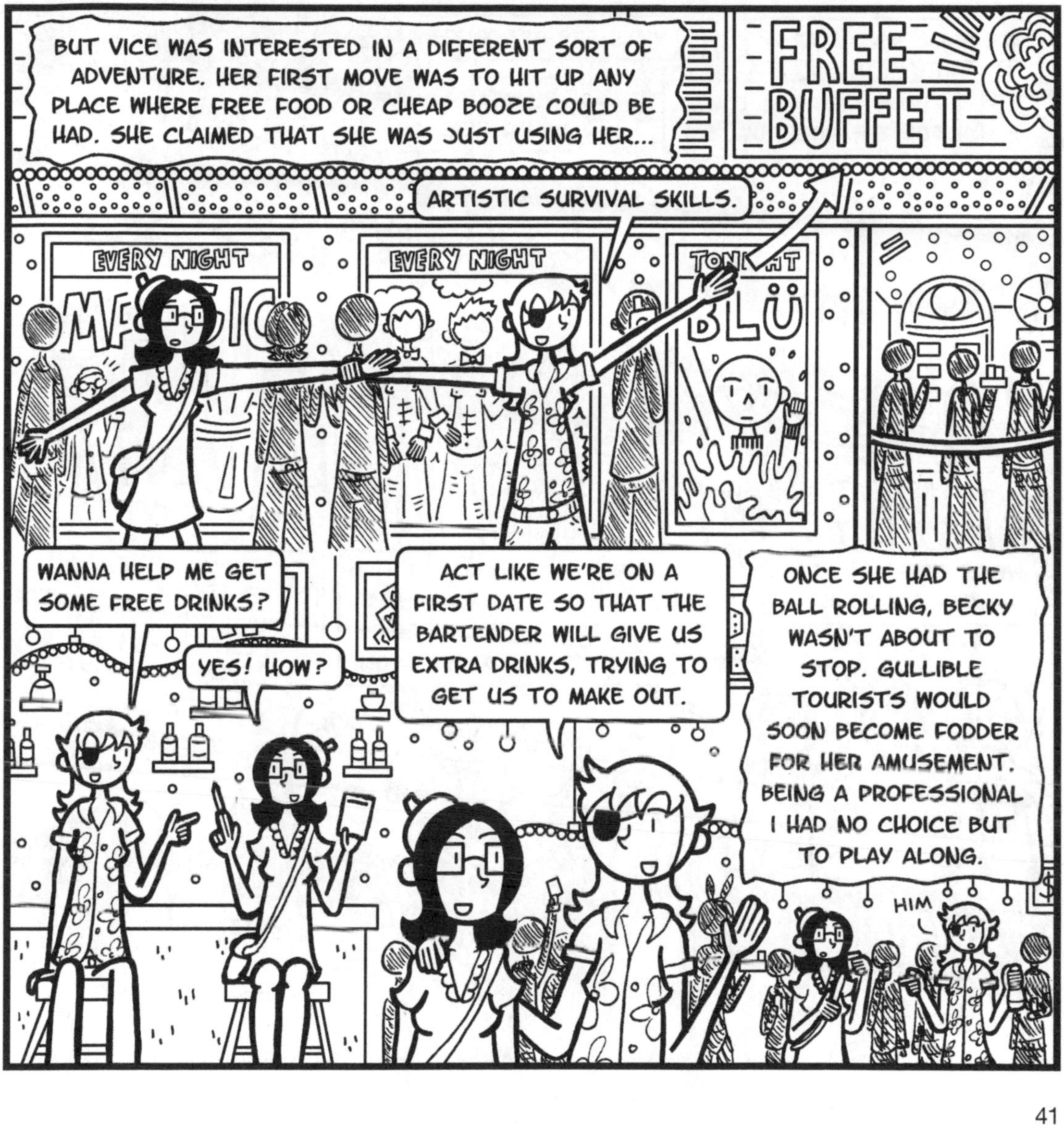
BUT VICE WAS INTERESTED IN A DIFFERENT SORT OF ADVENTURE. HER FIRST MOVE WAS TO HIT UP ANY PLACE WHERE FREE FOOD OR CHEAP BOOZE COULD BE HAD. SHE CLAIMED THAT SHE WAS JUST USING HER...
FREE BUFFET
ARTISTIC SURVIVAL SKILLS.
EVERY NIGHT
EVERY NIGHT
BLÜ
WANNA HELP ME GET SOME FREE DRINKS?
YES! HOW?
ACT LIKE WE'RE ON A FIRST DATE SO THAT THE BARTENDER WILL GIVE US EXTRA DRINKS, TRYING TO GET US TO MAKE OUT.
ONCE SHE HAD THE BALL ROLLING, BECKY WASN'T ABOUT TO STOP. GULLIBLE TOURISTS WOULD SOON BECOME FODDER FOR HER AMUSEMENT. BEING A PROFESSIONAL I HAD NO CHOICE BUT TO PLAY ALONG.
HIM

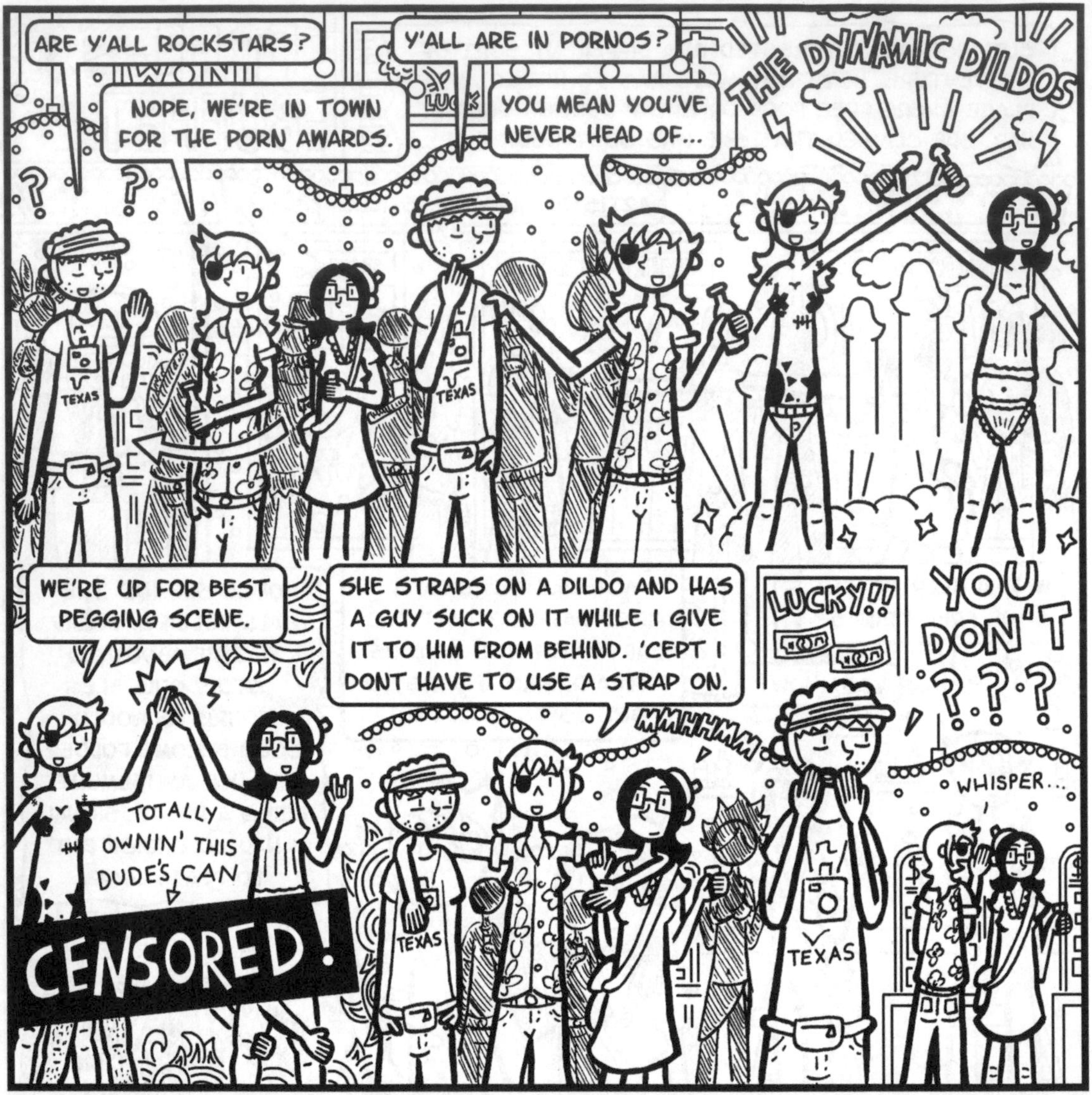
ARE Y'ALL ROCKSTARS?
NOPE, WE'RE IN TOWN FOR THE PORN AWARDS.
Y'ALL ARE IN PORNOS?
YOU MEAN YOU'VE NEVER HEAD OF...
THE DYNAMIC DILDOS
LUCK
WE'RE UP FOR BEST PEGGING SCENE.
TOTALLY OWNIN' THIS DUDE'S CAN
CENSORED!
SHE STRAPS ON A DILDO AND HAS A GUY SUCK ON IT WHILE I GIVE IT TO HIM FROM BEHIND. 'CEPT I DONT HAVE TO USE A STRAP ON.
MMHHMM
LUCKY!!
YOU DON'T ???
WHISPER...
TEXAS

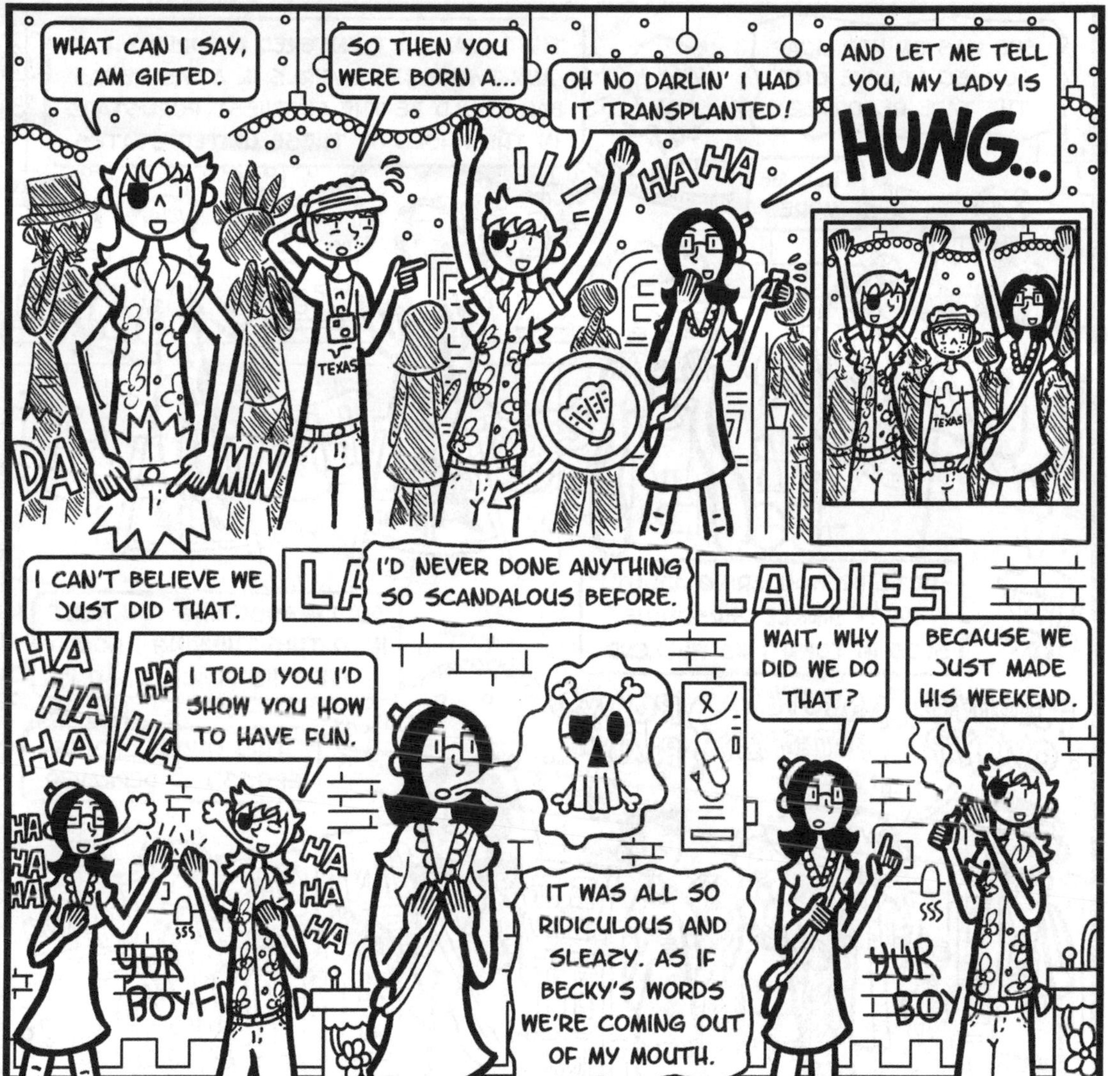
WHAT CAN I SAY, I AM GIFTED.
DA MN
SO THEN YOU WERE BORN A...
OH NO DARLIN' I HAD IT TRANSPLANTED!
HAHA
AND LET ME TELL YOU, MY LADY IS HUNG...
TEXAS
LADIES
I CAN'T BELIEVE WE JUST DID THAT.
HA HA HA
I TOLD YOU I'D SHOW YOU HOW TO HAVE FUN.
HA HA HA
I'D NEVER DONE ANYTHING SO SCANDALOUS BEFORE.
IT WAS ALL SO RIDICULOUS AND SLEAZY. AS IF BECKY'S WORDS WE'RE COMING OUT OF MY MOUTH.
WAIT, WHY DID WE DO THAT?
BECAUSE WE JUST MADE HIS WEEKEND.
YUR BOYFR D
YUR BOY

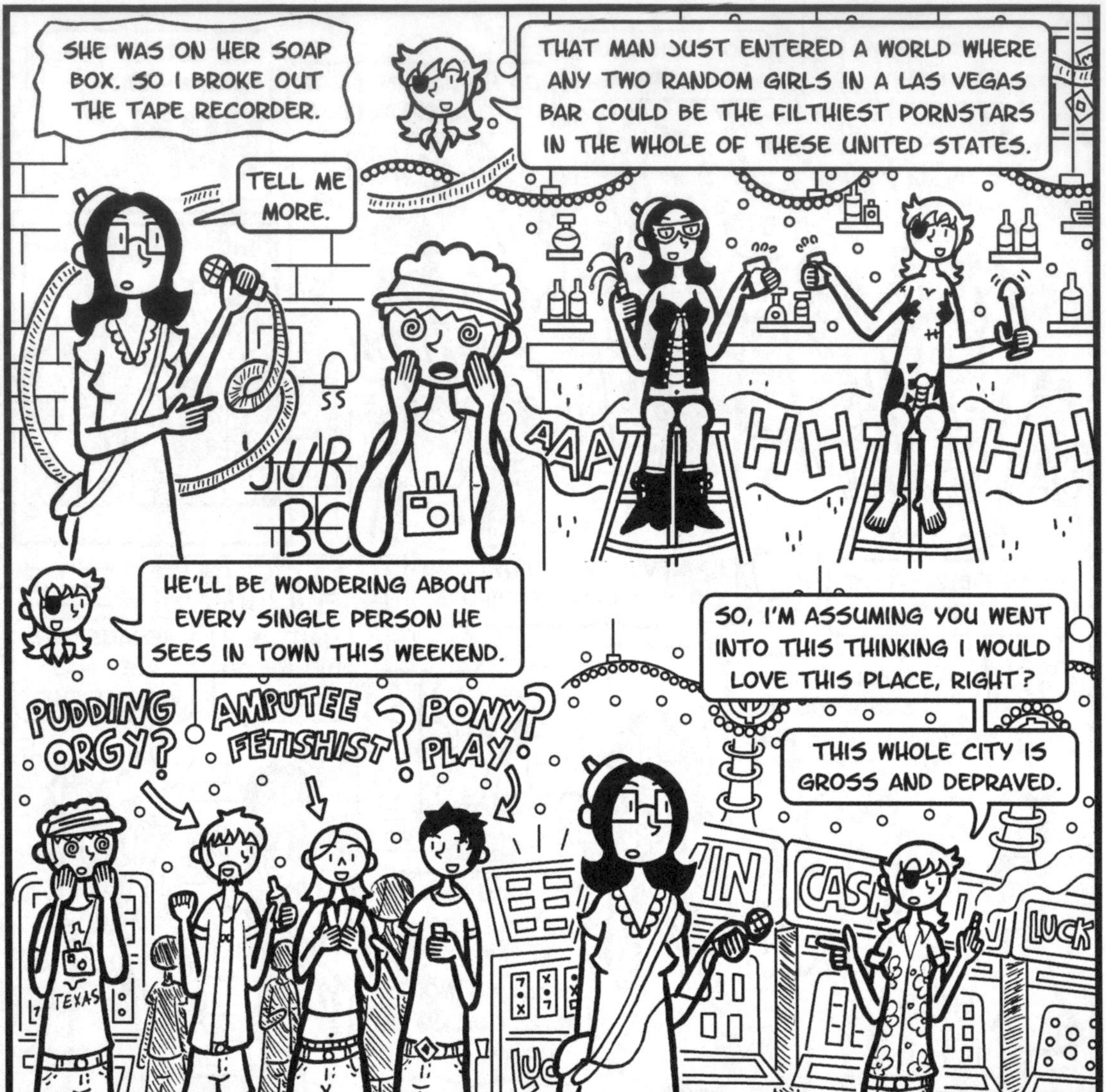
SHE WAS ON HER SOAP BOX. SO I BROKE OUT THE TAPE RECORDER.
THAT MAN JUST ENTERED A WORLD WHERE ANY TWO RANDOM GIRLS IN A LAS VEGAS BAR COULD BE THE FILTHIEST PORNSTARS IN THE WHOLE OF THESE UNITED STATES.
TELL ME MORE.
AAAHHHH
HE'LL BE WONDERING ABOUT EVERY SINGLE PERSON HE SEES IN TOWN THIS WEEKEND.
PUDDING ORGY?
AMPUTEE FETISHIST?
PONY PLAY?
TEXAS
SO, I'M ASSUMING YOU WENT INTO THIS THINKING I WOULD LOVE THIS PLACE, RIGHT?
THIS WHOLE CITY IS GROSS AND DEPRAVED.
WIN
CASH
LUCK

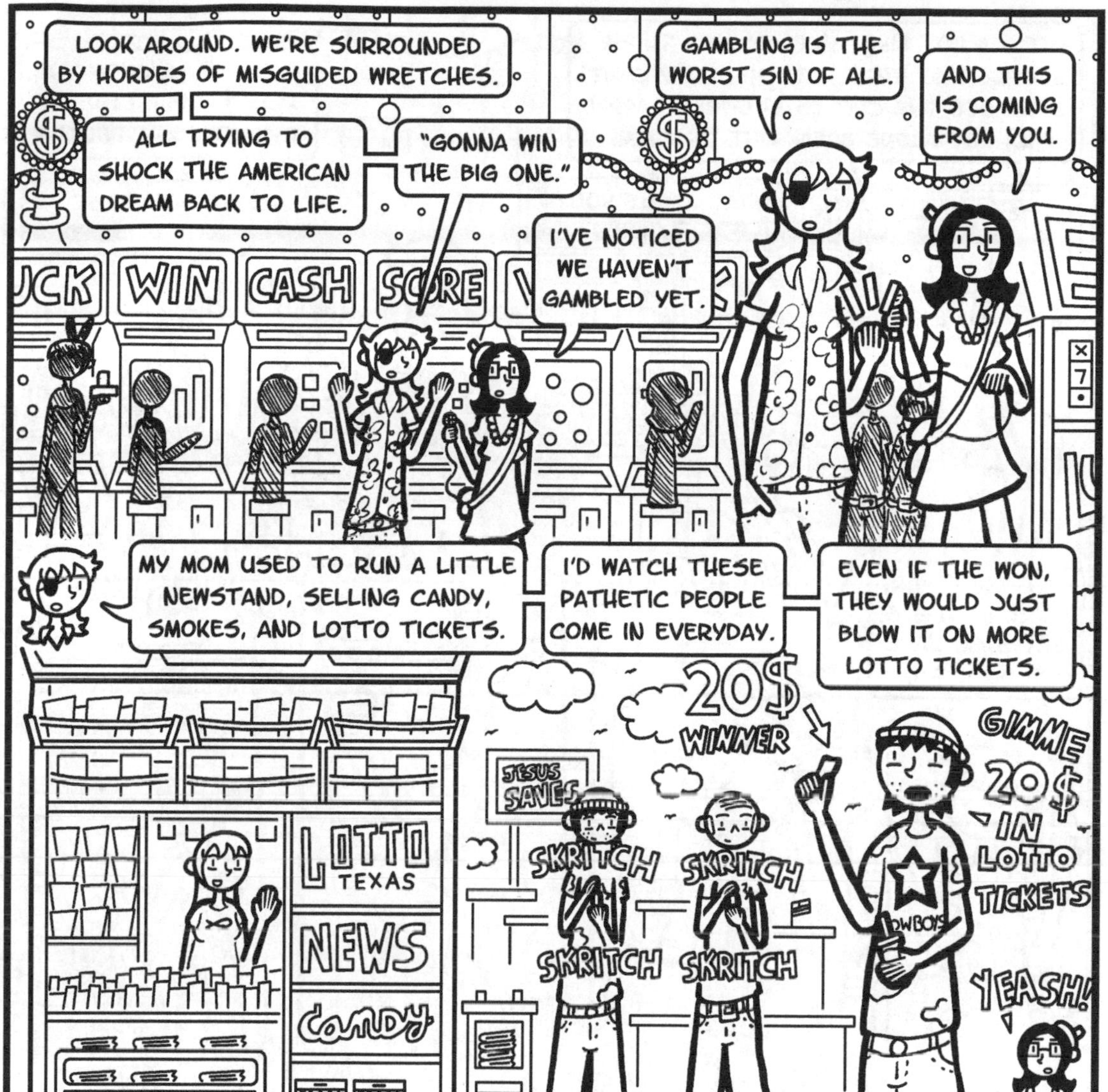

LOOK AROUND. WE'RE SURROUNDED BY HORDES OF MISGUIDED WRETCHES.
ALL TRYING TO SHOCK THE AMERICAN DREAM BACK TO LIFE.
"GONNA WIN THE BIG ONE."
GAMBLING IS THE WORST SIN OF ALL.
AND THIS IS COMING FROM YOU.
I'VE NOTICED WE HAVEN'T GAMBLED YET.
WIN
CASH
SCORE
MY MOM USED TO RUN A LITTLE NEWSTAND, SELLING CANDY, SMOKES, AND LOTTO TICKETS.
I'D WATCH THESE PATHETIC PEOPLE COME IN EVERYDAY.
EVEN IF THE WON, THEY WOULD JUST BLOW IT ON MORE LOTTO TICKETS.
20$ WINNER
GIMME 20$ IN LOTTO TICKETS
JESUS SAVES
LOTTO TEXAS
NEWS
Candy
SKRITCH
SKRITCH
SKRITCH
SKRITCH
YEASH!

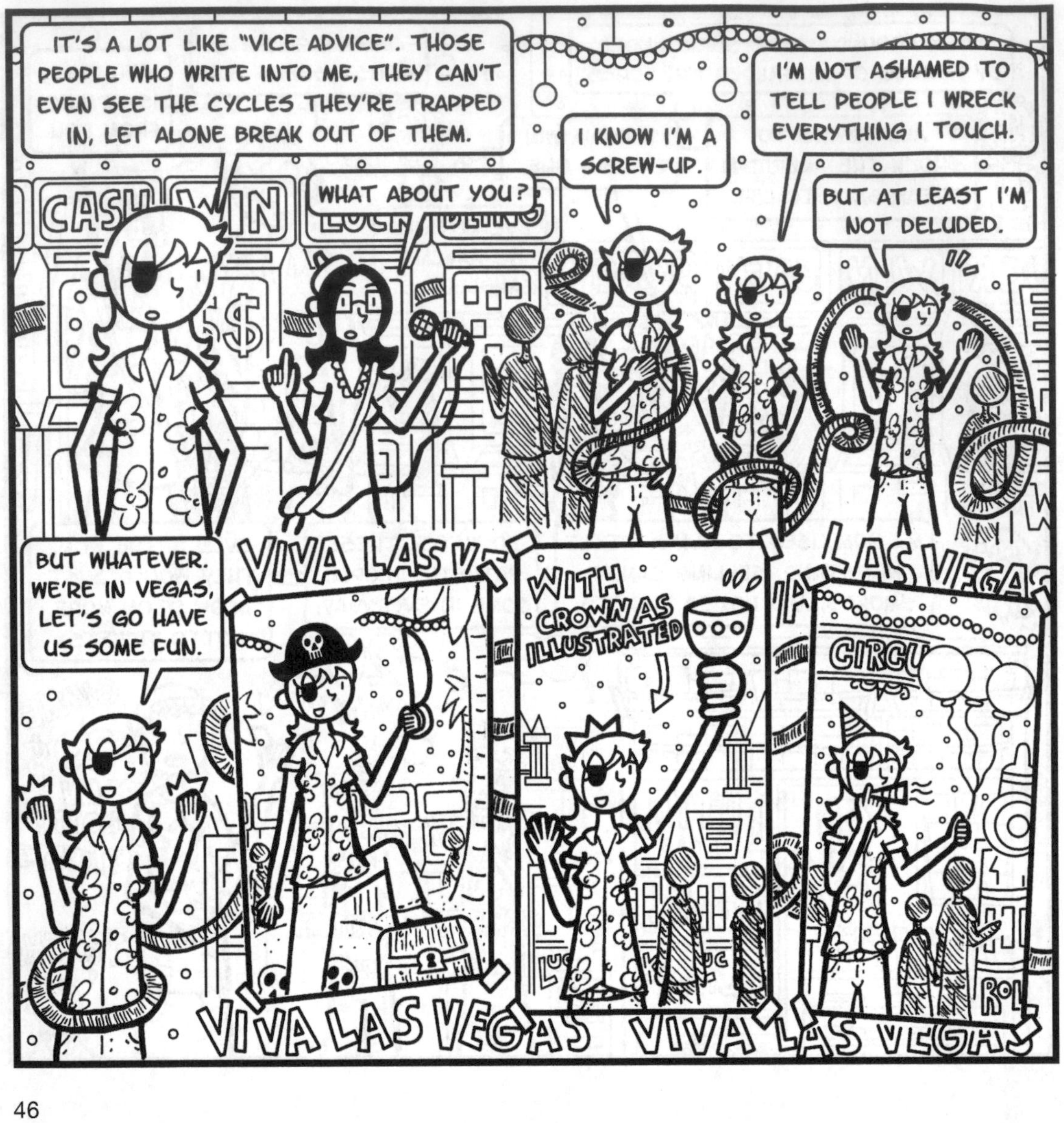
IT'S A LOT LIKE "VICE ADVICE". THOSE PEOPLE WHO WRITE INTO ME, THEY CAN'T EVEN SEE THE CYCLES THEY'RE TRAPPED IN, LET ALONE BREAK OUT OF THEM.
WHAT ABOUT YOU?
I KNOW I'M A SCREW-UP.
I'M NOT ASHAMED TO TELL PEOPLE I WRECK EVERYTHING I TOUCH.
BUT AT LEAST I'M NOT DELUDED.
CASH
WIN
BUT WHATEVER. WE'RE IN VEGAS, LET'S GO HAVE US SOME FUN.
WITH CROWN AS ILLUSTRATED
VIVA LAS VEGAS
VIVA LAS VEGAS

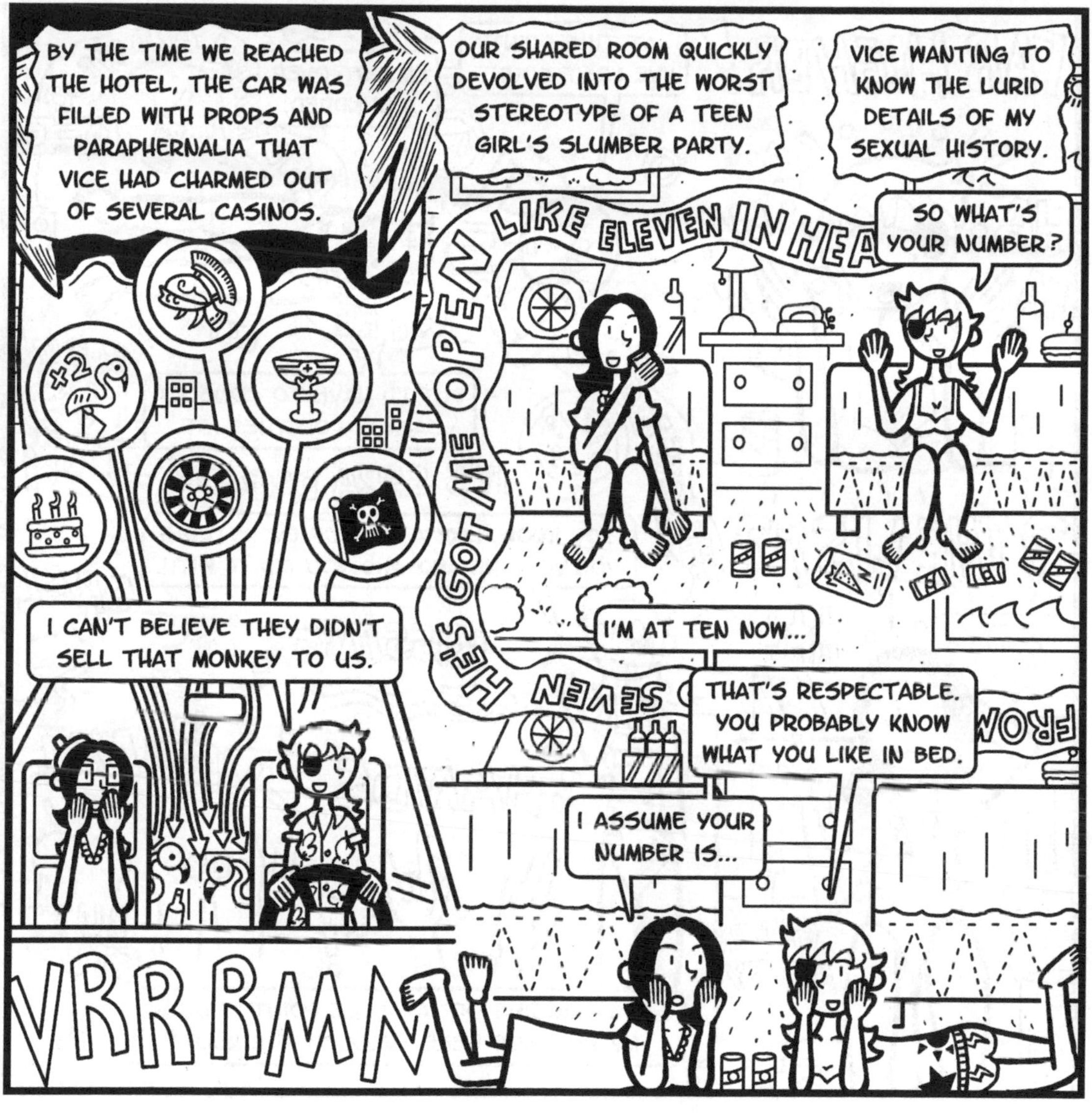
BY THE TIME WE REACHED THE HOTEL, THE CAR WAS FILLED WITH PROPS AND PARAPHERNALIA THAT VICE HAD CHARMED OUT OF SEVERAL CASINOS.
I CAN'T BELIEVE THEY DIDN'T SELL THAT MONKEY TO US.
VRRRMN
OUR SHARED ROOM QUICKLY DEVOLVED INTO THE WORST STEREOTYPE OF A TEEN GIRL'S SLUMBER PARTY.
VICE WANTING TO KNOW THE LURID DETAILS OF MY SEXUAL HISTORY.
HE'S GOT ME OPEN LIKE ELEVEN IN
SO WHAT'S YOUR NUMBER?
I'M AT TEN NOW...
SEVEN
FROM
THAT'S RESPECTABLE. YOU PROBABLY KNOW WHAT YOU LIKE IN BED.
I ASSUME YOUR NUMBER IS...

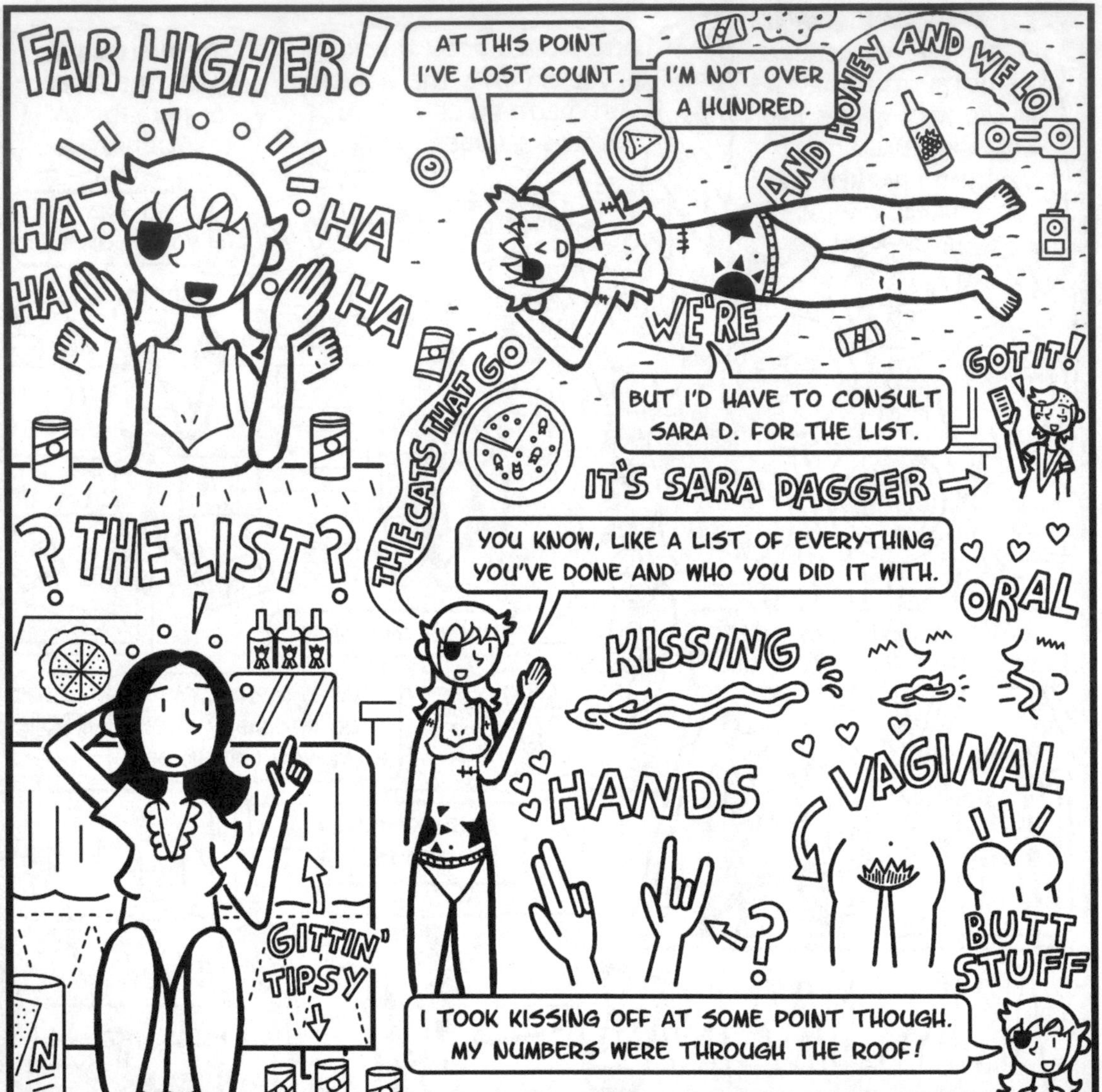
FAR HIGHER!
HA HA HA HA
AT THIS POINT I'VE LOST COUNT.
I'M NOT OVER A HUNDRED.
BUT I'D HAVE TO CONSULT SARA D. FOR THE LIST.
GOT IT!
IT'S SARA DAGGER
WE'RE THE CATS THAT GO AND HONEY AND WE LO
?THE LIST?
YOU KNOW, LIKE A LIST OF EVERYTHING YOU'VE DONE AND WHO YOU DID IT WITH.
KISSING
ORAL
HANDS
VAGINAL
BUTT STUFF
GITTIN' TIPSY
I TOOK KISSING OFF AT SOME POINT THOUGH. MY NUMBERS WERE THROUGH THE ROOF!

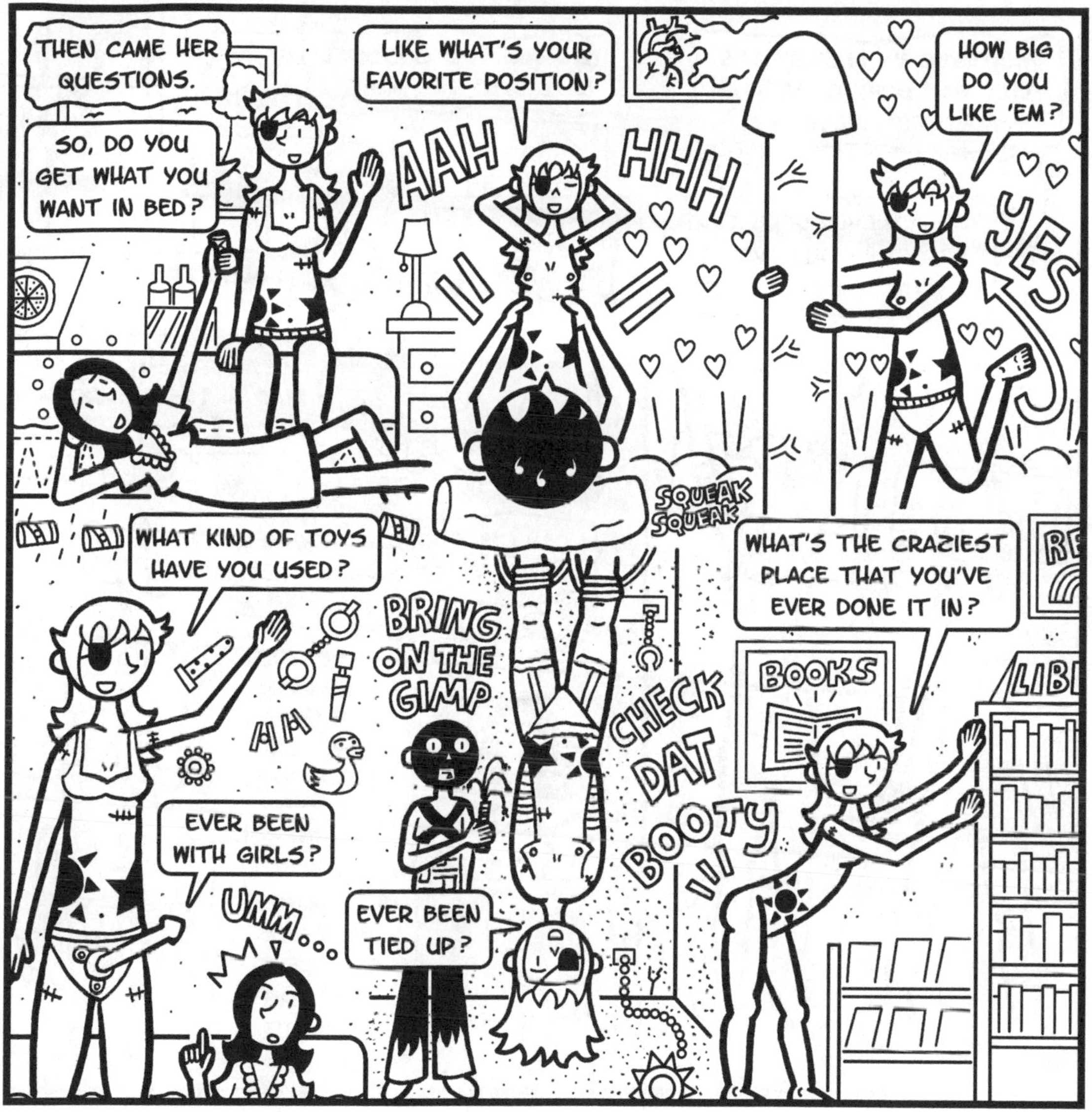
THEN CAME HER QUESTIONS.
SO, DO YOU GET WHAT YOU WANT IN BED?
LIKE WHAT'S YOUR FAVORITE POSITION?
AAH
HHH
HOW BIG DO YOU LIKE 'EM?
YES
SQUEAK SQUEAK
WHAT KIND OF TOYS HAVE YOU USED?
BRING ON THE GIMP
HA
WHAT'S THE CRAZIEST PLACE THAT YOU'VE EVER DONE IT IN?
BOOKS
CHECK DAT BOOTY
EVER BEEN WITH GIRLS?
UMM...
EVER BEEN TIED UP?

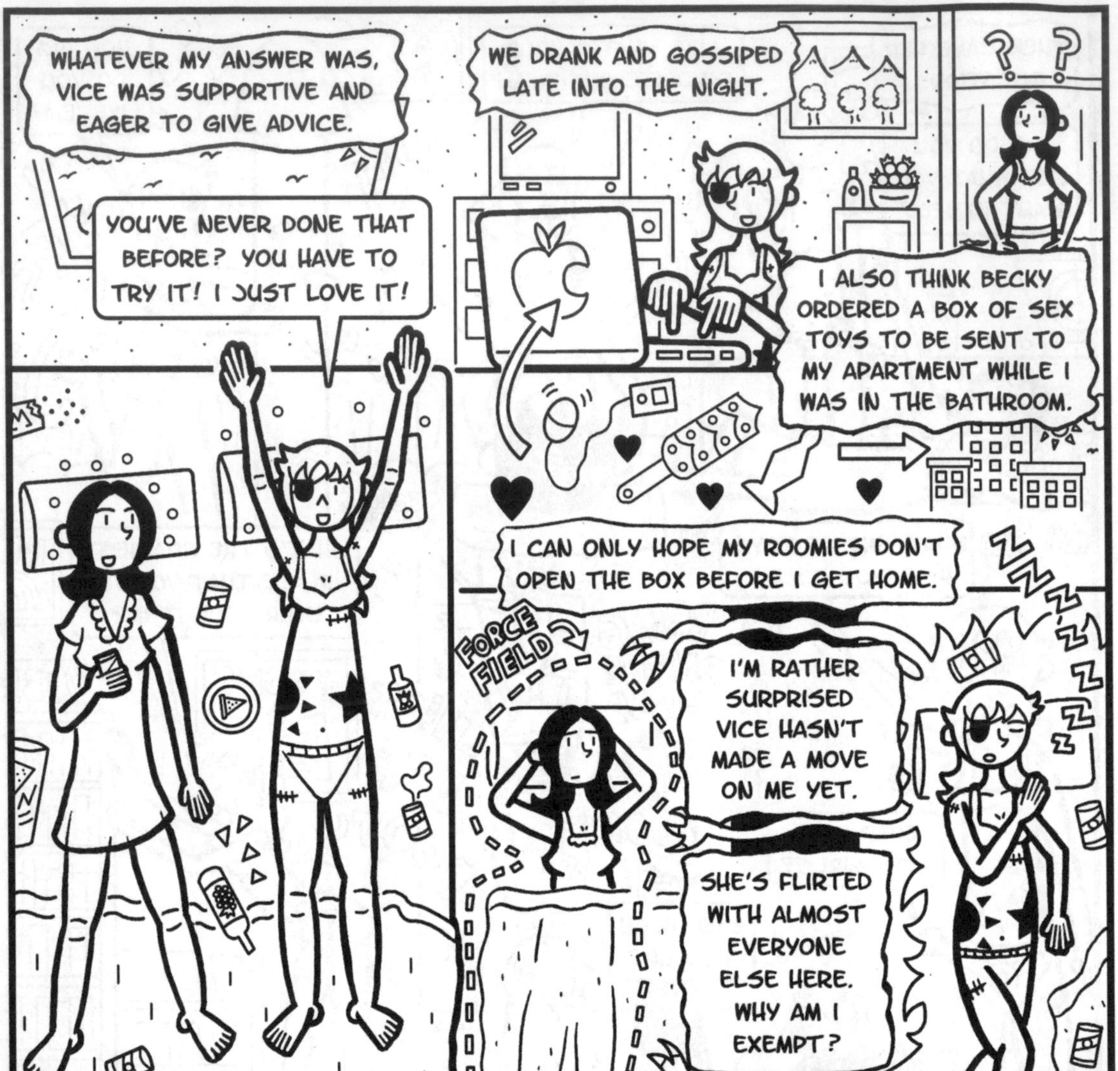
WHATEVER MY ANSWER WAS, VICE WAS SUPPORTIVE AND EAGER TO GIVE ADVICE.
YOU'VE NEVER DONE THAT BEFORE? YOU HAVE TO TRY IT! I JUST LOVE IT!
WE DRANK AND GOSSIPED LATE INTO THE NIGHT.
I ALSO THINK BECKY ORDERED A BOX OF SEX TOYS TO BE SENT TO MY APARTMENT WHILE I WAS IN THE BATHROOM.
I CAN ONLY HOPE MY ROOMIES DON'T OPEN THE BOX BEFORE I GET HOME.
FORCE FIELD
I'M RATHER SURPRISED VICE HASN'T MADE A MOVE ON ME YET.
SHE'S FLIRTED WITH ALMOST EVERYONE ELSE HERE. WHY AM I EXEMPT?
ZZZ

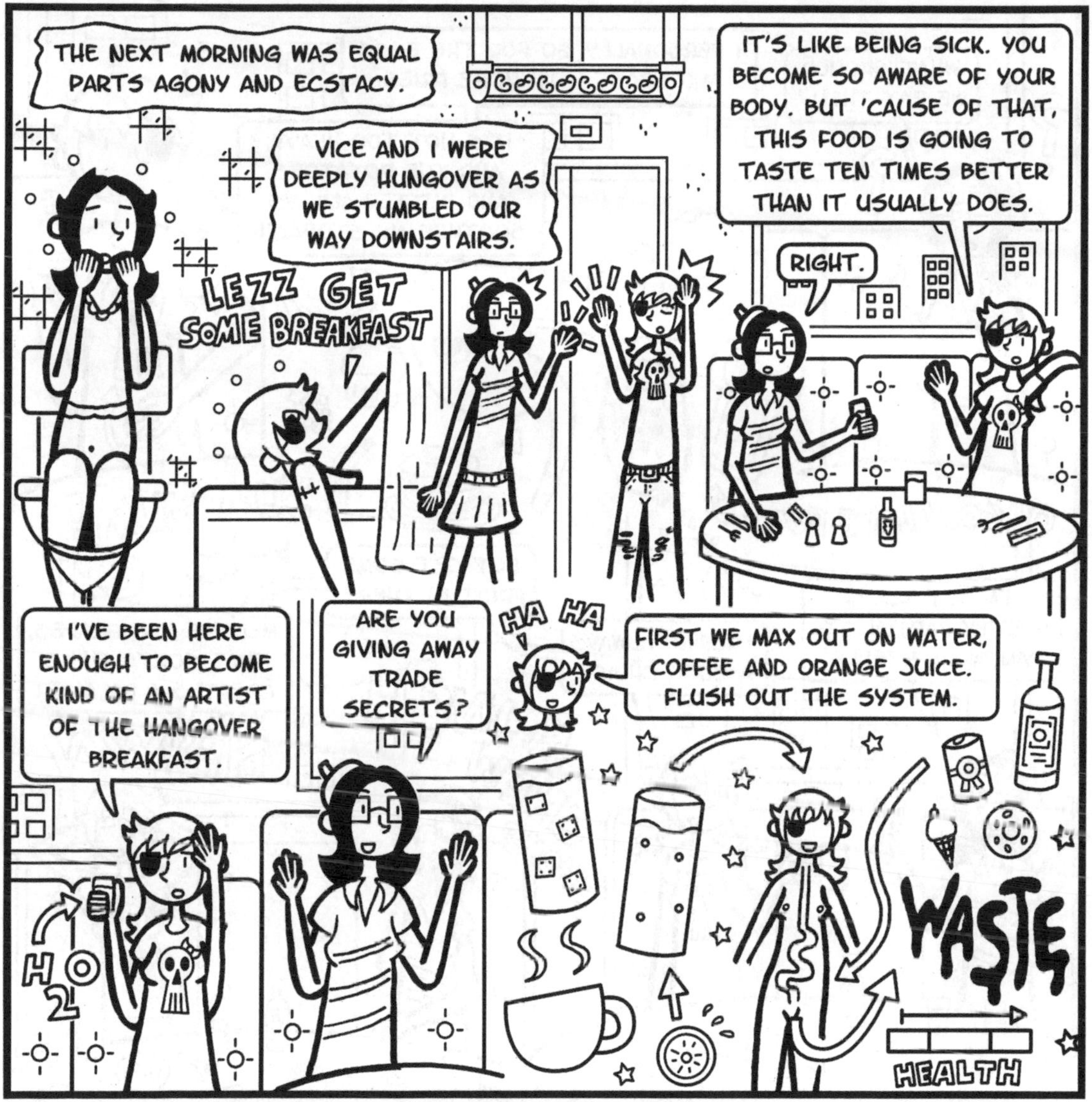

THE NEXT MORNING WAS EQUAL PARTS AGONY AND ECSTACY.
VICE AND I WERE DEEPLY HUNGOVER AS WE STUMBLED OUR WAY DOWNSTAIRS.
LEZZ GET SOME BREAKFAST!
IT'S LIKE BEING SICK. YOU BECOME SO AWARE OF YOUR BODY. BUT 'CAUSE OF THAT, THIS FOOD IS GOING TO TASTE TEN TIMES BETTER THAN IT USUALLY DOES.
RIGHT.
I'VE BEEN HERE ENOUGH TO BECOME KIND OF AN ARTIST OF THE HANGOVER BREAKFAST.
ARE YOU GIVING AWAY TRADE SECRETS?
HA HA!
FIRST WE MAX OUT ON WATER, COFFEE AND ORANGE JUICE. FLUSH OUT THE SYSTEM.
H_2O
WASTE
HEALTH

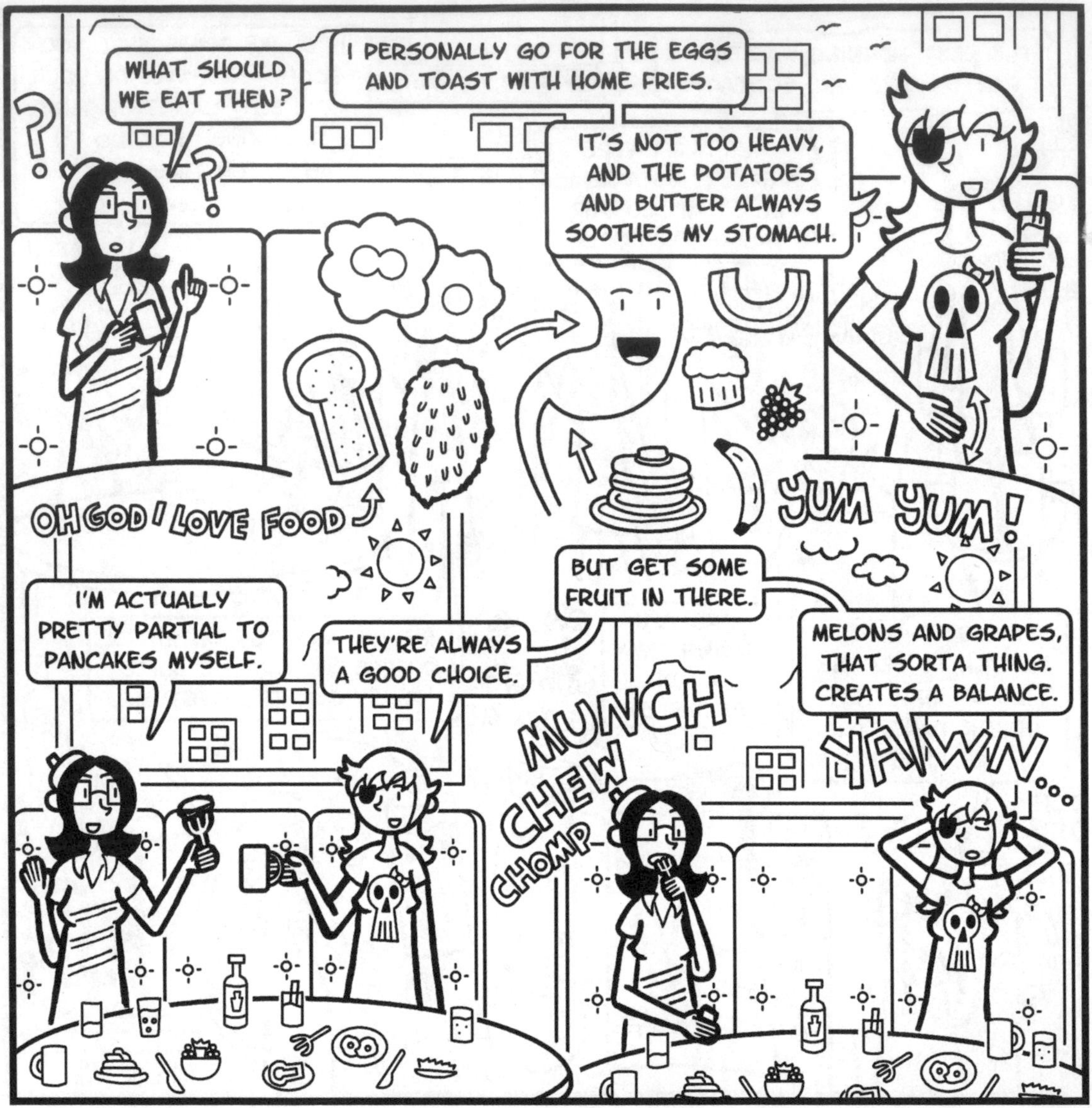
WHAT SHOULD WE EAT THEN?
I PERSONALLY GO FOR THE EGGS AND TOAST WITH HOME FRIES.
IT'S NOT TOO HEAVY, AND THE POTATOES AND BUTTER ALWAYS SOOTHES MY STOMACH.
OH GOD I LOVE FOOD
YUM YUM!
I'M ACTUALLY PRETTY PARTIAL TO PANCAKES MYSELF.
THEY'RE ALWAYS A GOOD CHOICE.
BUT GET SOME FRUIT IN THERE.
MELONS AND GRAPES, THAT SORTA THING. CREATES A BALANCE.
MUNCH
CHEW
CHOMP
YAWN...

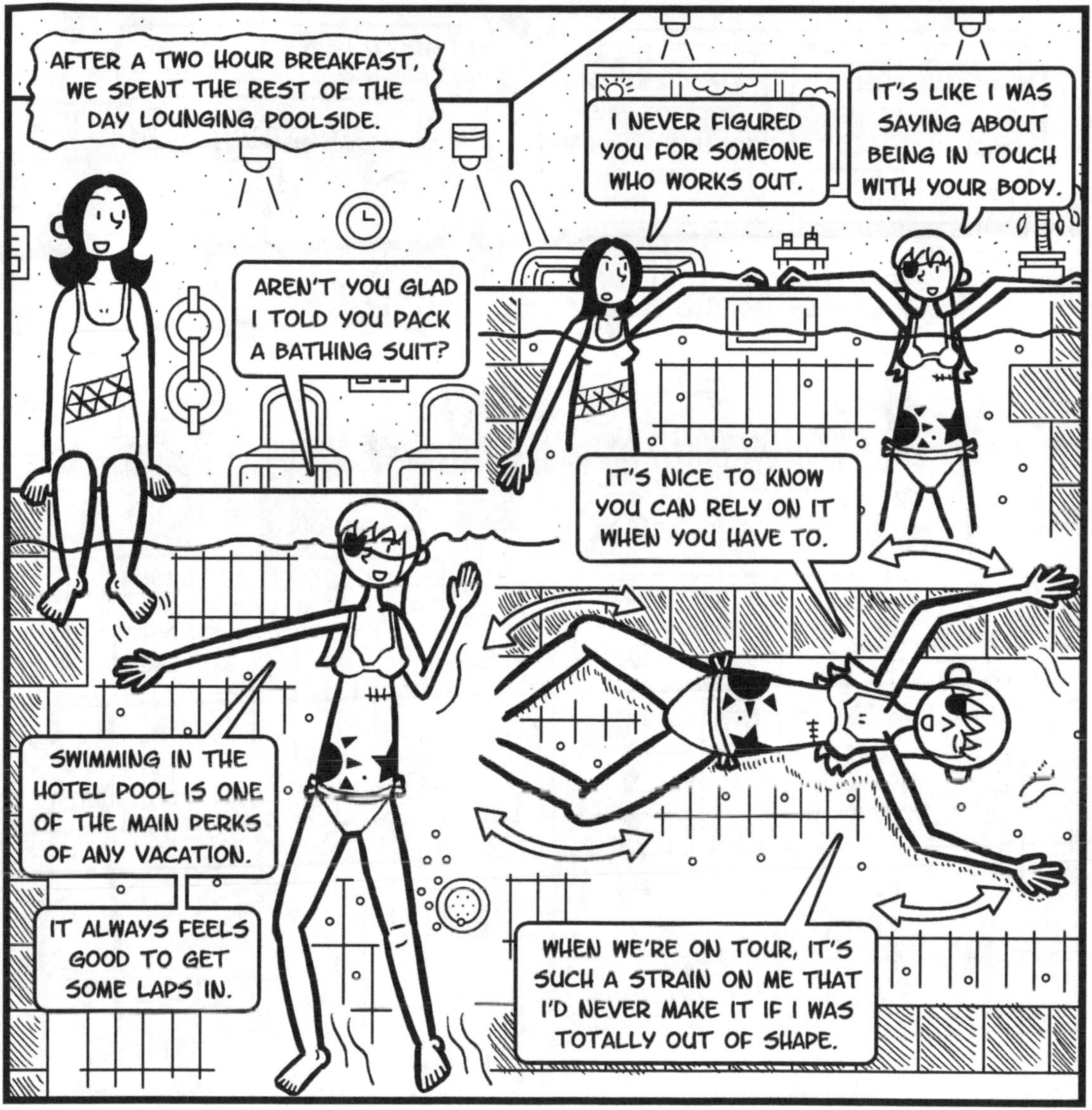
AFTER A TWO HOUR BREAKFAST, WE SPENT THE REST OF THE DAY LOUNGING POOLSIDE.
AREN'T YOU GLAD I TOLD YOU PACK A BATHING SUIT?
I NEVER FIGURED YOU FOR SOMEONE WHO WORKS OUT.
IT'S LIKE I WAS SAYING ABOUT BEING IN TOUCH WITH YOUR BODY.
IT'S NICE TO KNOW YOU CAN RELY ON IT WHEN YOU HAVE TO.
SWIMMING IN THE HOTEL POOL IS ONE OF THE MAIN PERKS OF ANY VACATION.
IT ALWAYS FEELS GOOD TO GET SOME LAPS IN.
WHEN WE'RE ON TOUR, IT'S SUCH A STRAIN ON ME THAT I'D NEVER MAKE IT IF I WAS TOTALLY OUT OF SHAPE.

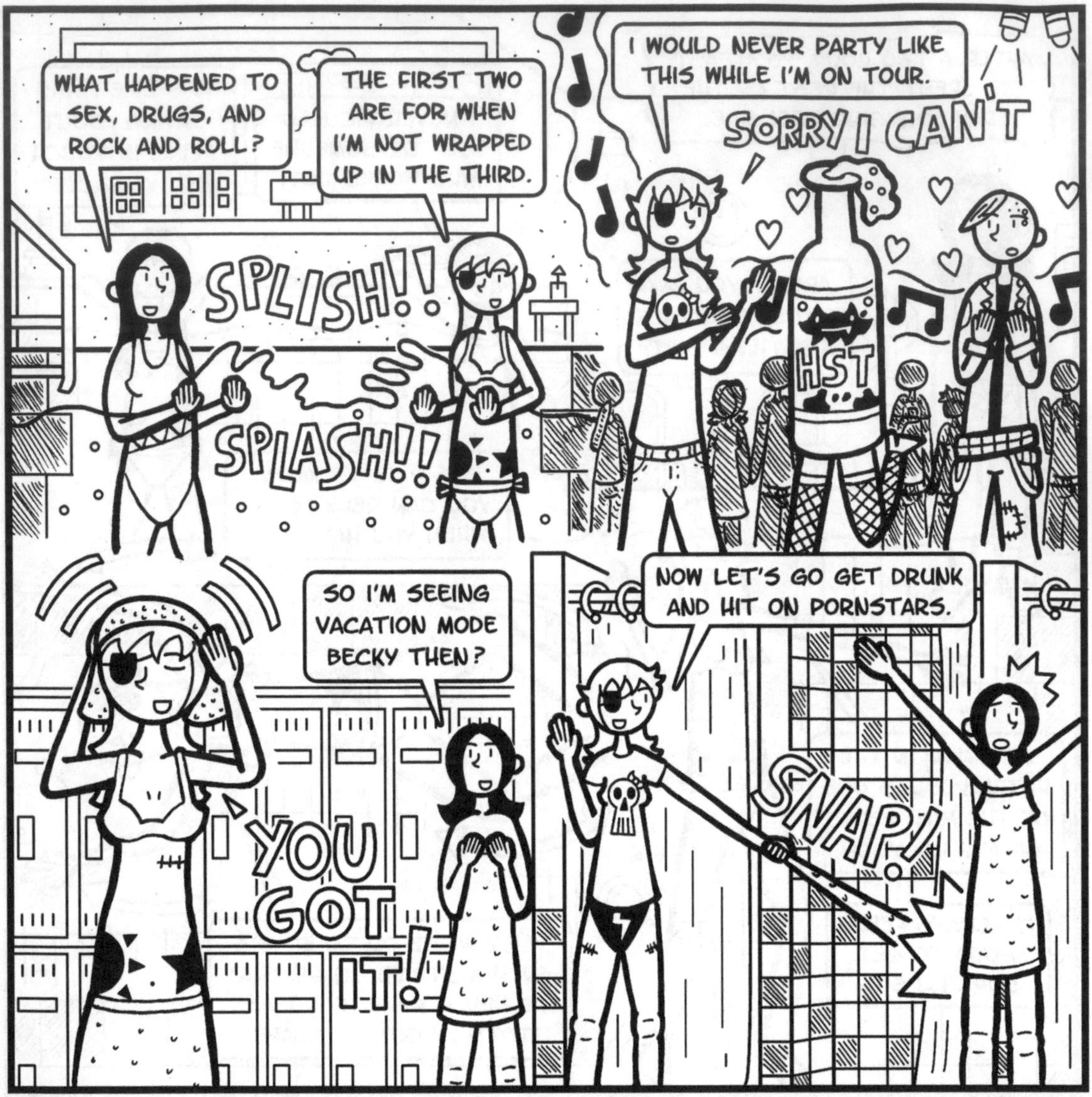
WHAT HAPPENED TO SEX, DRUGS, AND ROCK AND ROLL?
THE FIRST TWO ARE FOR WHEN I'M NOT WRAPPED UP IN THE THIRD.
SPLISH!!
SPLASH!!
I WOULD NEVER PARTY LIKE THIS WHILE I'M ON TOUR.
SORRY I CAN'T
HST
SO I'M SEEING VACATION MODE BECKY THEN?
YOU GOT IT!
NOW LET'S GO GET DRUNK AND HIT ON PORNSTARS.
SNAP!

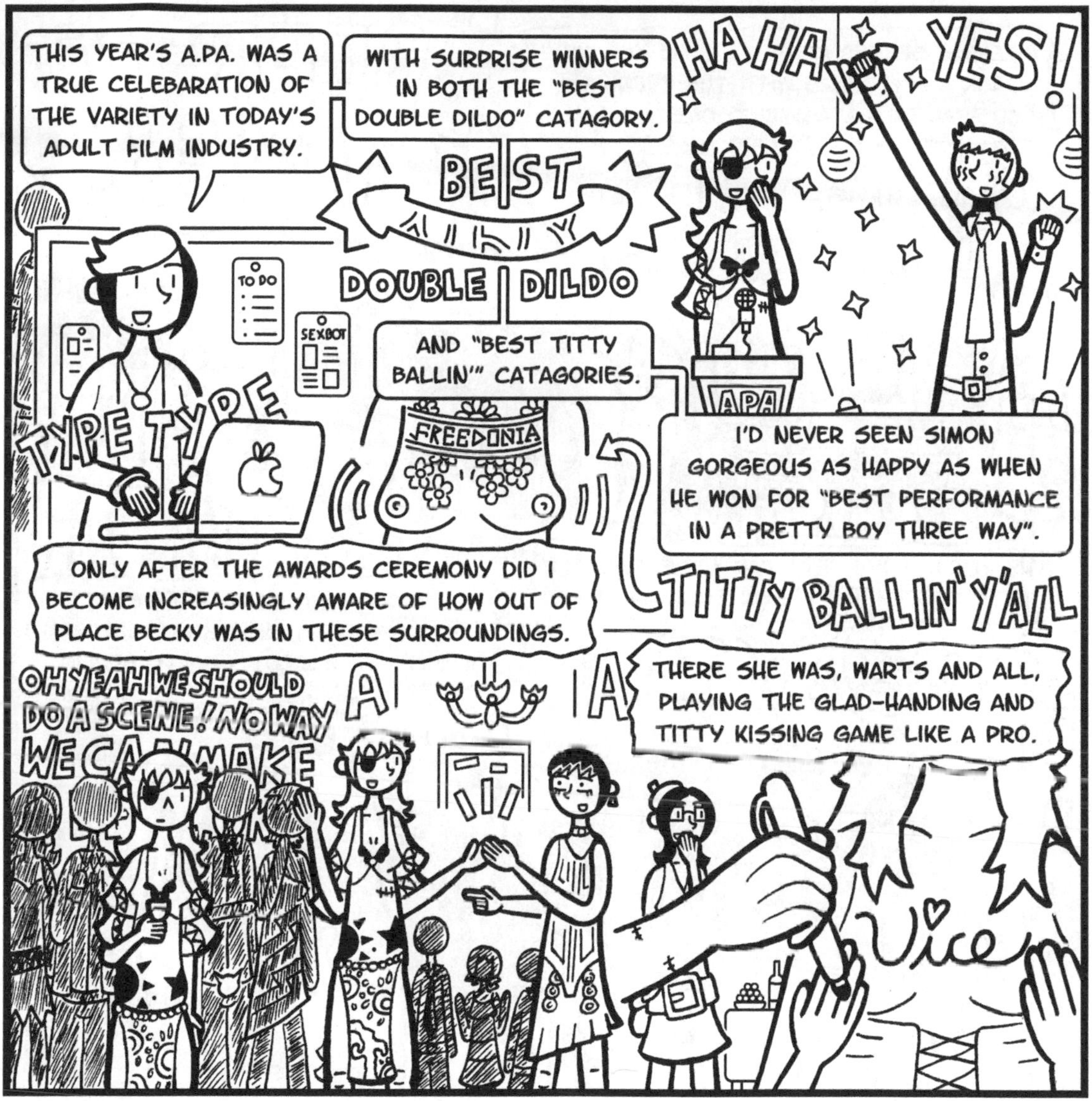
THIS YEAR'S A.PA. WAS A TRUE CELEBARATION OF THE VARIETY IN TODAY'S ADULT FILM INDUSTRY.
WITH SURPRISE WINNERS IN BOTH THE "BEST DOUBLE DILDO" CATAGORY.
HAHA
YES!
BEST
DOUBLE DILDO
TO DO
SEXBOT
AND "BEST TITTY BALLIN'" CATAGORIES.
APA
TYPE TYPE
FREEDONIA
I'D NEVER SEEN SIMON GORGEOUS AS HAPPY AS WHEN HE WON FOR "BEST PERFORMANCE IN A PRETTY BOY THREE WAY".
ONLY AFTER THE AWARDS CEREMONY DID I BECOME INCREASINGLY AWARE OF HOW OUT OF PLACE BECKY WAS IN THESE SURROUNDINGS.
TITTY BALLIN' Y'ALL
A
A
THERE SHE WAS, WARTS AND ALL, PLAYING THE GLAD-HANDING AND TITTY KISSING GAME LIKE A PRO.
OH YEAH WE SHOULD DO A SCENE! NO WAY WE CAN MAKE
Vice

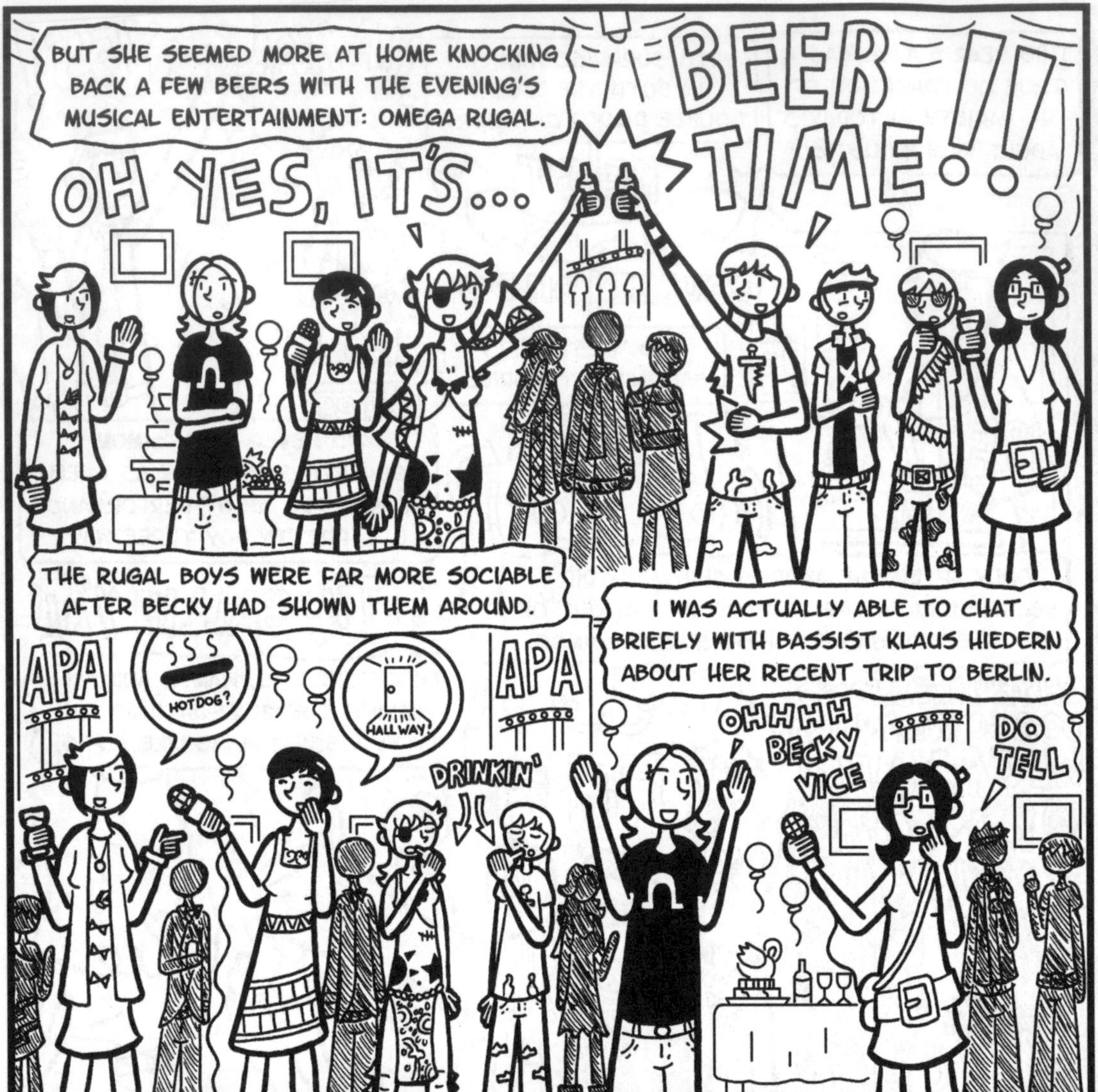
BUT SHE SEEMED MORE AT HOME KNOCKING BACK A FEW BEERS WITH THE EVENING'S MUSICAL ENTERTAINMENT: OMEGA RUGAL.
OH YES, IT'S...
BEER TIME!!
THE RUGAL BOYS WERE FAR MORE SOCIABLE AFTER BECKY HAD SHOWN THEM AROUND.
I WAS ACTUALLY ABLE TO CHAT BRIEFLY WITH BASSIST KLAUS HIEDERN ABOUT HER RECENT TRIP TO BERLIN.
APA
HOT DOG?
HALLWAY
APA
DRINKIN'
OHHHH BECKY VICE
DO TELL

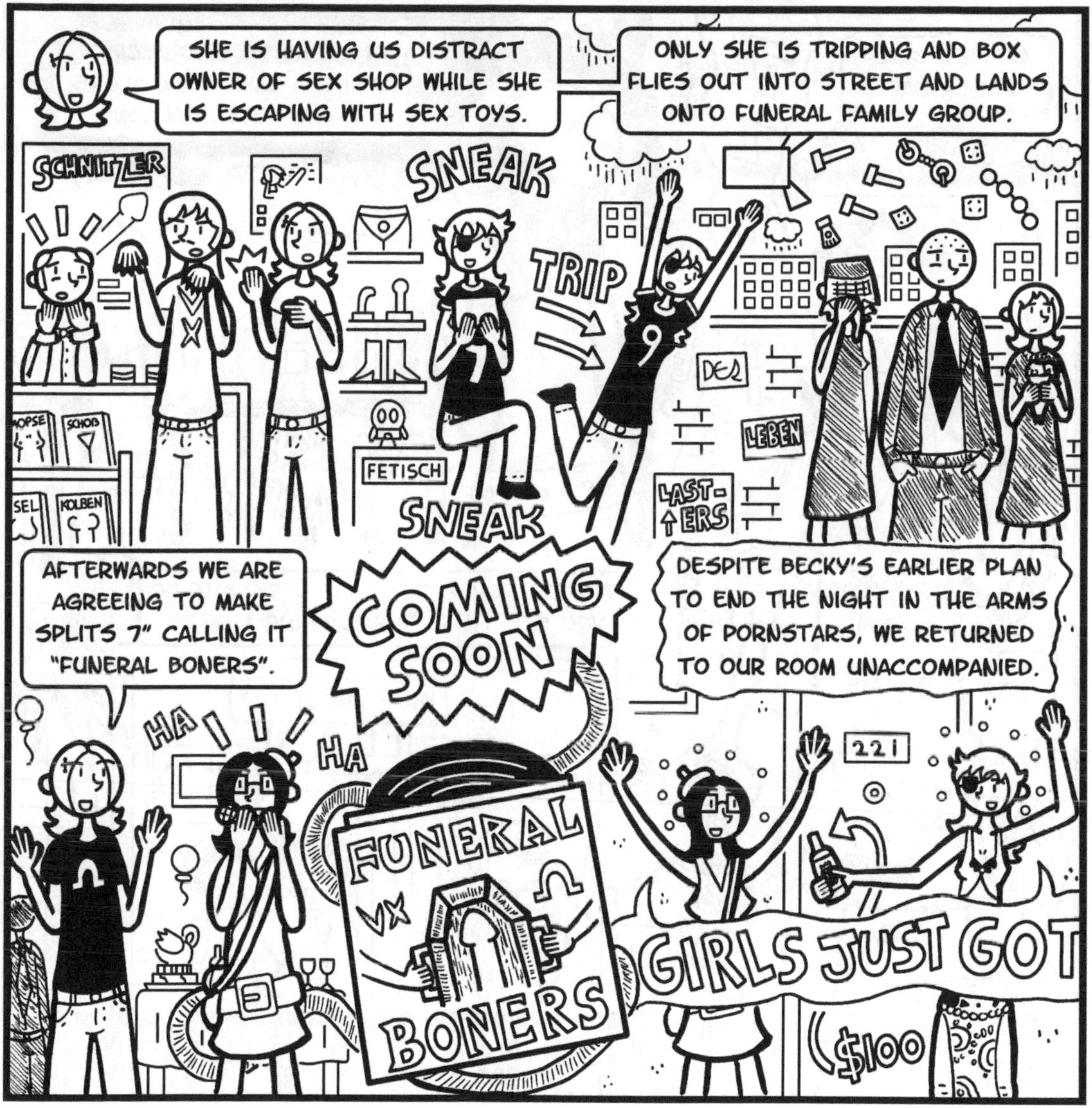
SHE IS HAVING US DISTRACT OWNER OF SEX SHOP WHILE SHE IS ESCAPING WITH SEX TOYS.
ONLY SHE IS TRIPPING AND BOX FLIES OUT INTO STREET AND LANDS ONTO FUNERAL FAMILY GROUP.
SCHNITZLER
SNEAK
TRIP
SNEAK
FETISCH
SCHOB
KOLBEN
DER
LEBEN
LAST- ERS
AFTERWARDS WE ARE AGREEING TO MAKE SPLITS 7" CALLING IT "FUNERAL BONERS".
COMING SOON
DESPITE BECKY'S EARLIER PLAN TO END THE NIGHT IN THE ARMS OF PORNSTARS, WE RETURNED TO OUR ROOM UNACCOMPANIED.
HA
HA
FUNERAL BONERS
221
GIRLS JUST GOT
($100

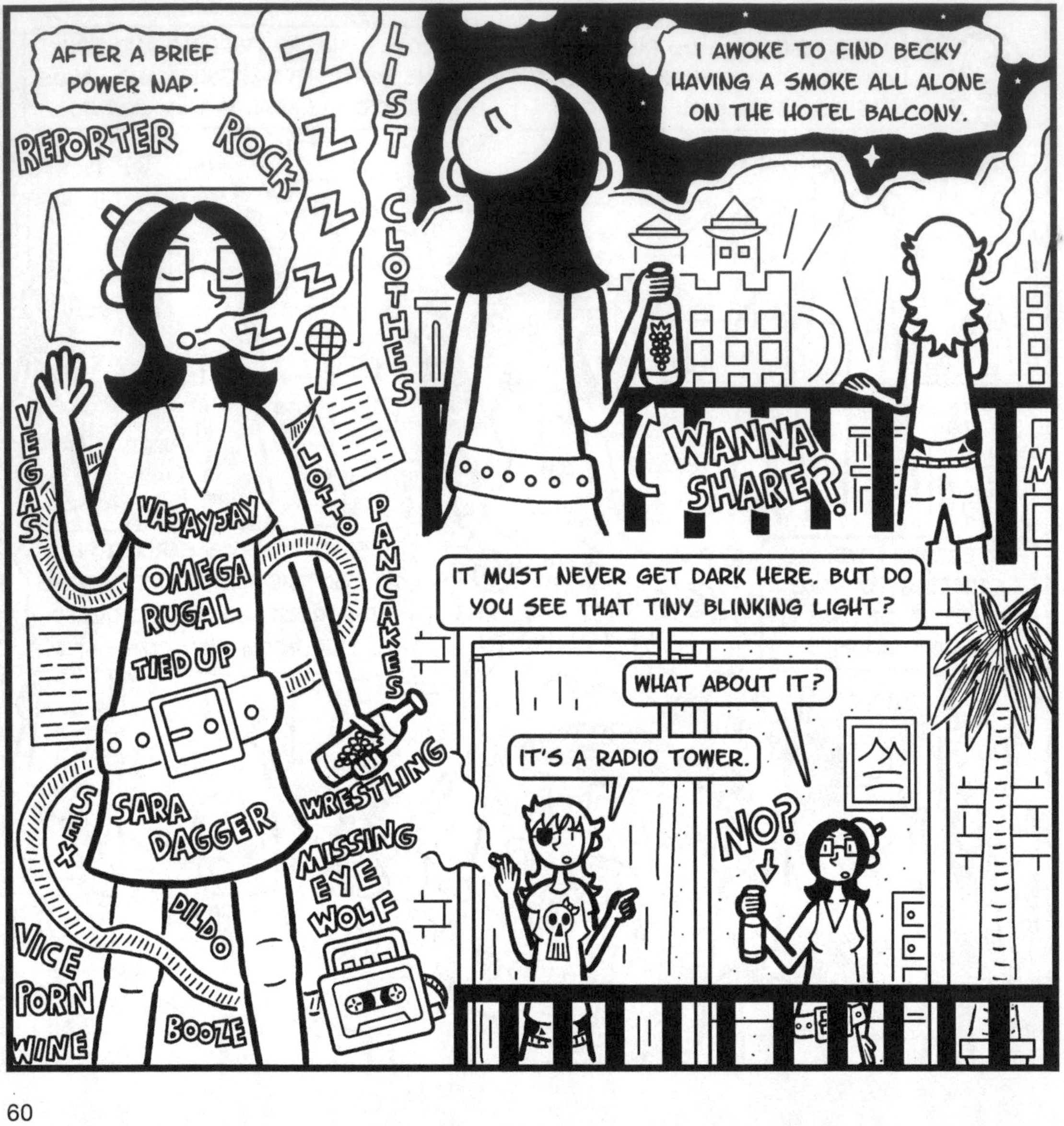
AFTER A BRIEF POWER NAP.
ZZZZZZ
REPORTER
ROCK
LIST
CLOTHES
VEGAS
VAJAYJAY
OMEGA
RUGAL
TIED UP
LOTTO
PANCAKES
SARA DAGGER
SEX
WRESTLING
MISSING EYE WOLF
DILDO
VICE
PORN
WINE
BOOZE
I AWOKE TO FIND BECKY HAVING A SMOKE ALL ALONE ON THE HOTEL BALCONY.
WANNA SHARE?
IT MUST NEVER GET DARK HERE. BUT DO YOU SEE THAT TINY BLINKING LIGHT?
WHAT ABOUT IT?
IT'S A RADIO TOWER.
NO?

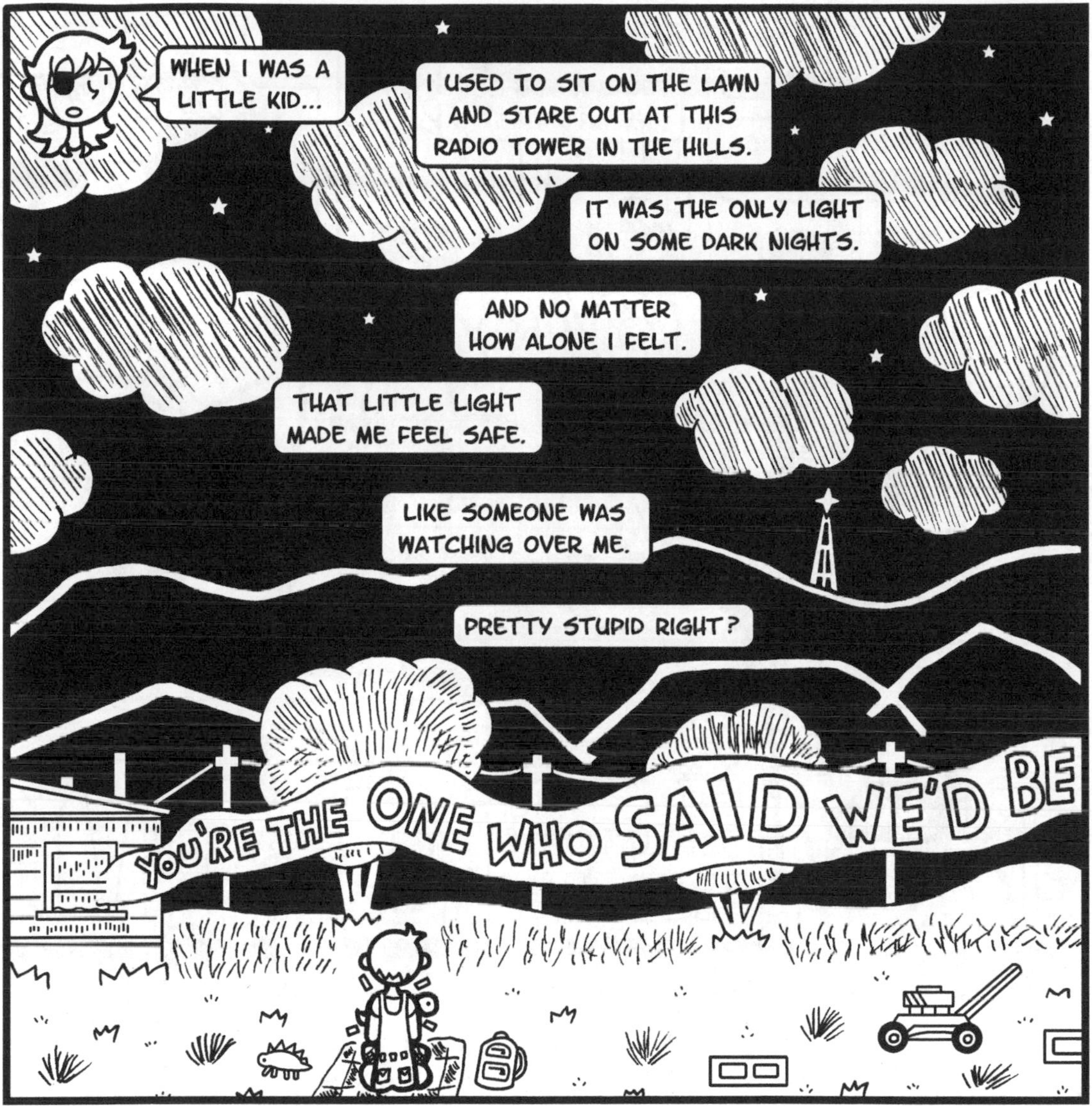
WHEN I WAS A LITTLE KID...
I USED TO SIT ON THE LAWN AND STARE OUT AT THIS RADIO TOWER IN THE HILLS.
IT WAS THE ONLY LIGHT ON SOME DARK NIGHTS.
AND NO MATTER HOW ALONE I FELT.
THAT LITTLE LIGHT MADE ME FEEL SAFE.
LIKE SOMEONE WAS WATCHING OVER ME.
PRETTY STUPID RIGHT?
YOU'RE THE ONE WHO SAID WE'D BE

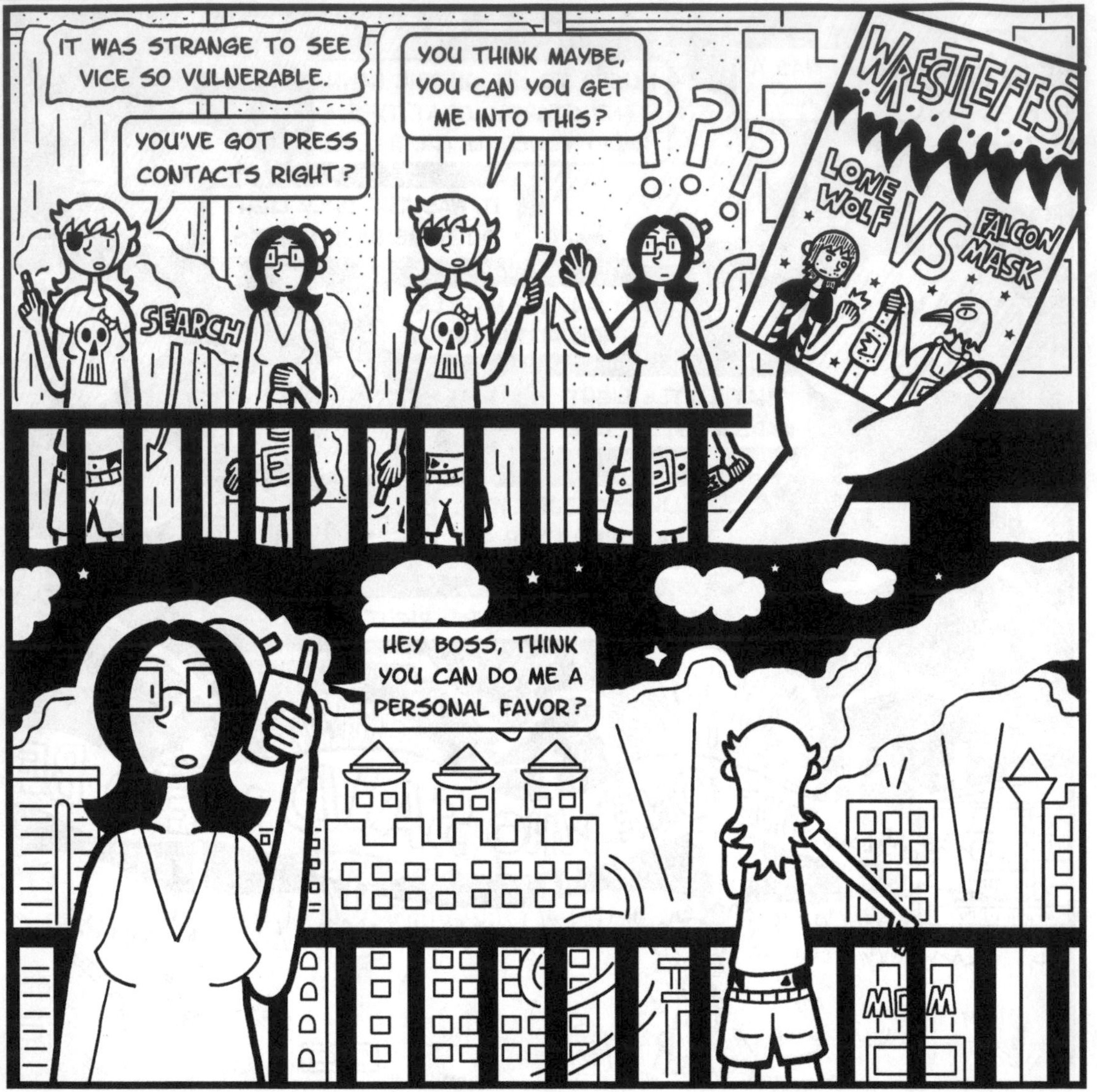
IT WAS STRANGE TO SEE VICE SO VULNERABLE.
YOU'VE GOT PRESS CONTACTS RIGHT?
SEARCH
YOU THINK MAYBE, YOU CAN YOU GET ME INTO THIS?
???
WRESTLEFEST
LONE WOLF VS FALCON MASK
HEY BOSS, THINK YOU CAN DO ME A PERSONAL FAVOR?
MGM

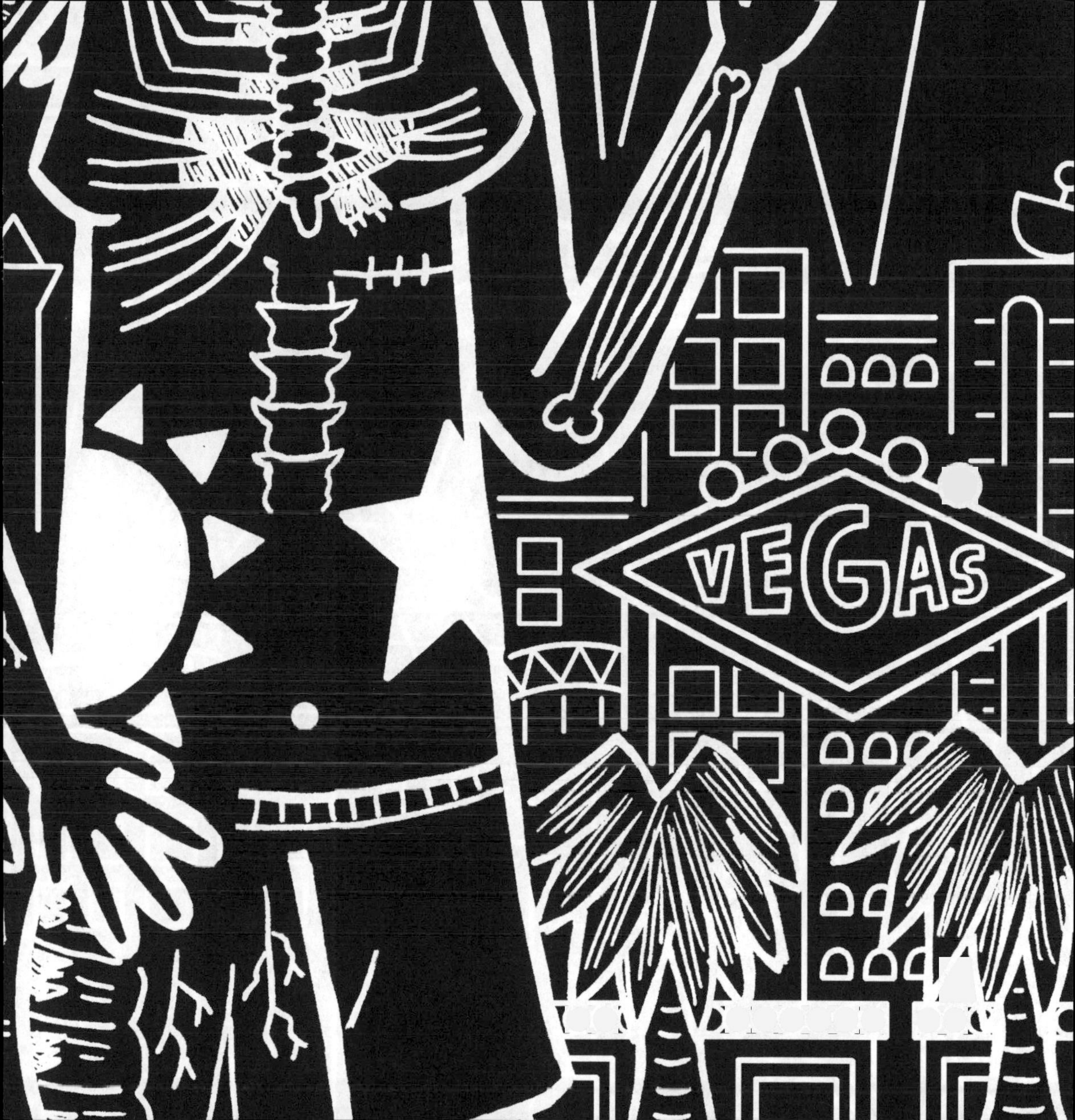
vEGAs

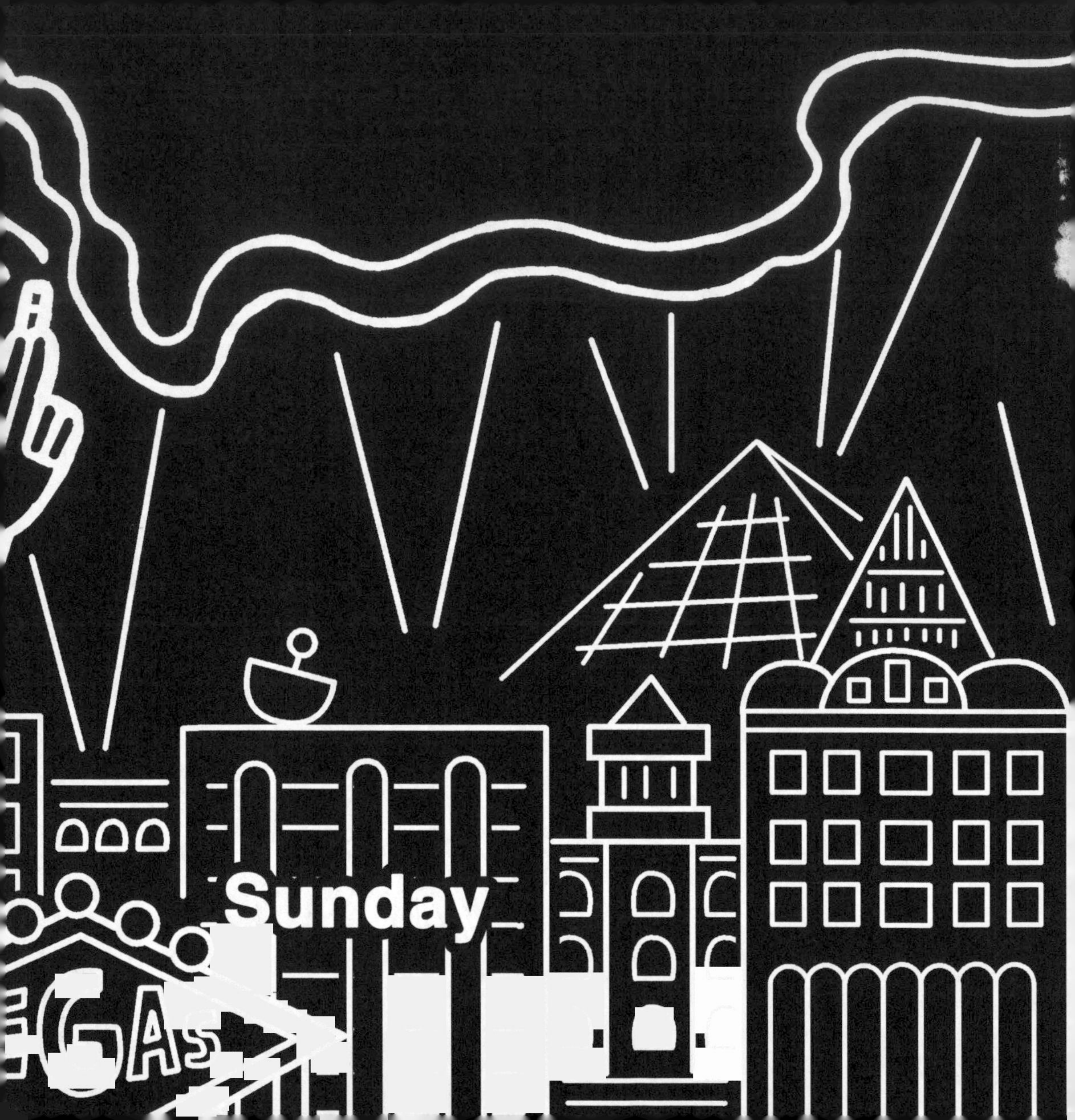
Sunday
GAS

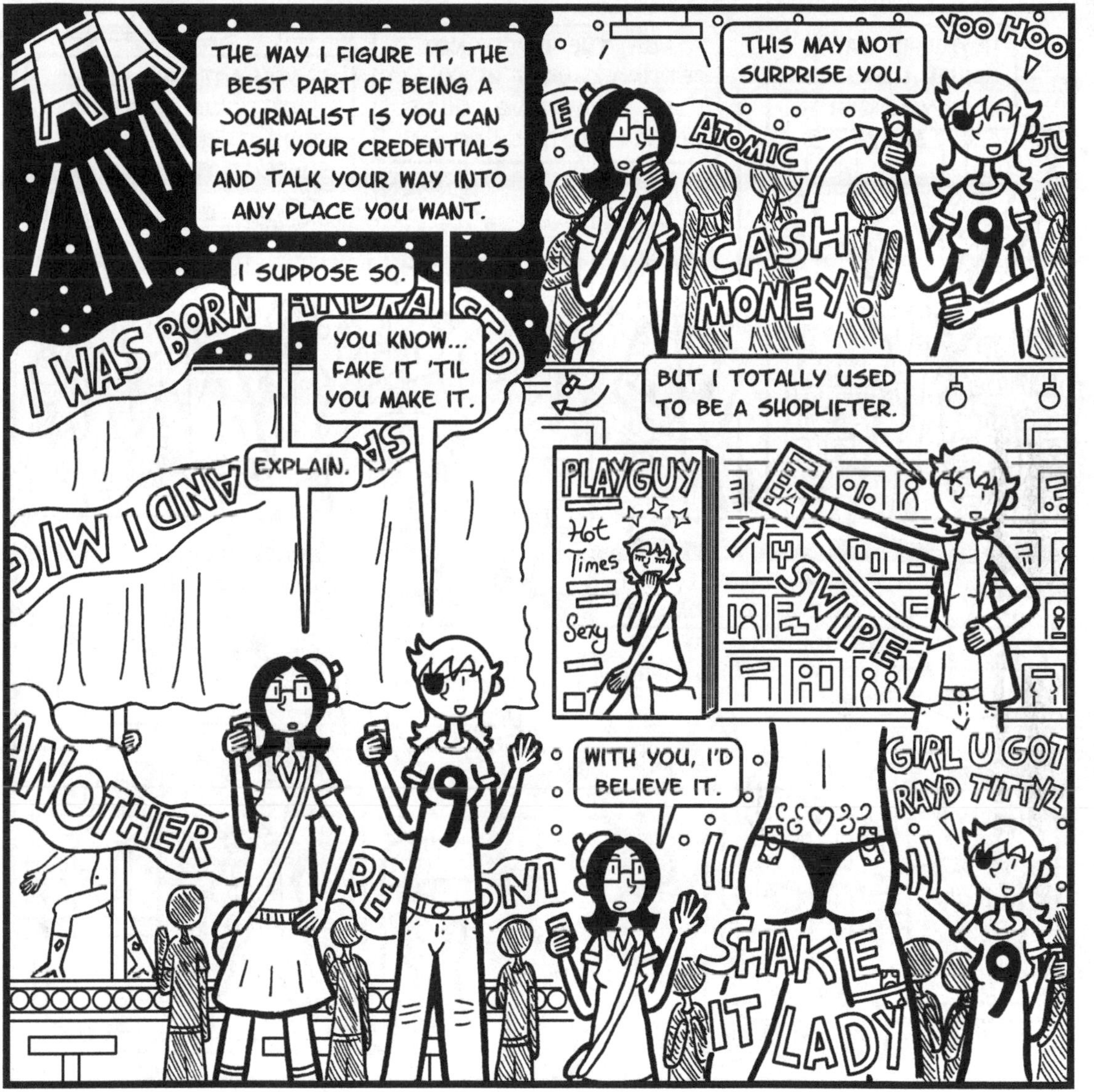
THE WAY I FIGURE IT, THE BEST PART OF BEING A JOURNALIST IS YOU CAN FLASH YOUR CREDENTIALS AND TALK YOUR WAY INTO ANY PLACE YOU WANT.
I SUPPOSE SO.
YOU KNOW... FAKE IT 'TIL YOU MAKE IT.
EXPLAIN.
THIS MAY NOT SURPRISE YOU.
YOO HOO
ATOMIC
CASH MONEY!
BUT I TOTALLY USED TO BE A SHOPLIFTER.
PLAYGUY
Hot Times
Sexy
SWIPE
WITH YOU, I'D BELIEVE IT.
GIRL U GOT RAYD TITTYZ
SHAKE IT LADY

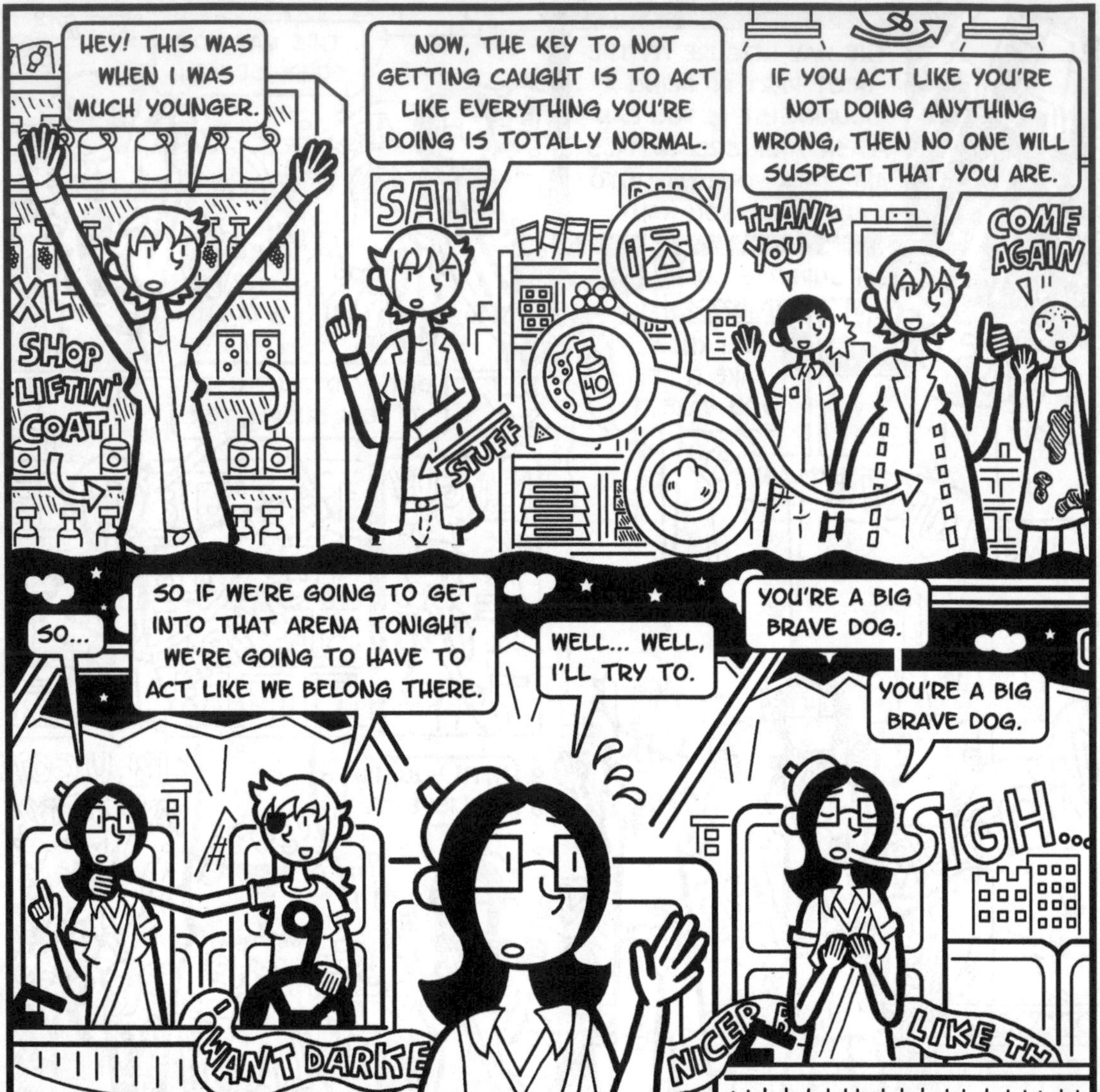
HEY! THIS WAS WHEN I WAS MUCH YOUNGER.
XL
SHOP LIFTIN' COAT
NOW, THE KEY TO NOT GETTING CAUGHT IS TO ACT LIKE EVERYTHING YOU'RE DOING IS TOTALLY NORMAL.
SALE
STUFF
40
IF YOU ACT LIKE YOU'RE NOT DOING ANYTHING WRONG, THEN NO ONE WILL SUSPECT THAT YOU ARE.
THANK YOU
COME AGAIN
SO...
SO IF WE'RE GOING TO GET INTO THAT ARENA TONIGHT, WE'RE GOING TO HAVE TO ACT LIKE WE BELONG THERE.
WELL... WELL, I'LL TRY TO.
YOU'RE A BIG BRAVE DOG.
YOU'RE A BIG BRAVE DOG.
SIGH...

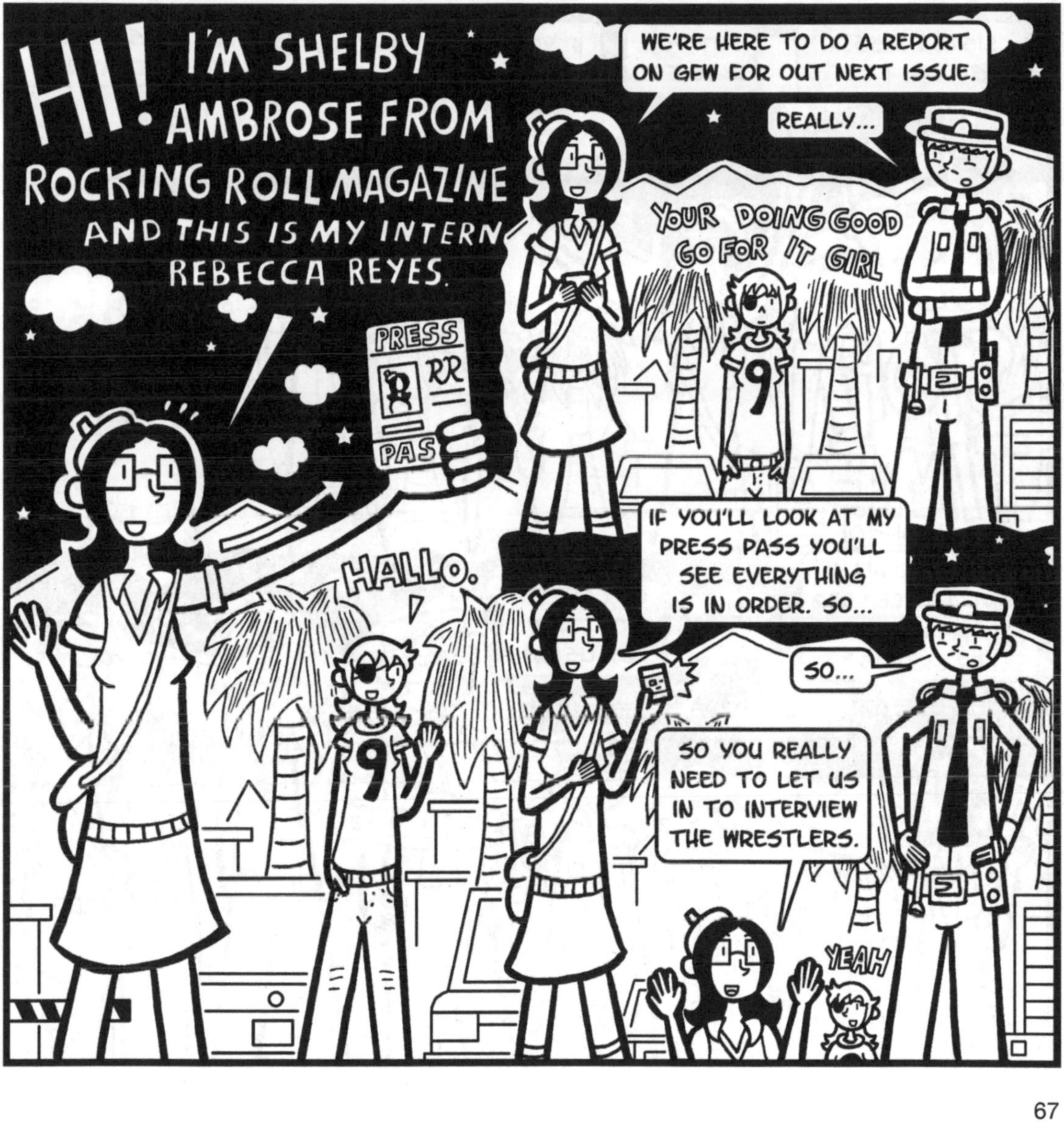
HI! I'M SHELBY AMBROSE FROM ROCKING ROLL MAGAZINE AND THIS IS MY INTERN REBECCA REYES.
PRESS
RR
PAS
HALLO.
WE'RE HERE TO DO A REPORT ON GFW FOR OUT NEXT ISSUE.
REALLY...
YOUR DOING GOOD GO FOR IT GIRL
IF YOU'LL LOOK AT MY PRESS PASS YOU'LL SEE EVERYTHING IS IN ORDER. SO...
SO...
SO YOU REALLY NEED TO LET US IN TO INTERVIEW THE WRESTLERS.
YEAH

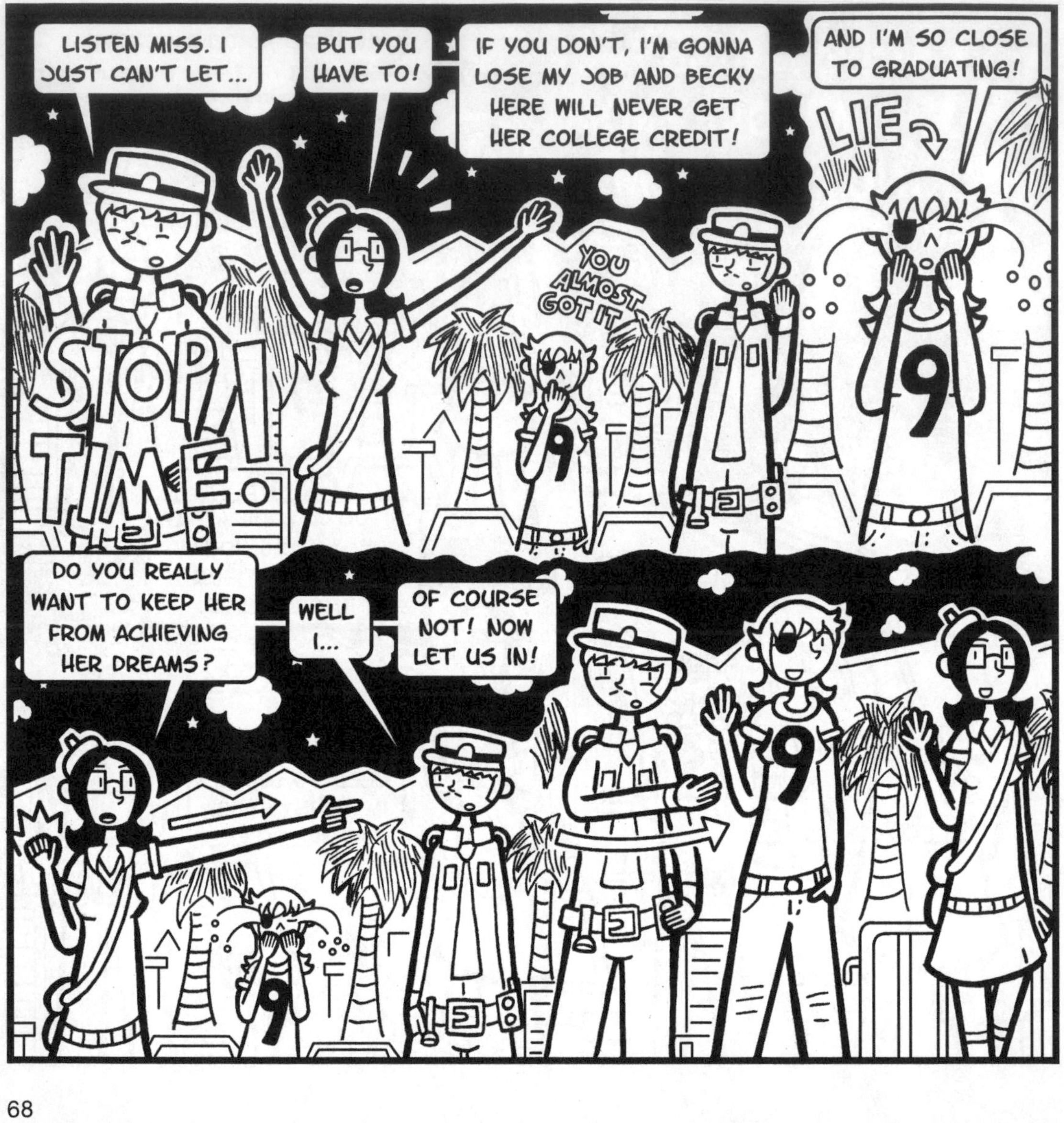
LISTEN MISS. I JUST CAN'T LET...
BUT YOU HAVE TO!
IF YOU DON'T, I'M GONNA LOSE MY JOB AND BECKY HERE WILL NEVER GET HER COLLEGE CREDIT!
AND I'M SO CLOSE TO GRADUATING!
LIE
STOP TIME!
YOU ALMOST GOT IT
9
DO YOU REALLY WANT TO KEEP HER FROM ACHIEVING HER DREAMS?
WELL I...
OF COURSE NOT! NOW LET US IN!

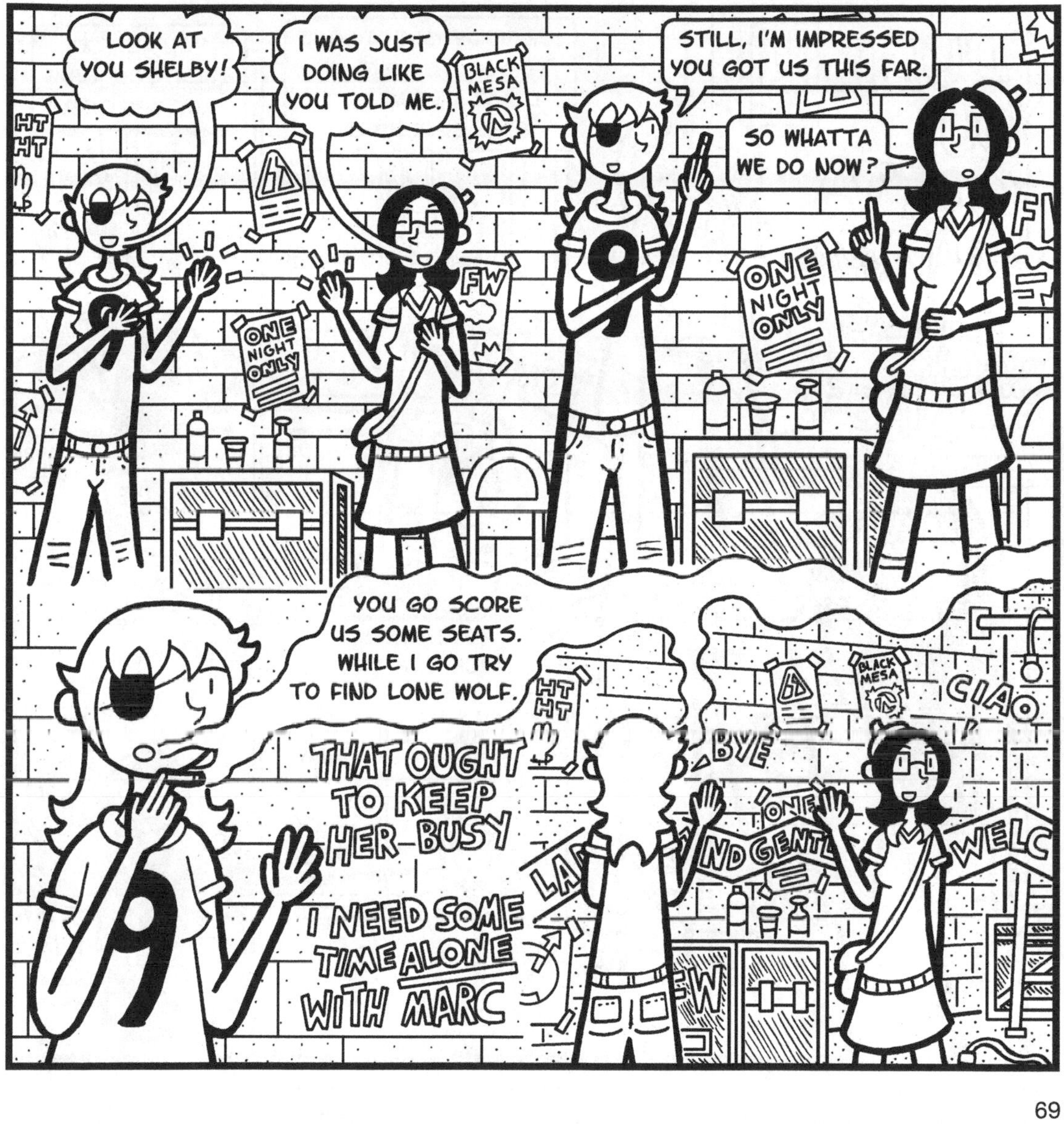
LOOK AT YOU SHELBY!
I WAS JUST DOING LIKE YOU TOLD ME.
STILL, I'M IMPRESSED YOU GOT US THIS FAR.
SO WHATTA WE DO NOW?
YOU GO SCORE US SOME SEATS. WHILE I GO TRY TO FIND LONE WOLF.
THAT OUGHT TO KEEP HER BUSY
I NEED SOME TIME ALONE WITH MARC
BYE
CIAO

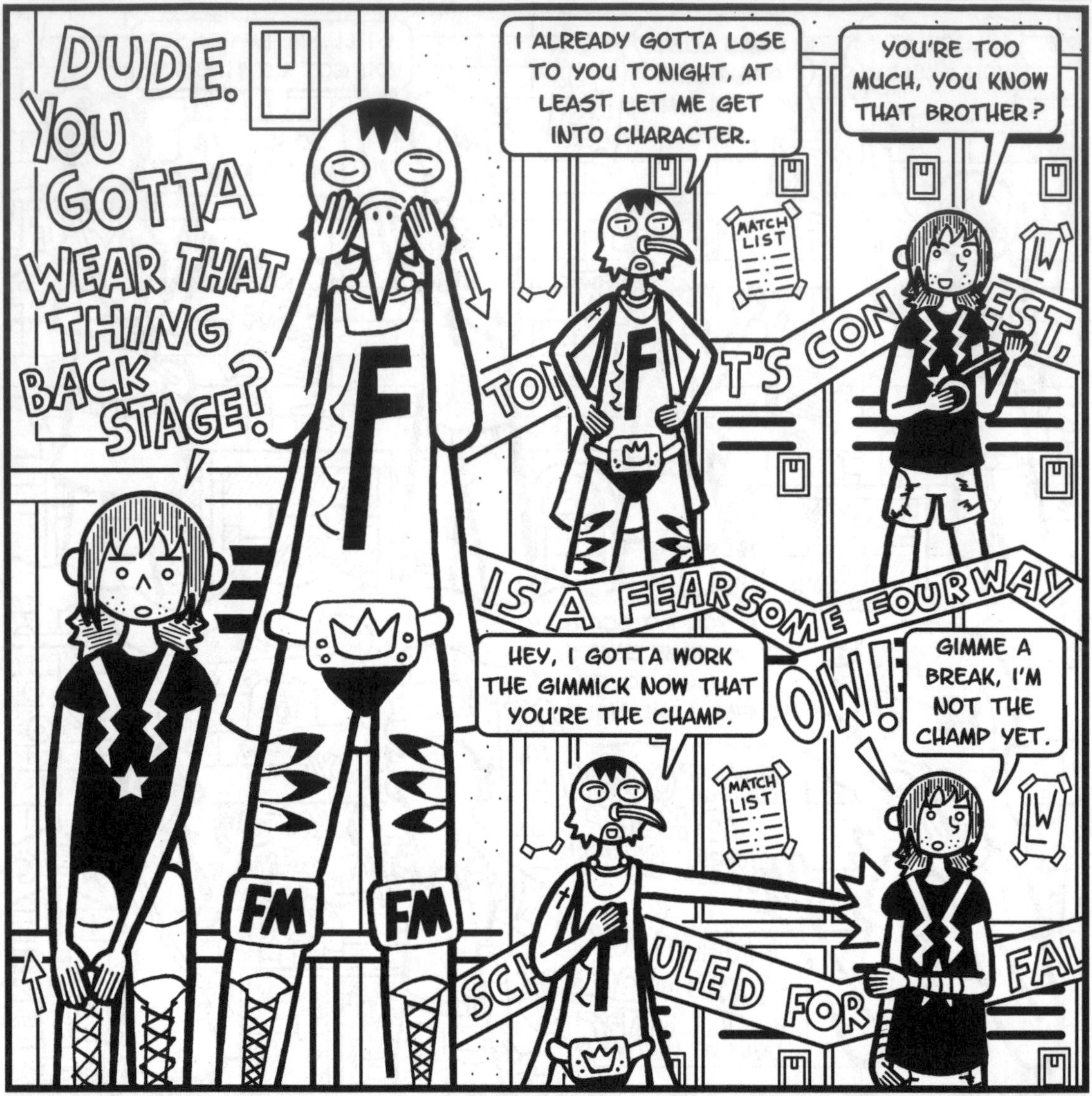
DUDE. YOU GOTTA WEAR THAT THING BACK STAGE?
I ALREADY GOTTA LOSE TO YOU TONIGHT, AT LEAST LET ME GET INTO CHARACTER.
YOU'RE TOO MUCH, YOU KNOW THAT BROTHER?
MATCH LIST
TON T'S CON EST,
IS A FEARSOME FOURWAY
HEY, I GOTTA WORK THE GIMMICK NOW THAT YOU'RE THE CHAMP.
OW!
GIMME A BREAK, I'M NOT THE CHAMP YET.
MATCH LIST
FM
FM
SCH ULED FOR FAL

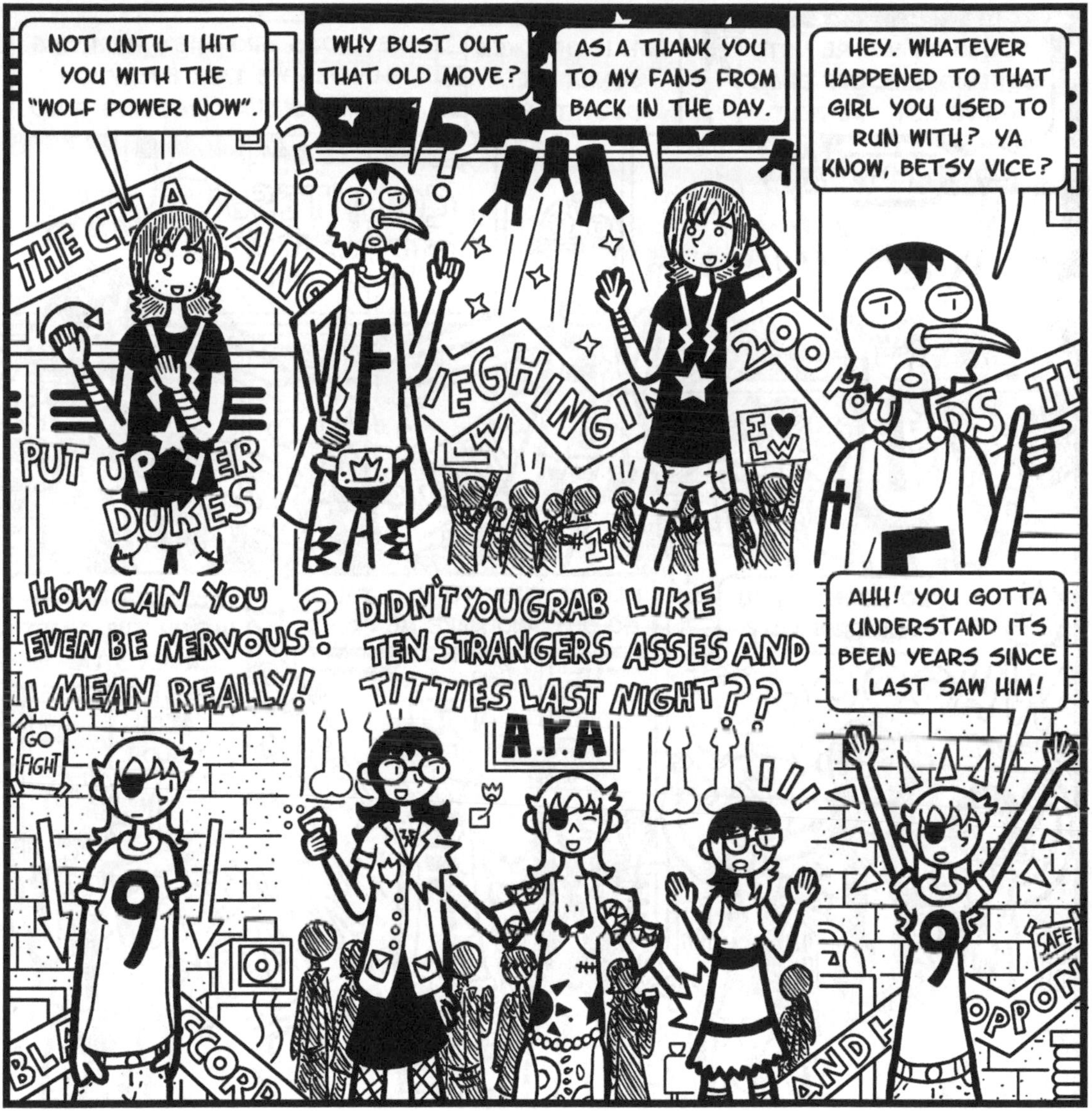
NOT UNTIL I HIT YOU WITH THE "WOLF POWER NOW".
WHY BUST OUT THAT OLD MOVE?
AS A THANK YOU TO MY FANS FROM BACK IN THE DAY.
HEY. WHATEVER HAPPENED TO THAT GIRL YOU USED TO RUN WITH? YA KNOW, BETSY VICE?
PUT UP YER DUKES
HOW CAN YOU EVEN BE NERVOUS? I MEAN REALLY!
DIDN'T YOU GRAB LIKE TEN STRANGERS ASSES AND TITTIES LAST NIGHT??
AHH! YOU GOTTA UNDERSTAND ITS BEEN YEARS SINCE I LAST SAW HIM!
GO FIGHT
A.P.A
SAFE

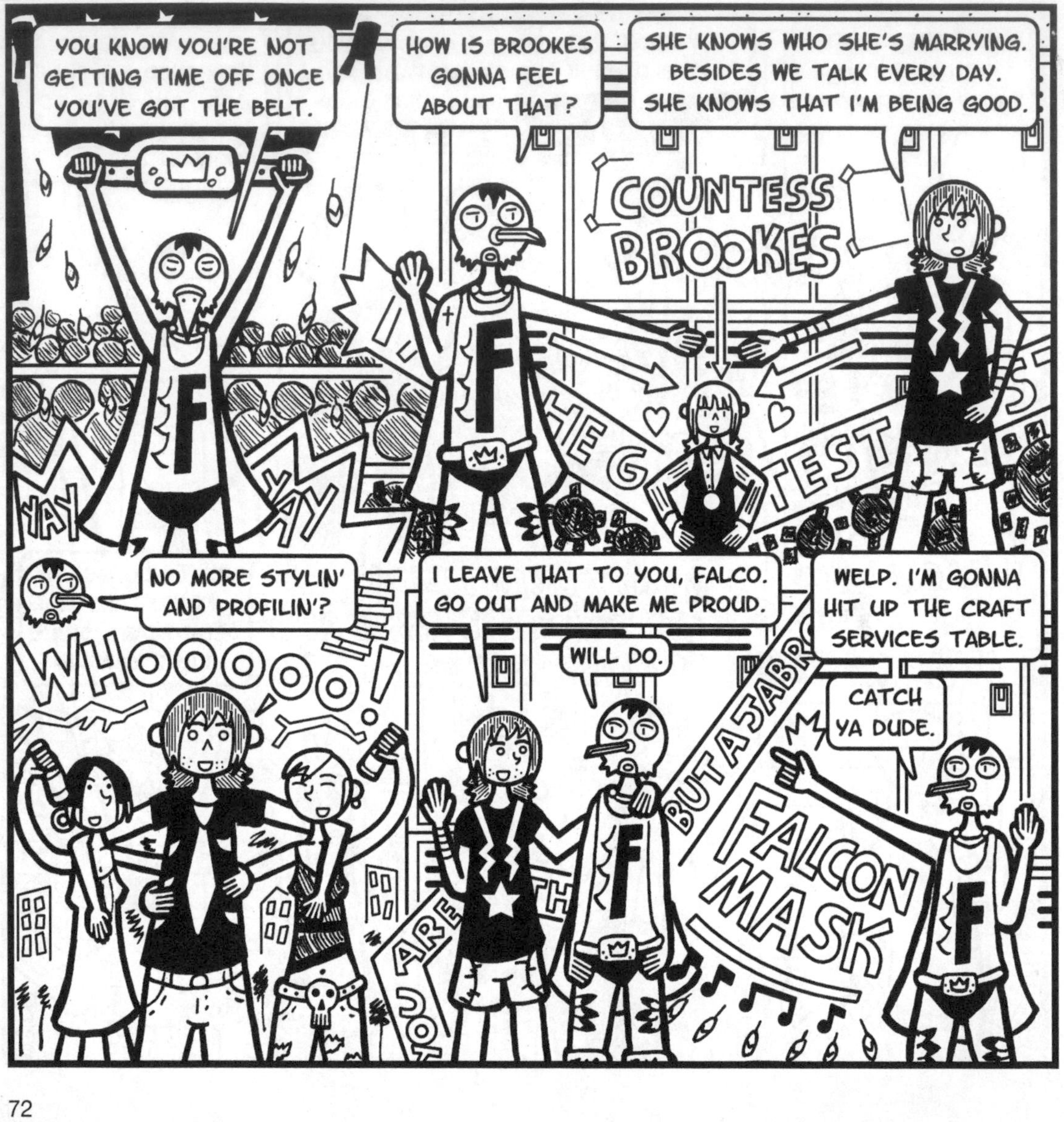
YOU KNOW YOU'RE NOT GETTING TIME OFF ONCE YOU'VE GOT THE BELT.
HOW IS BROOKES GONNA FEEL ABOUT THAT?
SHE KNOWS WHO SHE'S MARRYING. BESIDES WE TALK EVERY DAY. SHE KNOWS THAT I'M BEING GOOD.
COUNTESS BROOKES
YAY
YAY
NO MORE STYLIN' AND PROFILIN'?
WHOOOOO!
I LEAVE THAT TO YOU, FALCO. GO OUT AND MAKE ME PROUD.
WILL DO.
WELP. I'M GONNA HIT UP THE CRAFT SERVICES TABLE.
CATCH YA DUDE.
FALCON MASK

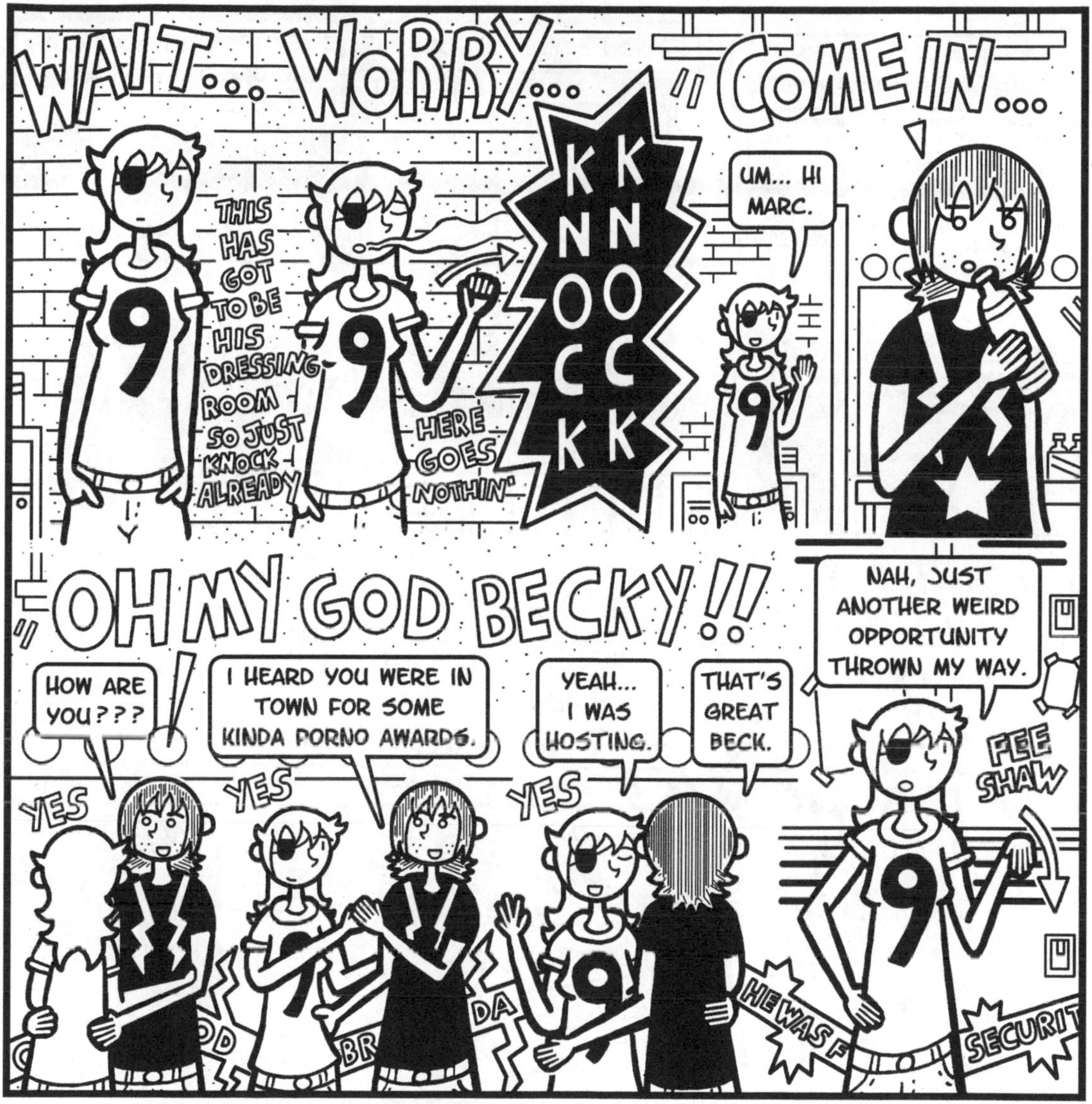

WAIT... WORRY... "COME IN..."
THIS HAS GOT TO BE HIS DRESSING ROOM SO JUST KNOCK ALREADY
HERE GOES NOTHIN'
KNOCK KNOCK
UM... HI MARC.
"OH MY GOD BECKY!!"
HOW ARE YOU???
YES
I HEARD YOU WERE IN TOWN FOR SOME KINDA PORNO AWARDS.
YES
YEAH... I WAS HOSTING.
YES
THAT'S GREAT BECK.
NAH, JUST ANOTHER WEIRD OPPORTUNITY THROWN MY WAY.
FEE SHAW
DA
HE WAS F
SECURIT

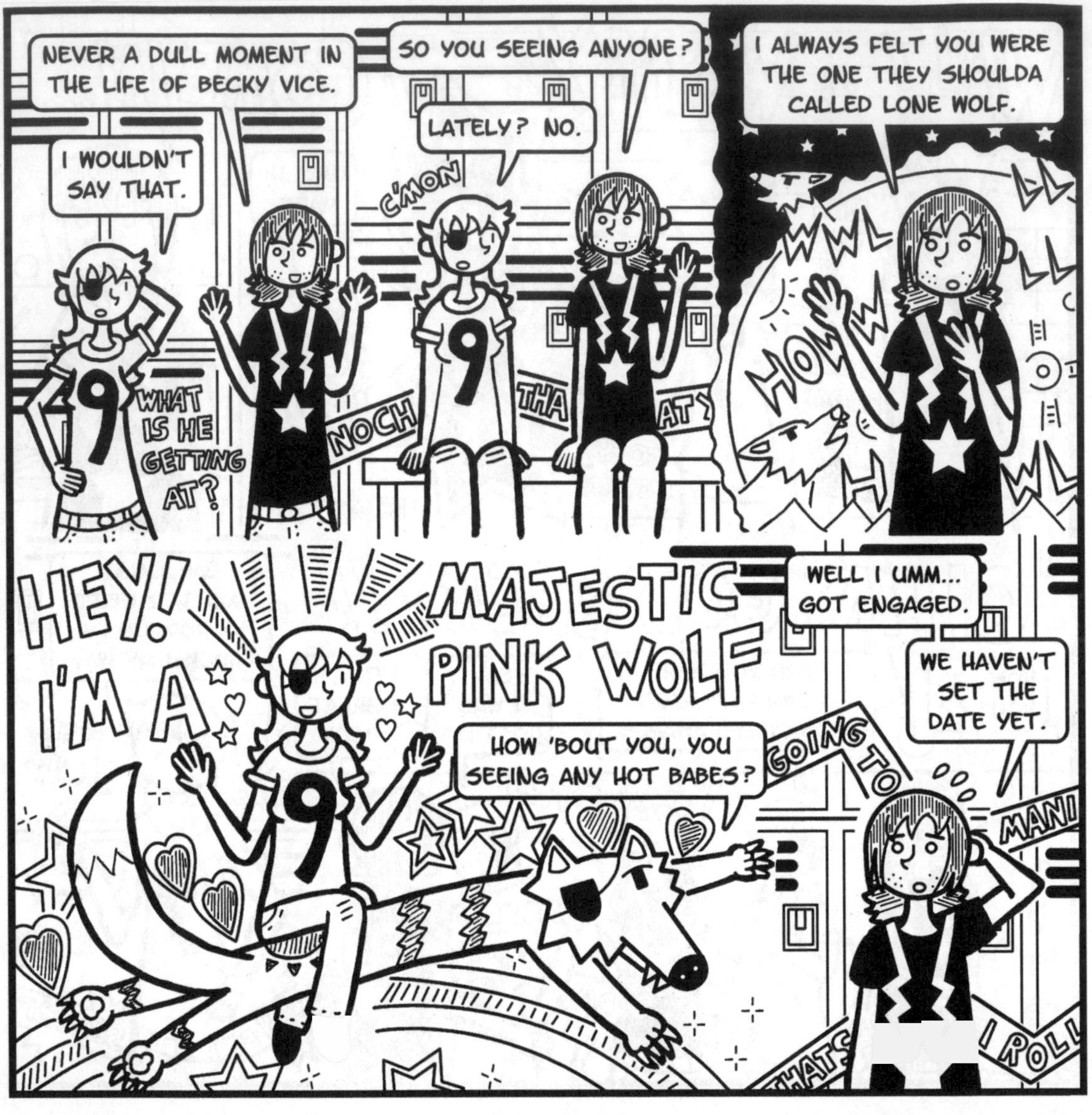
NEVER A DULL MOMENT IN THE LIFE OF BECKY VICE.
I WOULDN'T SAY THAT.
WHAT IS HE GETTING AT?
SO YOU SEEING ANYONE?
C'MON
LATELY? NO.
I ALWAYS FELT YOU WERE THE ONE THEY SHOULDA CALLED LONE WOLF.
HEY! I'M A MAJESTIC PINK WOLF
HOW 'BOUT YOU, YOU SEEING ANY HOT BABES?
WELL I UMM... GOT ENGAGED.
WE HAVEN'T SET THE DATE YET.

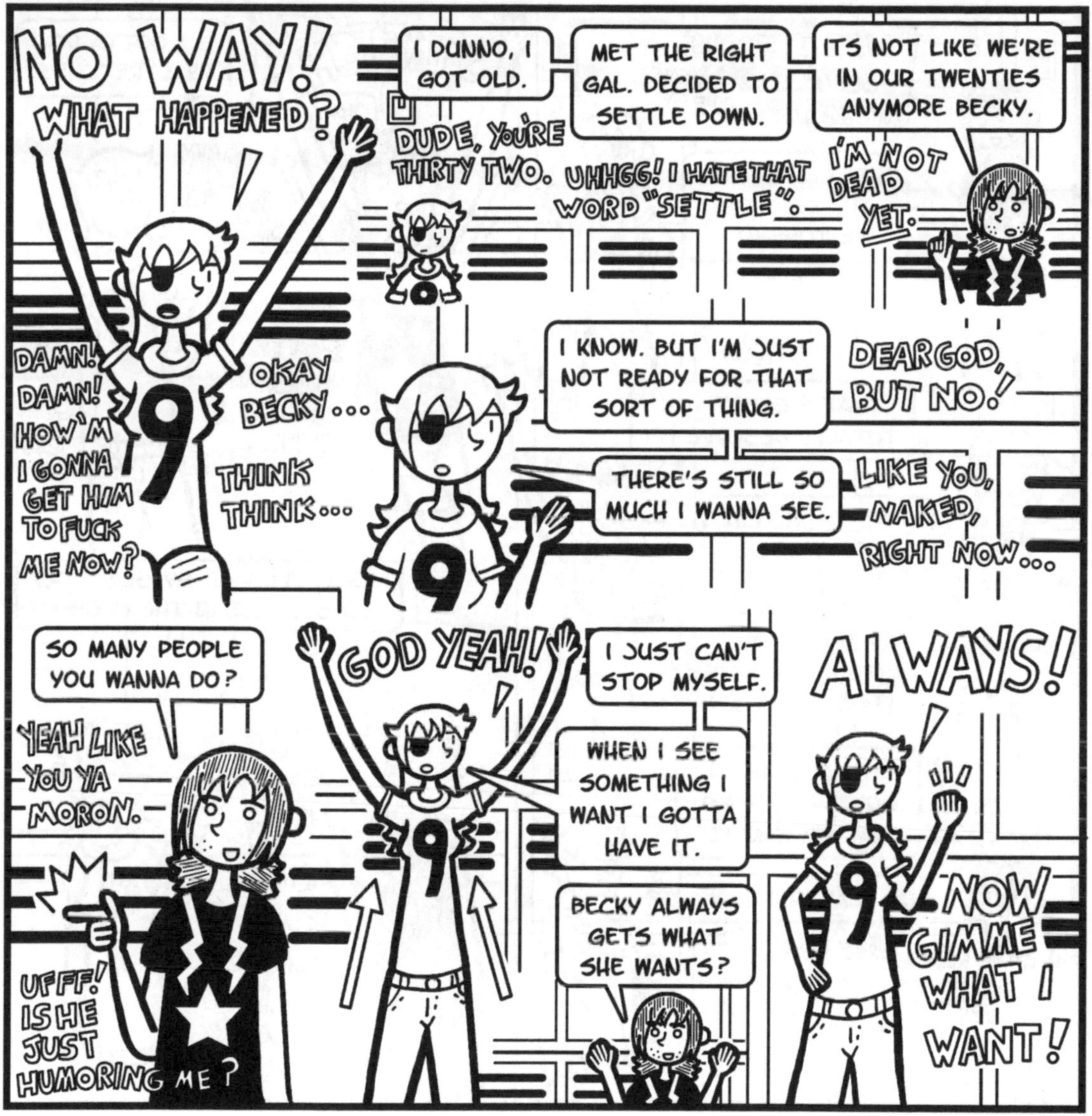
NO WAY! WHAT HAPPENED?
I DUNNO, I GOT OLD.
DUDE, YOU'RE THIRTY TWO.
MET THE RIGHT GAL. DECIDED TO SETTLE DOWN.
UHHGG! I HATE THAT WORD "SETTLE".
ITS NOT LIKE WE'RE IN OUR TWENTIES ANYMORE BECKY.
I'M NOT DEAD YET.
DAMN! DAMN! HOW'M I GONNA GET HIM TO FUCK ME NOW?
OKAY BECKY...
THINK THINK...
I KNOW. BUT I'M JUST NOT READY FOR THAT SORT OF THING.
DEAR GOD, BUT NO!
THERE'S STILL SO MUCH I WANNA SEE.
LIKE YOU, NAKED, RIGHT NOW...
SO MANY PEOPLE YOU WANNA DO?
YEAH LIKE YOU YA MORON.
UFFF! IS HE JUST HUMORING ME?
GOD YEAH!
I JUST CAN'T STOP MYSELF.
WHEN I SEE SOMETHING I WANT I GOTTA HAVE IT.
BECKY ALWAYS GETS WHAT SHE WANTS?
ALWAYS!
NOW GIMME WHAT I WANT!

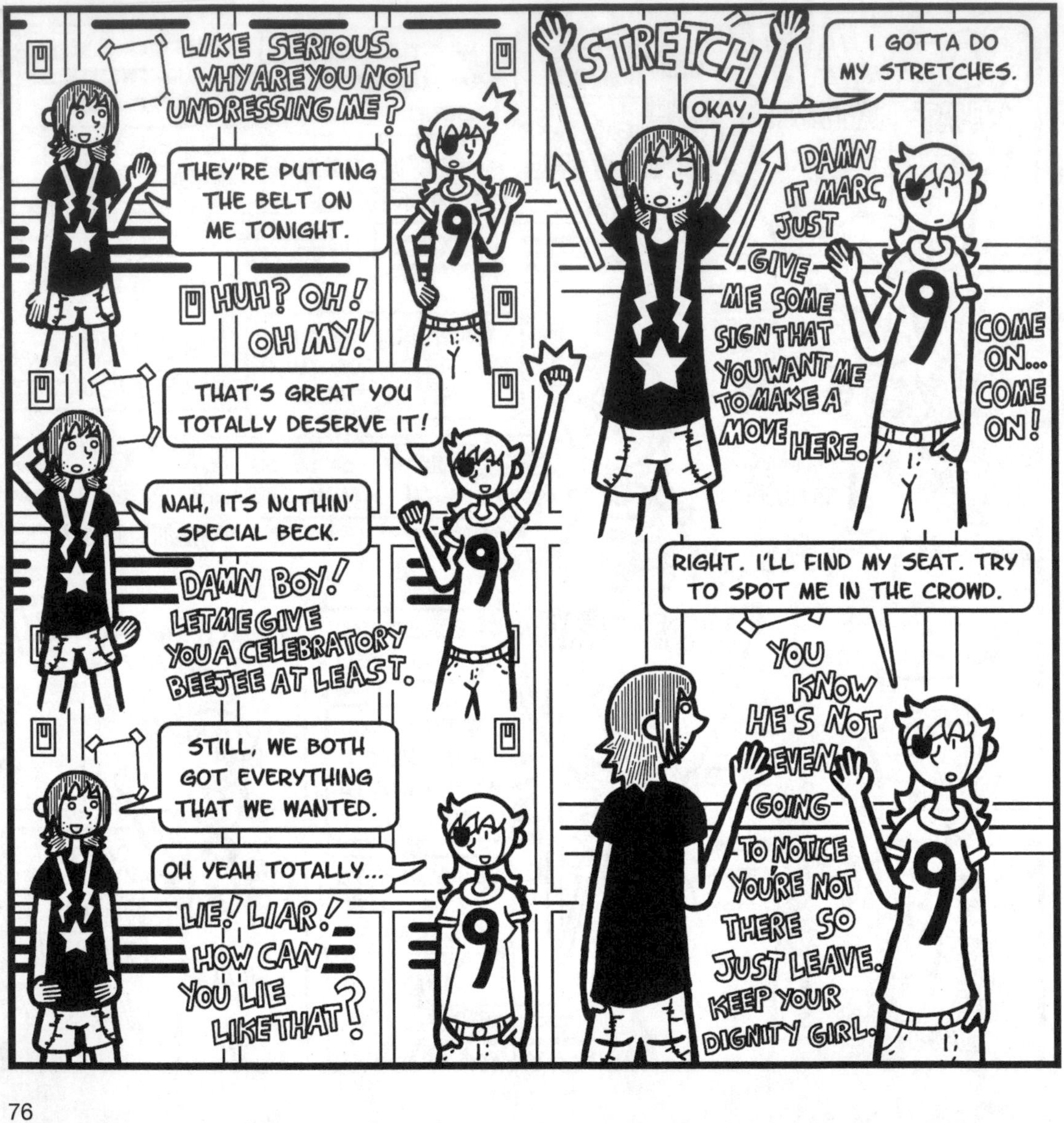
LIKE SERIOUS. WHY ARE YOU NOT UNDRESSING ME?
THEY'RE PUTTING THE BELT ON ME TONIGHT.
HUH? OH! OH MY!
THAT'S GREAT YOU TOTALLY DESERVE IT!
NAH, ITS NUTHIN' SPECIAL BECK.
DAMN BOY! LET ME GIVE YOU A CELEBRATORY BEEJEE AT LEAST.
STILL, WE BOTH GOT EVERYTHING THAT WE WANTED.
OH YEAH TOTALLY...
LIE! LIAR! HOW CAN YOU LIE LIKE THAT?
STRETCH
I GOTTA DO MY STRETCHES.
OKAY,
DAMN IT MARC, JUST GIVE ME SOME SIGN THAT YOU WANT ME TO MAKE A MOVE HERE.
COME ON... COME ON!
RIGHT. I'LL FIND MY SEAT. TRY TO SPOT ME IN THE CROWD.
YOU KNOW HE'S NOT EVEN GOING TO NOTICE YOU'RE NOT THERE SO JUST LEAVE. KEEP YOUR DIGNITY GIRL.

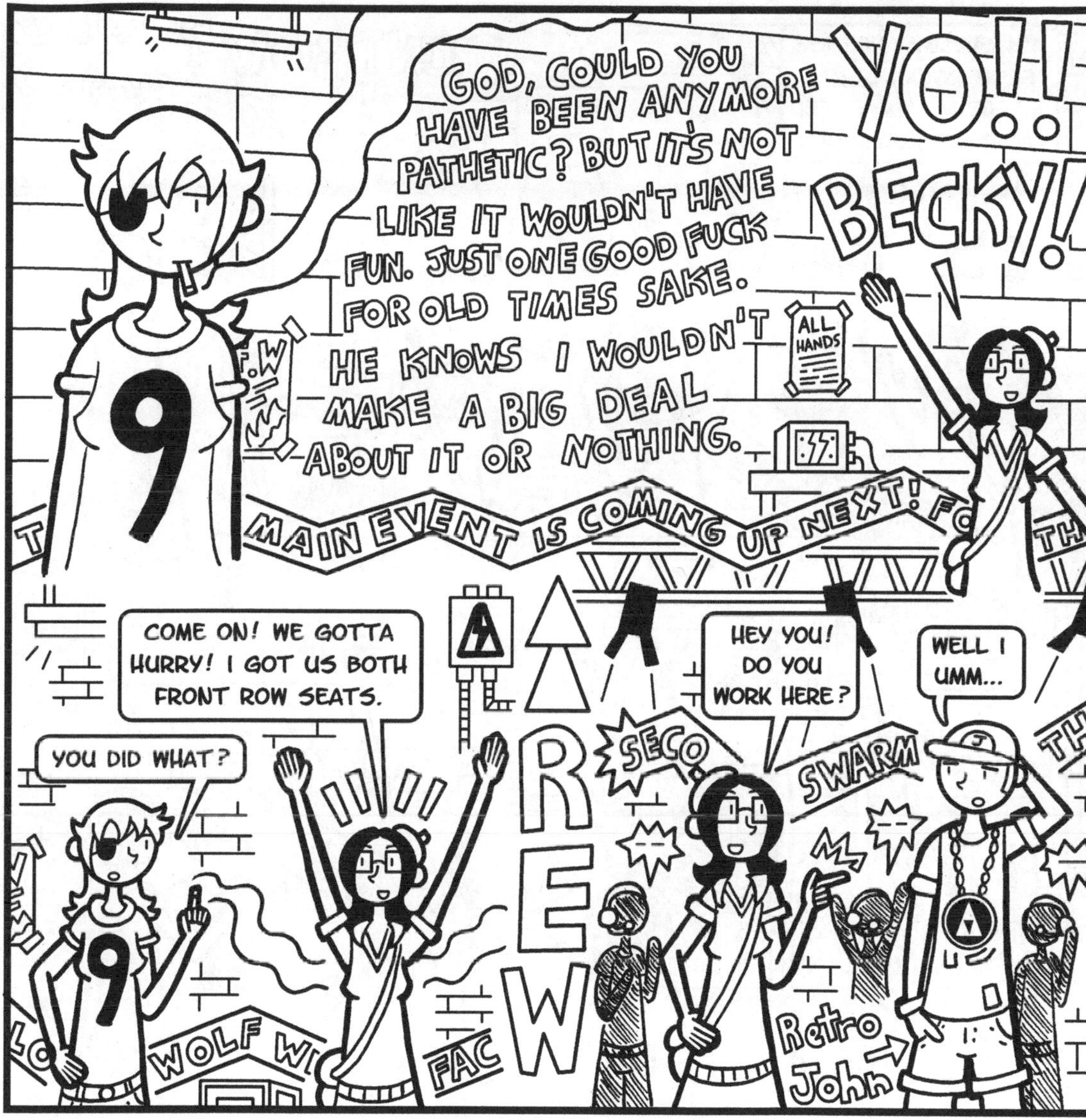
GOD, COULD YOU HAVE BEEN ANYMORE PATHETIC? BUT IT'S NOT LIKE IT WOULDN'T HAVE FUN. JUST ONE GOOD FUCK FOR OLD TIMES SAKE.
HE KNOWS I WOULDN'T MAKE A BIG DEAL ABOUT IT OR NOTHING.
YO!! BECKY!
ALL HANDS
MAIN EVENT IS COMING UP NEXT!
COME ON! WE GOTTA HURRY! I GOT US BOTH FRONT ROW SEATS.
YOU DID WHAT?
HEY YOU! DO YOU WORK HERE?
WELL I UMM...
SWARM
WOLF
Retro John

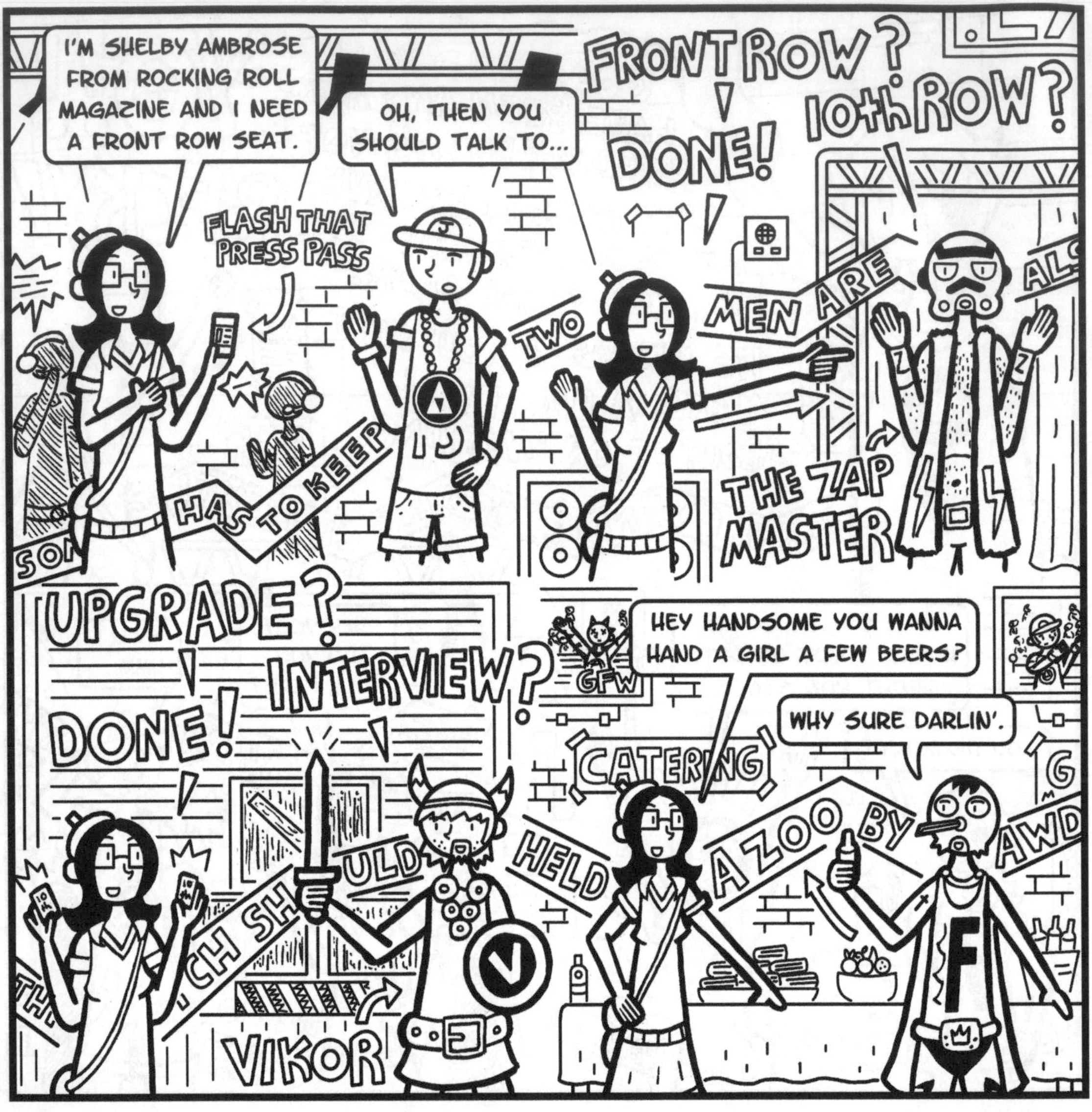
I'M SHELBY AMBROSE FROM ROCKING ROLL MAGAZINE AND I NEED A FRONT ROW SEAT.
OH, THEN YOU SHOULD TALK TO...
FRONT ROW?
10th ROW?
DONE!
FLASH THAT PRESS PASS
TWO
MEN ARE
HAS TO KEEP
THE ZAP MASTER
UPGRADE?
DONE!
INTERVIEW?
GFW
HEY HANDSOME YOU WANNA HAND A GIRL A FEW BEERS?
WHY SURE DARLIN'.
CATERING
ULD
HELD
AZOO BY
AWD
CH SH
VIKOR

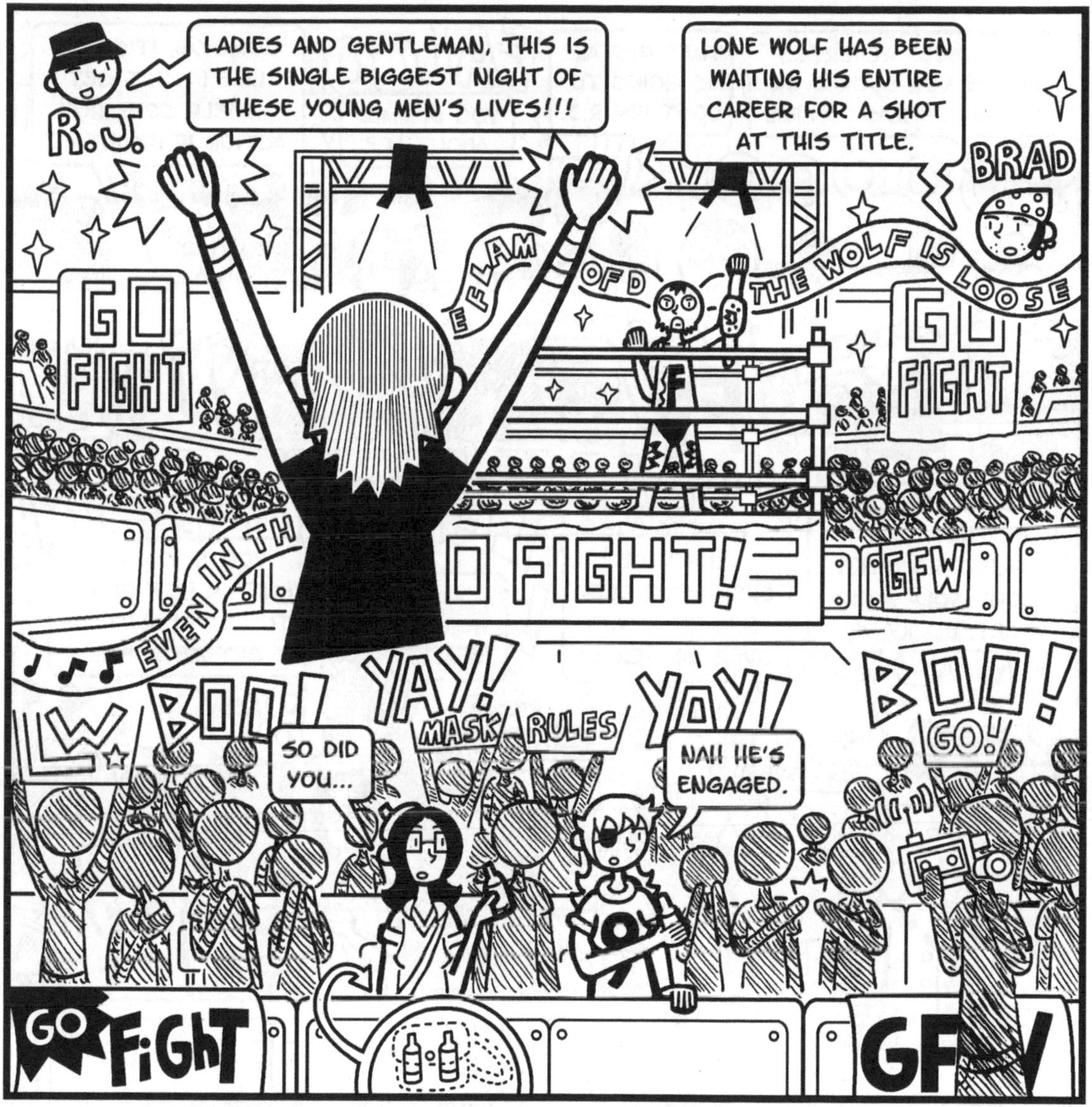
R.J.
LADIES AND GENTLEMAN, THIS IS THE SINGLE BIGGEST NIGHT OF THESE YOUNG MEN'S LIVES!!!
BRAD
LONE WOLF HAS BEEN WAITING HIS ENTIRE CAREER FOR A SHOT AT THIS TITLE.
GO FIGHT
FLAME OF D
THE WOLF IS LOOSE
GO FIGHT
EVEN IN TH
O FIGHT!
GFW
LW
BOO!
YAY!
MASK RULES
YAY!
BOO!
GO!
SO DID YOU...
NAH HE'S ENGAGED.
GO FIGHT
GF V

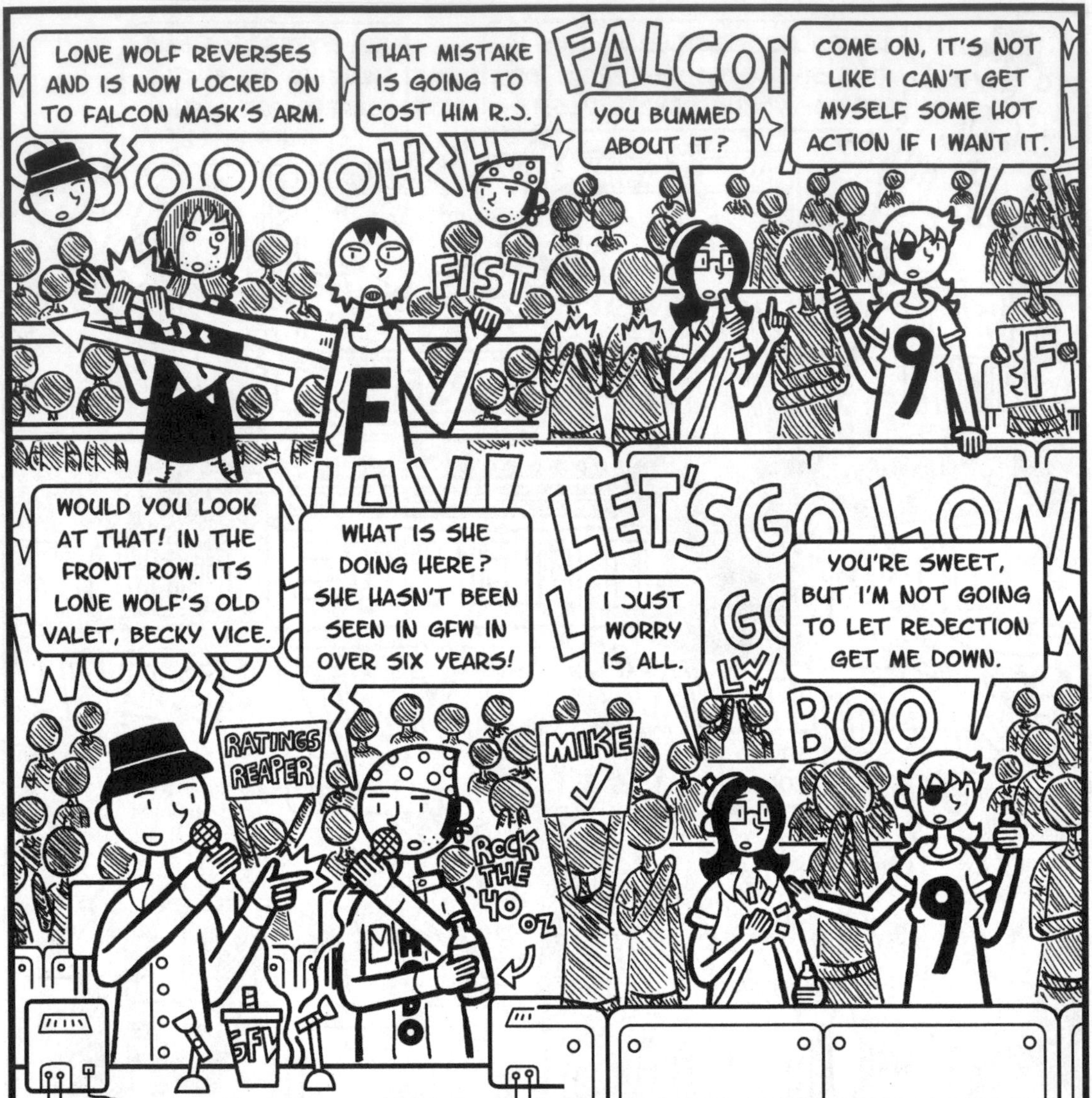
LONE WOLF REVERSES AND IS NOW LOCKED ON TO FALCON MASK'S ARM.
THAT MISTAKE IS GOING TO COST HIM R.J.
OOOOOOH
FALCON
YOU BUMMED ABOUT IT?
COME ON, IT'S NOT LIKE I CAN'T GET MYSELF SOME HOT ACTION IF I WANT IT.
FIST
F
9
F
WOULD YOU LOOK AT THAT! IN THE FRONT ROW. ITS LONE WOLF'S OLD VALET, BECKY VICE.
WHAT IS SHE DOING HERE? SHE HASN'T BEEN SEEN IN GFW IN OVER SIX YEARS!
LET'S GO LONE
I JUST WORRY IS ALL.
YOU'RE SWEET, BUT I'M NOT GOING TO LET REJECTION GET ME DOWN.
LW
BOO
RATINGS REAPER
MIKE
ROCK THE 40 OZ
9
GFW

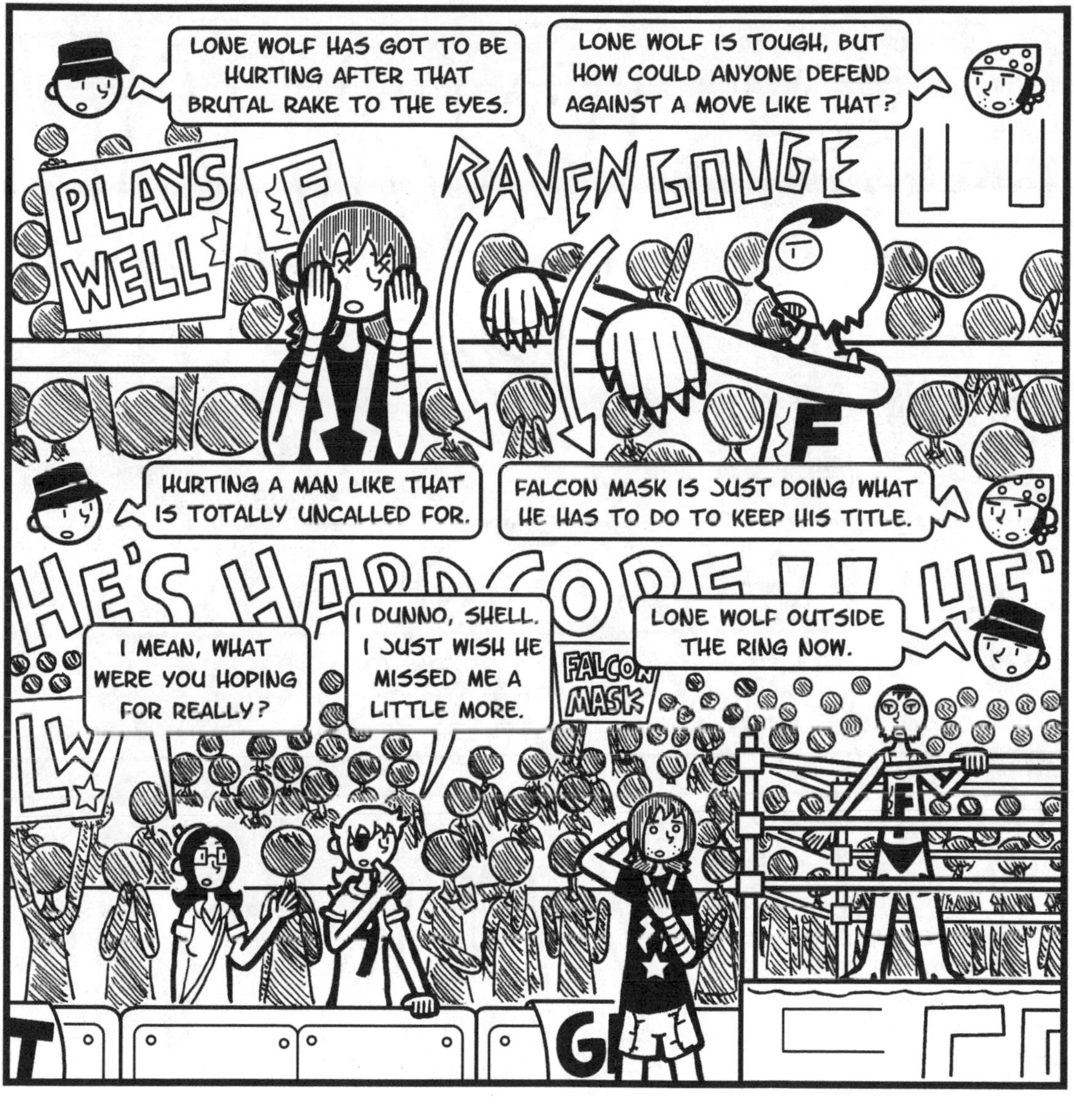
LONE WOLF HAS GOT TO BE HURTING AFTER THAT BRUTAL RAKE TO THE EYES.
LONE WOLF IS TOUGH, BUT HOW COULD ANYONE DEFEND AGAINST A MOVE LIKE THAT?
PLAYS WELL
RAVEN GOUGE
HURTING A MAN LIKE THAT IS TOTALLY UNCALLED FOR.
FALCON MASK IS JUST DOING WHAT HE HAS TO DO TO KEEP HIS TITLE.
I MEAN, WHAT WERE YOU HOPING FOR REALLY?
I DUNNO, SHELL. I JUST WISH HE MISSED ME A LITTLE MORE.
FALCON MASK
LONE WOLF OUTSIDE THE RING NOW.

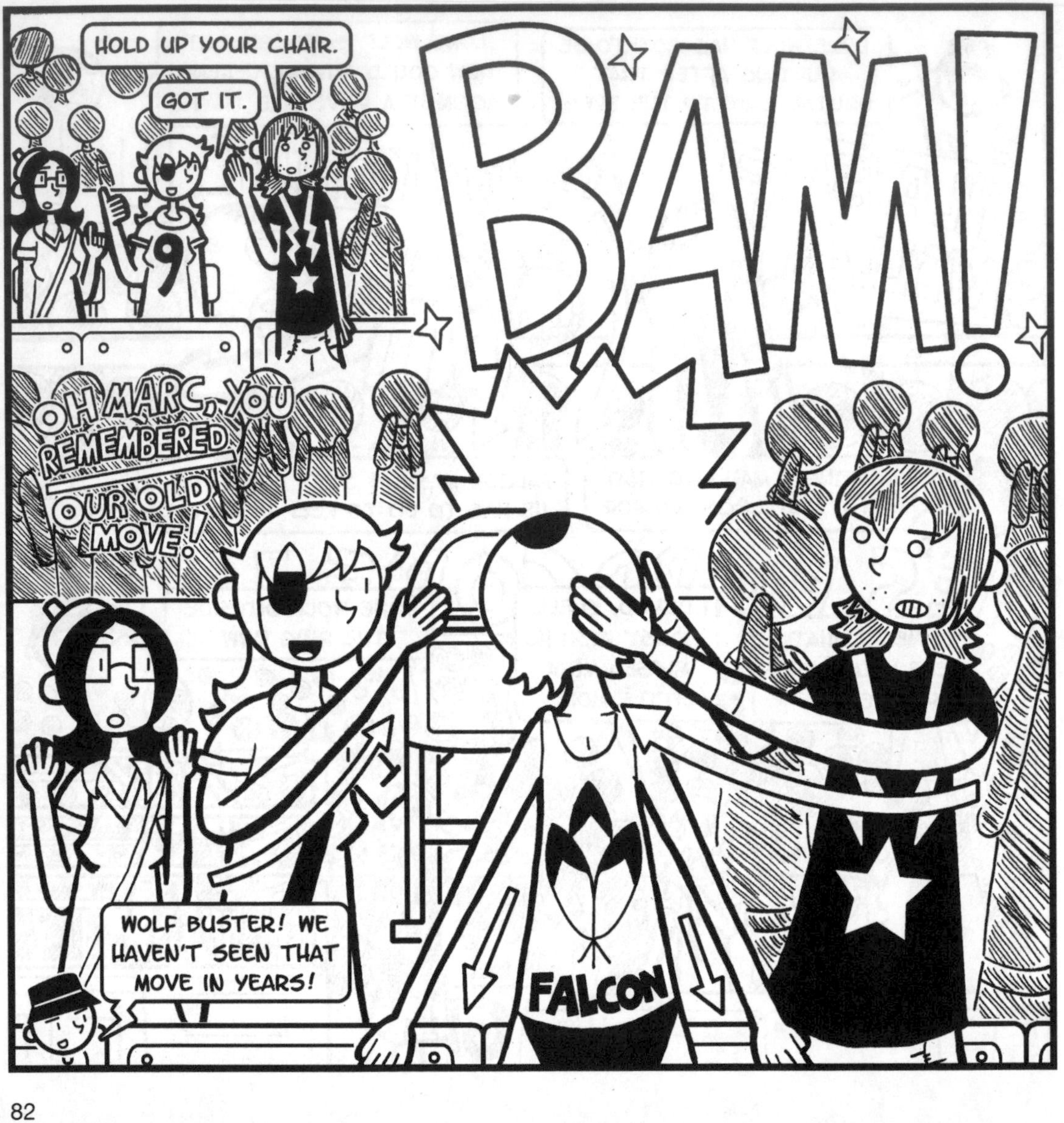
HOLD UP YOUR CHAIR.
GOT IT.
BAM!
OH MARC, YOU REMEMBERED OUR OLD MOVE!
WOLF BUSTER! WE HAVEN'T SEEN THAT MOVE IN YEARS!
FALCON
9

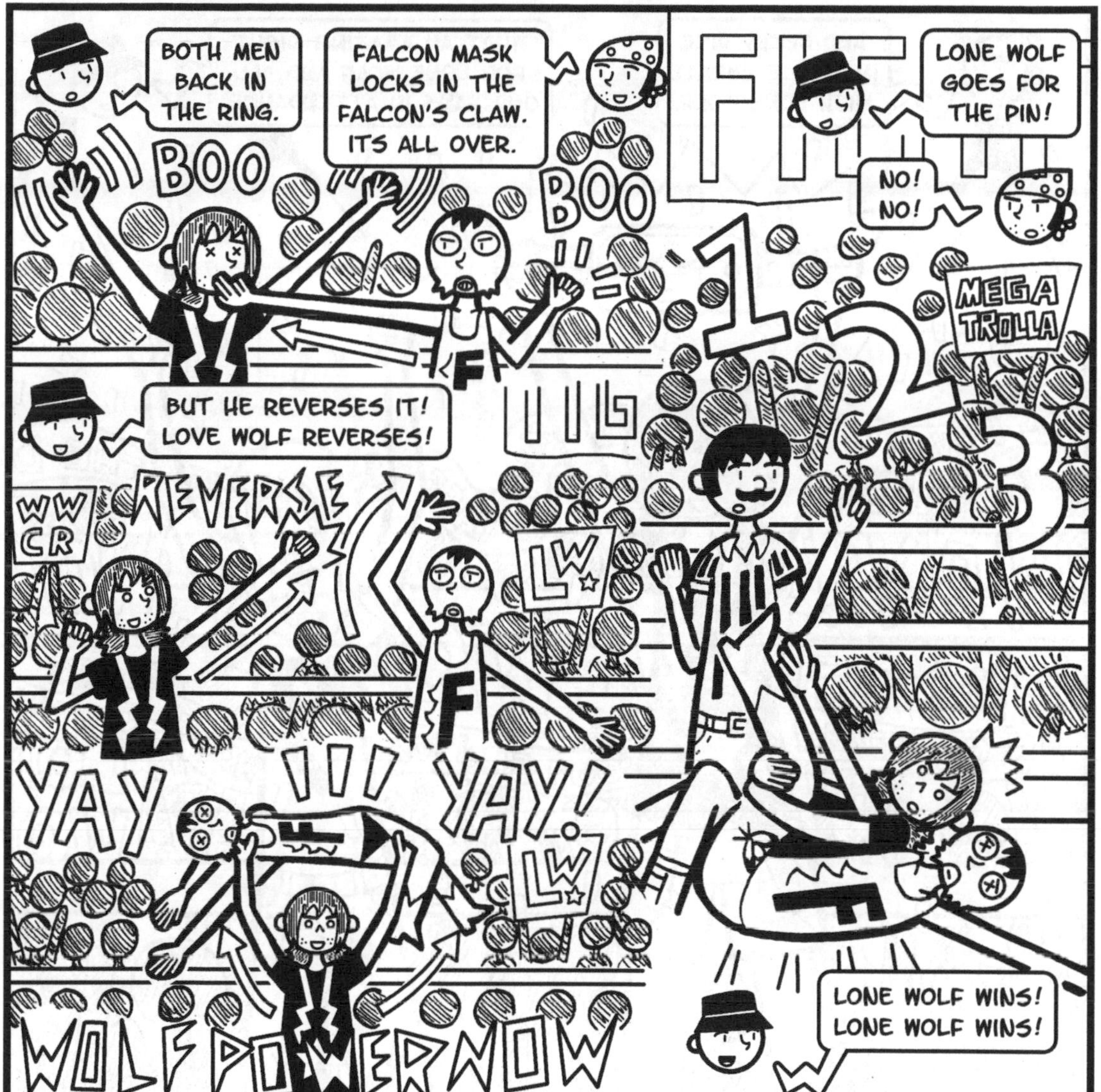
BOTH MEN BACK IN THE RING.
FALCON MASK LOCKS IN THE FALCON'S CLAW. IT'S ALL OVER.
LONE WOLF GOES FOR THE PIN!
NO! NO!
BOO
BOO
MEGA TROLLA
1
2
3
BUT HE REVERSES IT! LOVE WOLF REVERSES!
UG
WW CR
REVERSE
LW
YAY
YAY!
LW
WOLF POWER NOW
LONE WOLF WINS! LONE WOLF WINS!

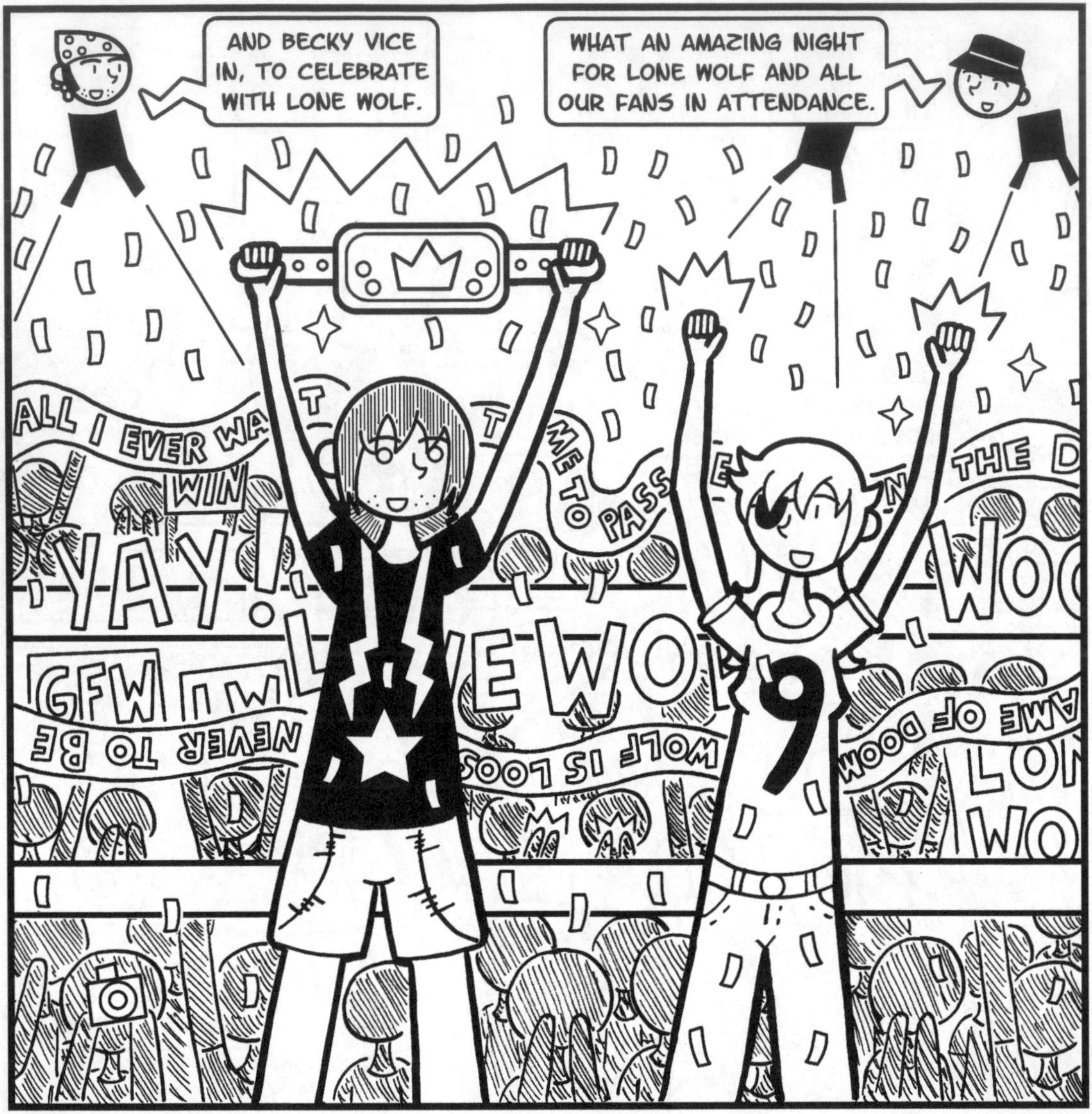
AND BECKY VICE IN, TO CELEBRATE WITH LONE WOLF.
WHAT AN AMAZING NIGHT FOR LONE WOLF AND ALL OUR FANS IN ATTENDANCE.
WIN
YAY!
GFW

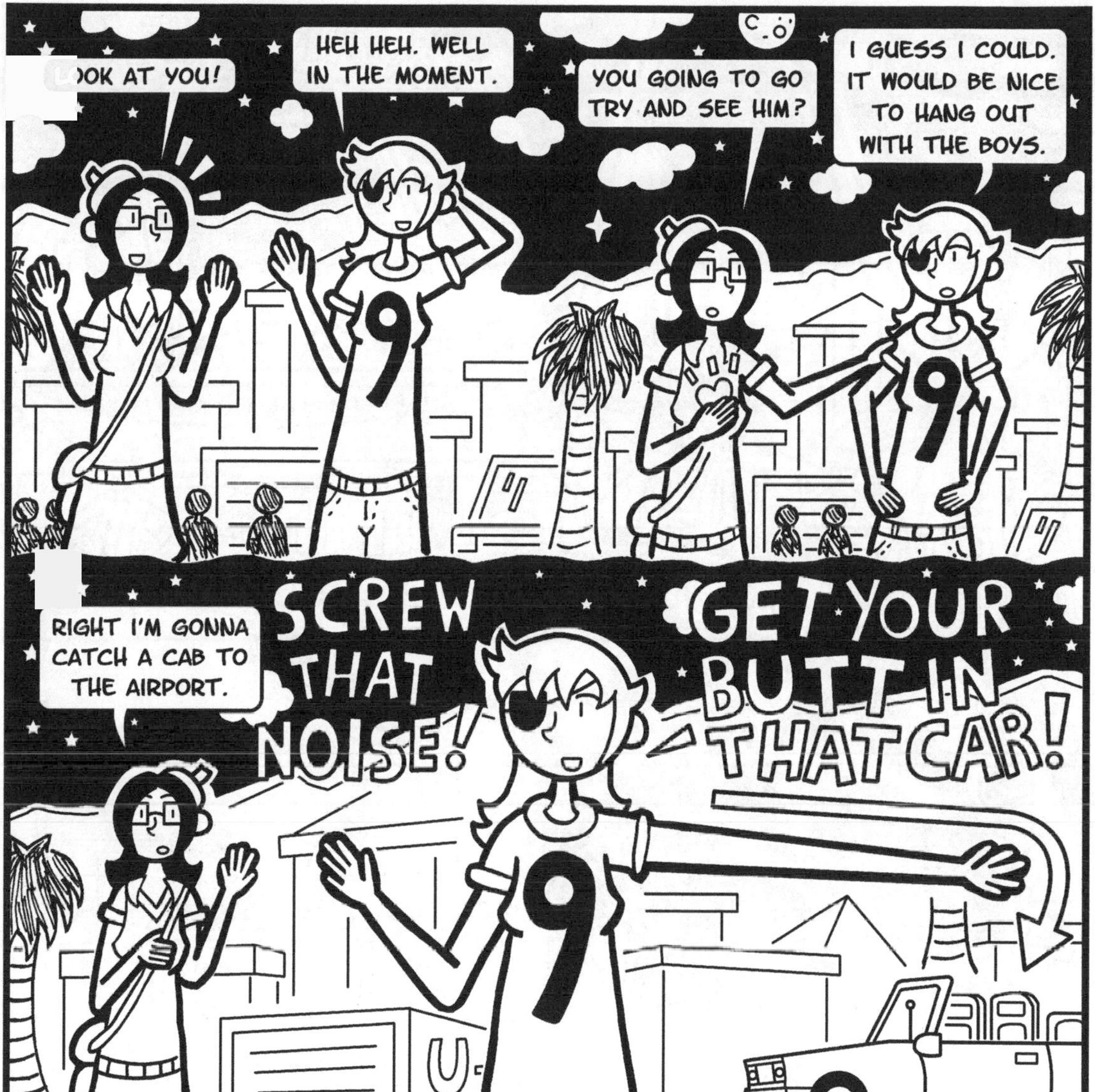

LOOK AT YOU!
HEH HEH. WELL IN THE MOMENT.
YOU GOING TO GO TRY AND SEE HIM?
I GUESS I COULD. IT WOULD BE NICE TO HANG OUT WITH THE BOYS.
RIGHT I'M GONNA CATCH A CAB TO THE AIRPORT.
SCREW THAT NOISE!
GET YOUR BUTT IN THAT CAR!

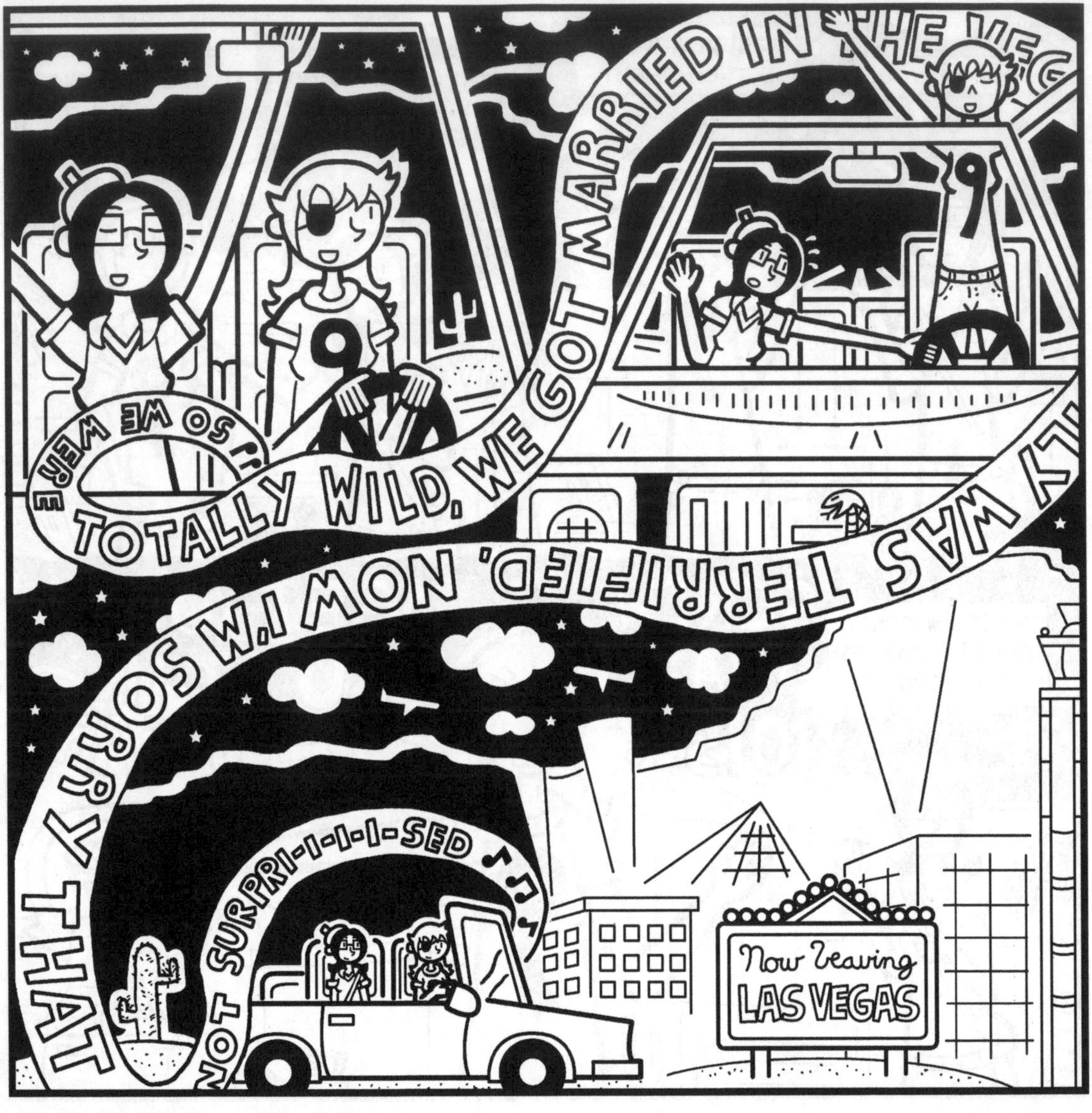
SO WE WERE
TOTALLY WILD, WE GOT MARRIED IN THE VEG
LY WAS TERRIFIED, NOW I'M SORRY THAT
NOT SURPRI-I-I-I-SED
Now Leaving
LAS VEGAS

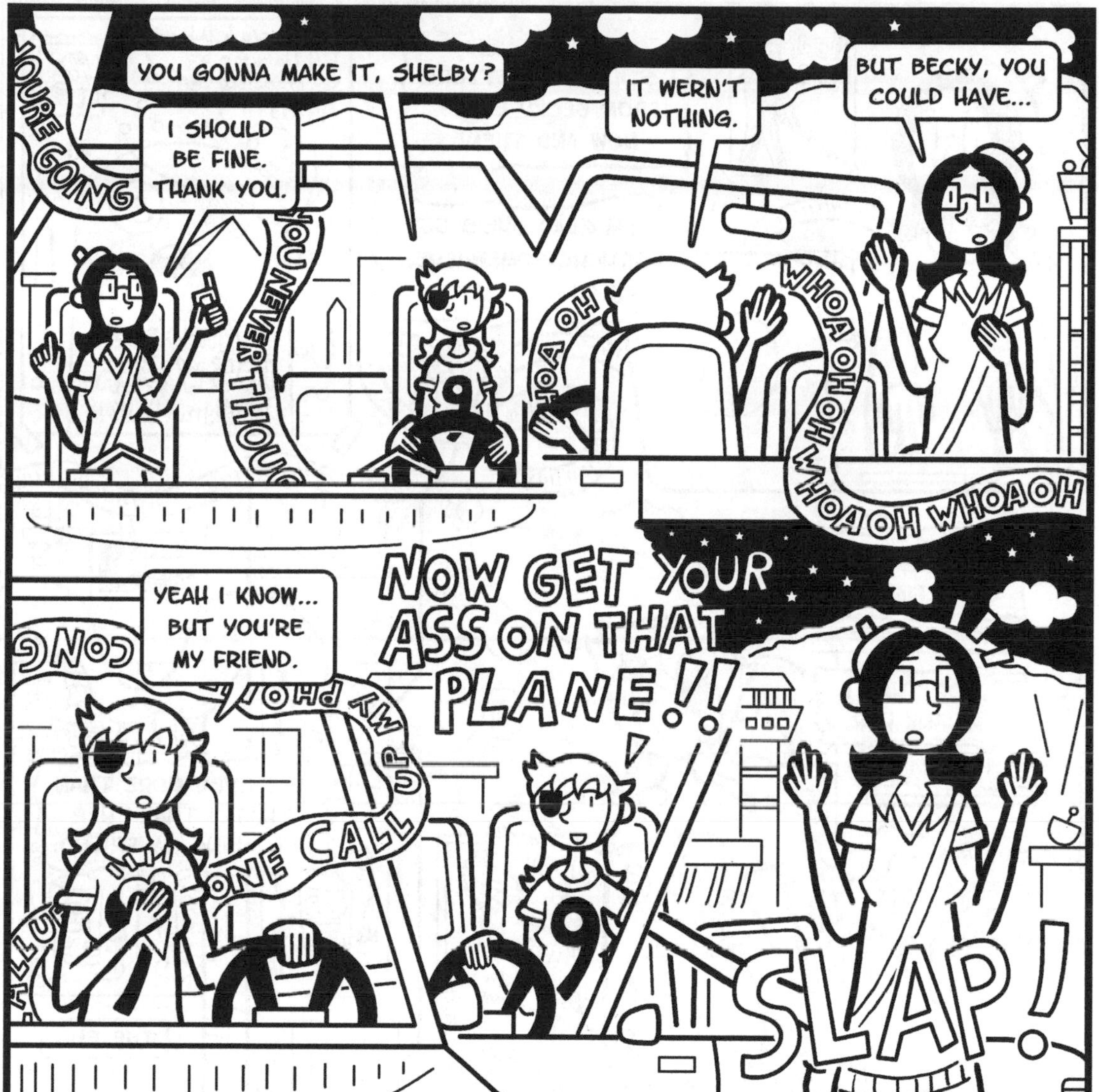
YOU'RE GOING
YOU GONNA MAKE IT, SHELBY?
I SHOULD BE FINE. THANK YOU.
YOU NEVER THOUG
IT WERN'T NOTHING.
WHOA OH
BUT BECKY, YOU COULD HAVE...
WHOA OH WHOA OH WHOA OH WHOA OH
YEAH I KNOW... BUT YOU'RE MY FRIEND.
CONG
MY PHO
ONE CALL UP
NOW GET YOUR ASS ON THAT PLANE!!
SLAP!

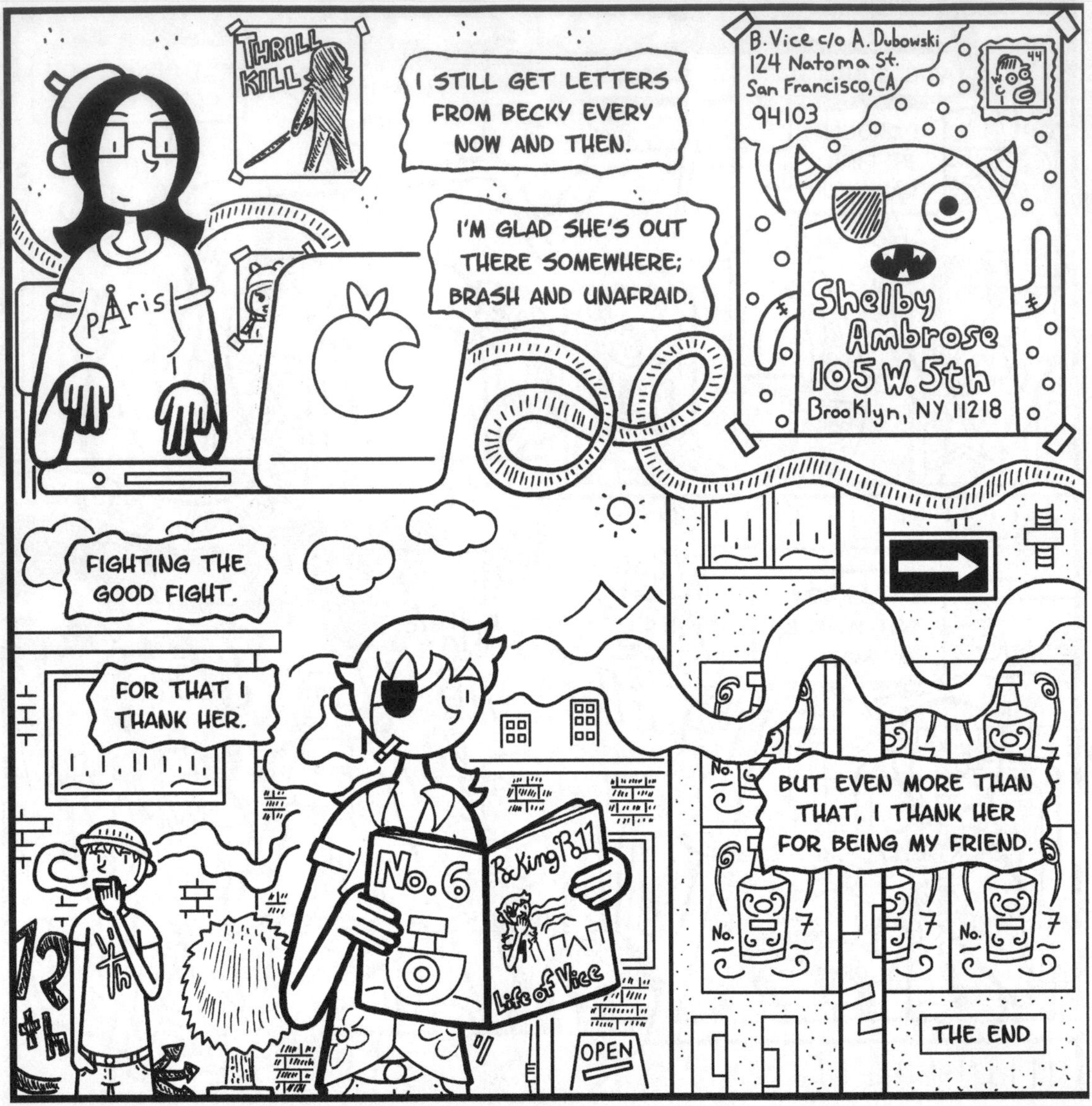
THRILL KILL
I STILL GET LETTERS FROM BECKY EVERY NOW AND THEN.
B. Vice c/o A. Dubowski
124 Natoma St.
San Francisco, CA
94103
I'M GLAD SHE'S OUT THERE SOMEWHERE; BRASH AND UNAFRAID.
pAris
Shelby Ambrose
105 W. 5th
Brooklyn, NY 11218
FIGHTING THE GOOD FIGHT.
FOR THAT I THANK HER.
No. 6
Life of Vice
BUT EVEN MORE THAN THAT, I THANK HER FOR BEING MY FRIEND.
OPEN
THE END

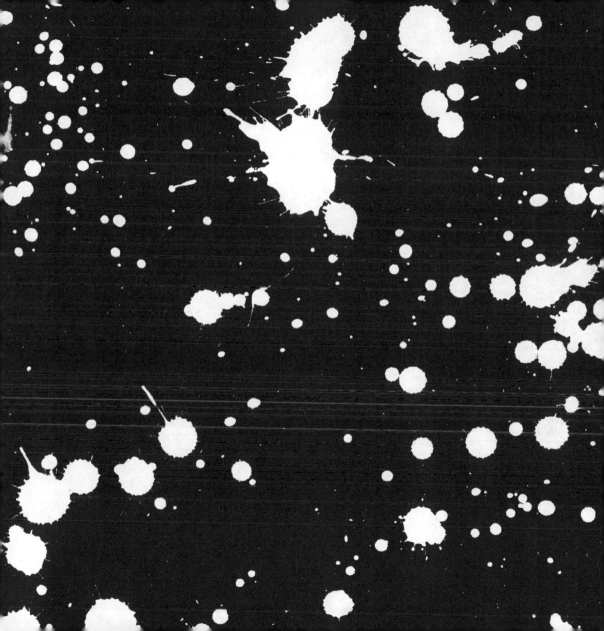

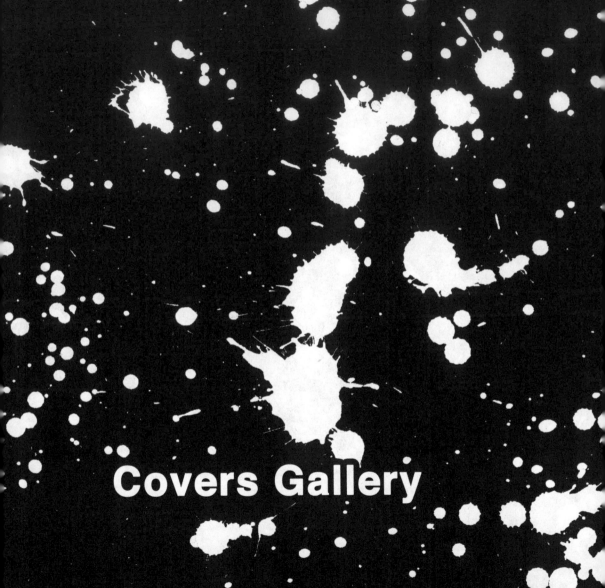

Covers Gallery

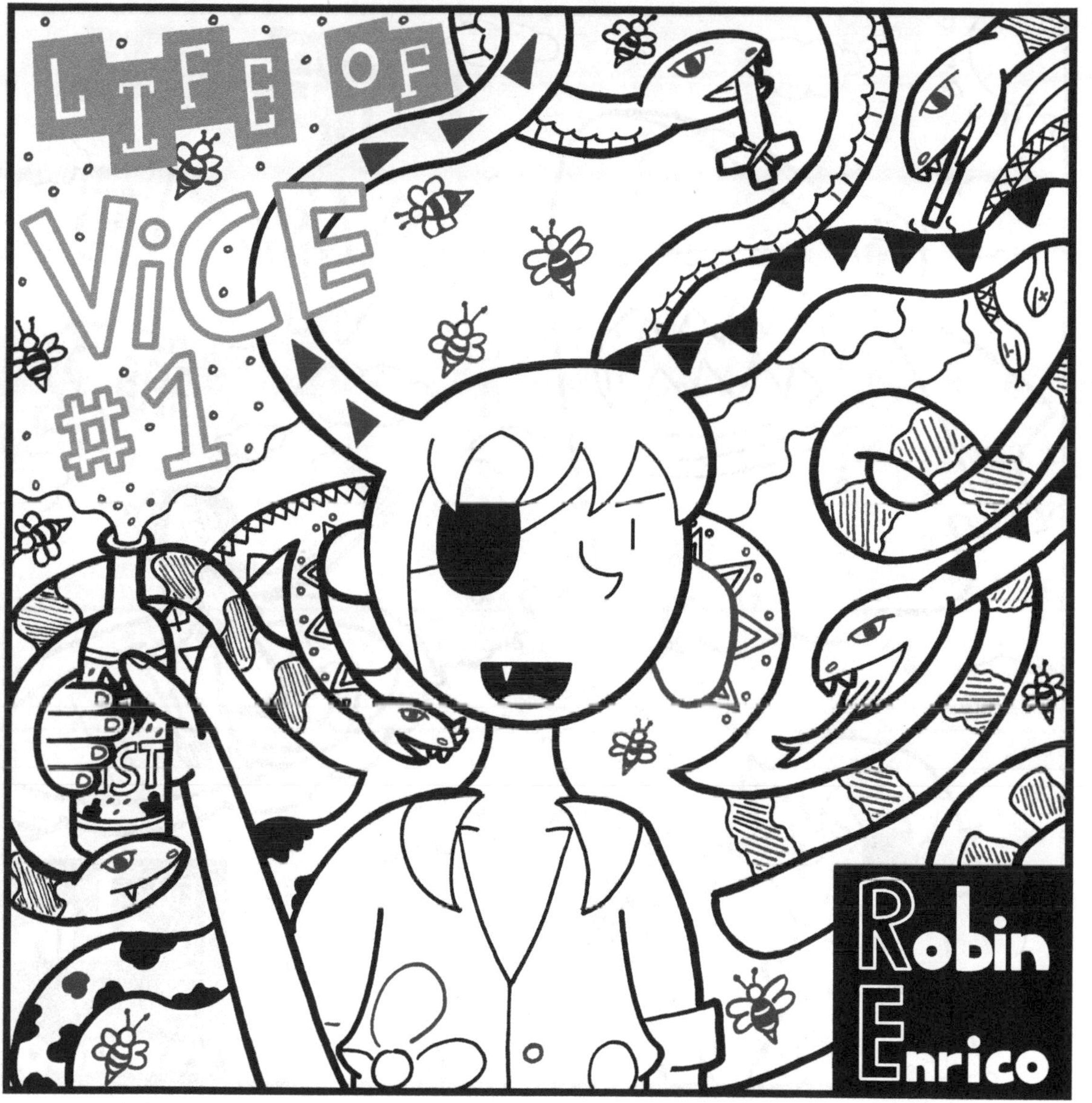
LIFE OF
ViCE
#1
DIST
Robin
Enrico

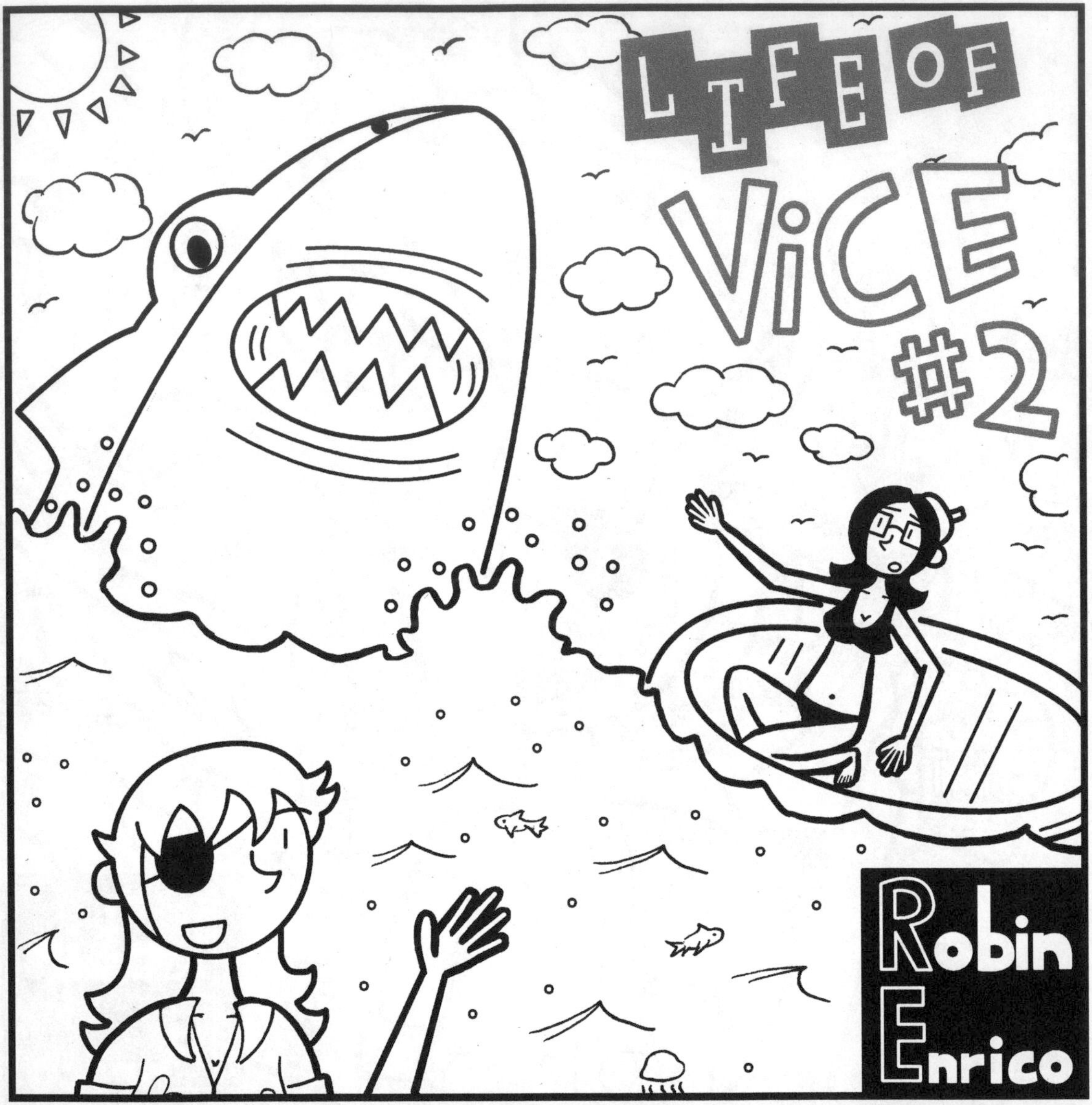
LIFE OF
ViCE
#2
Robin
Enrico

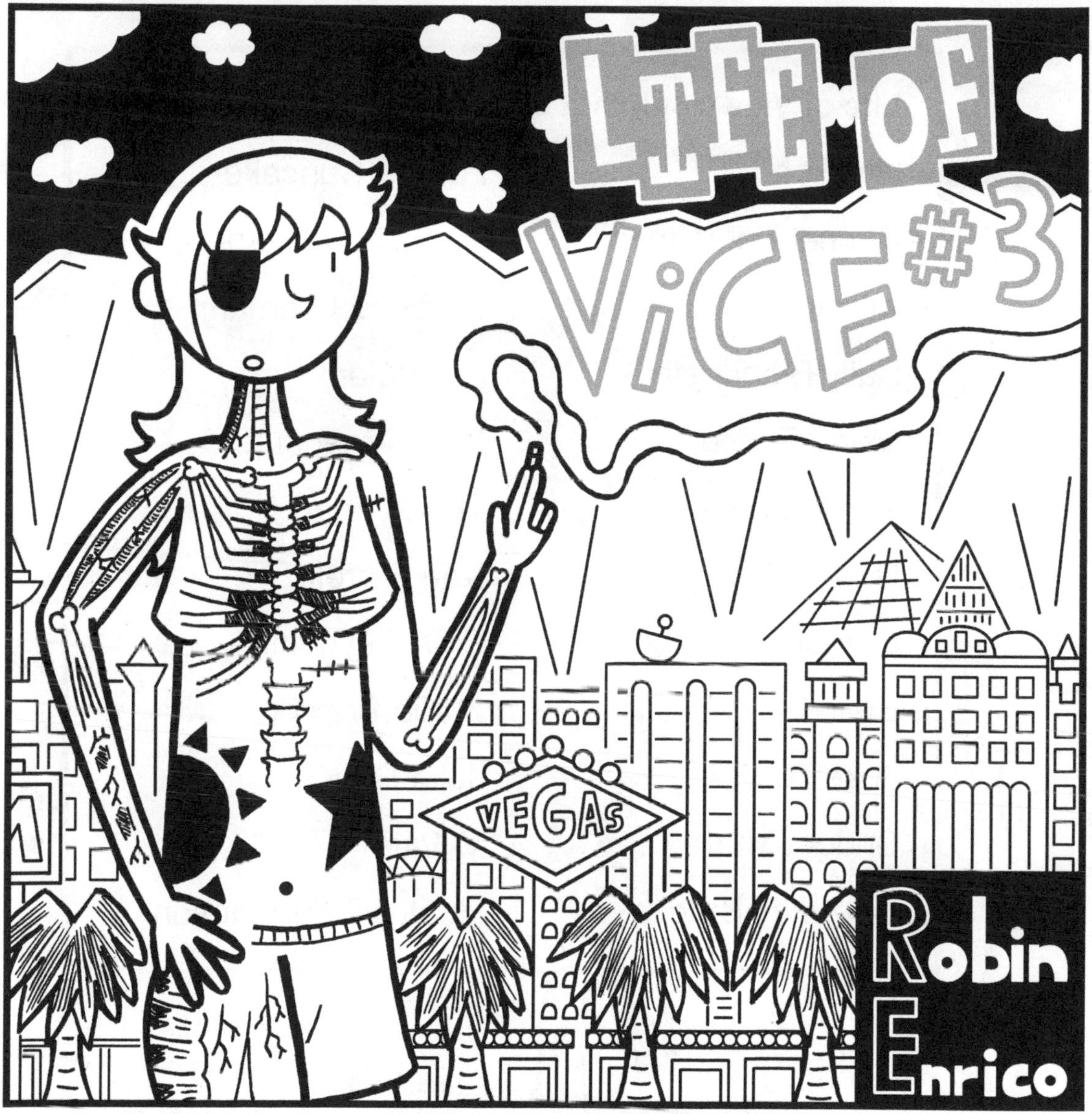

LIFE OF
ViCE #3
vEGAs
Robin
Enrico

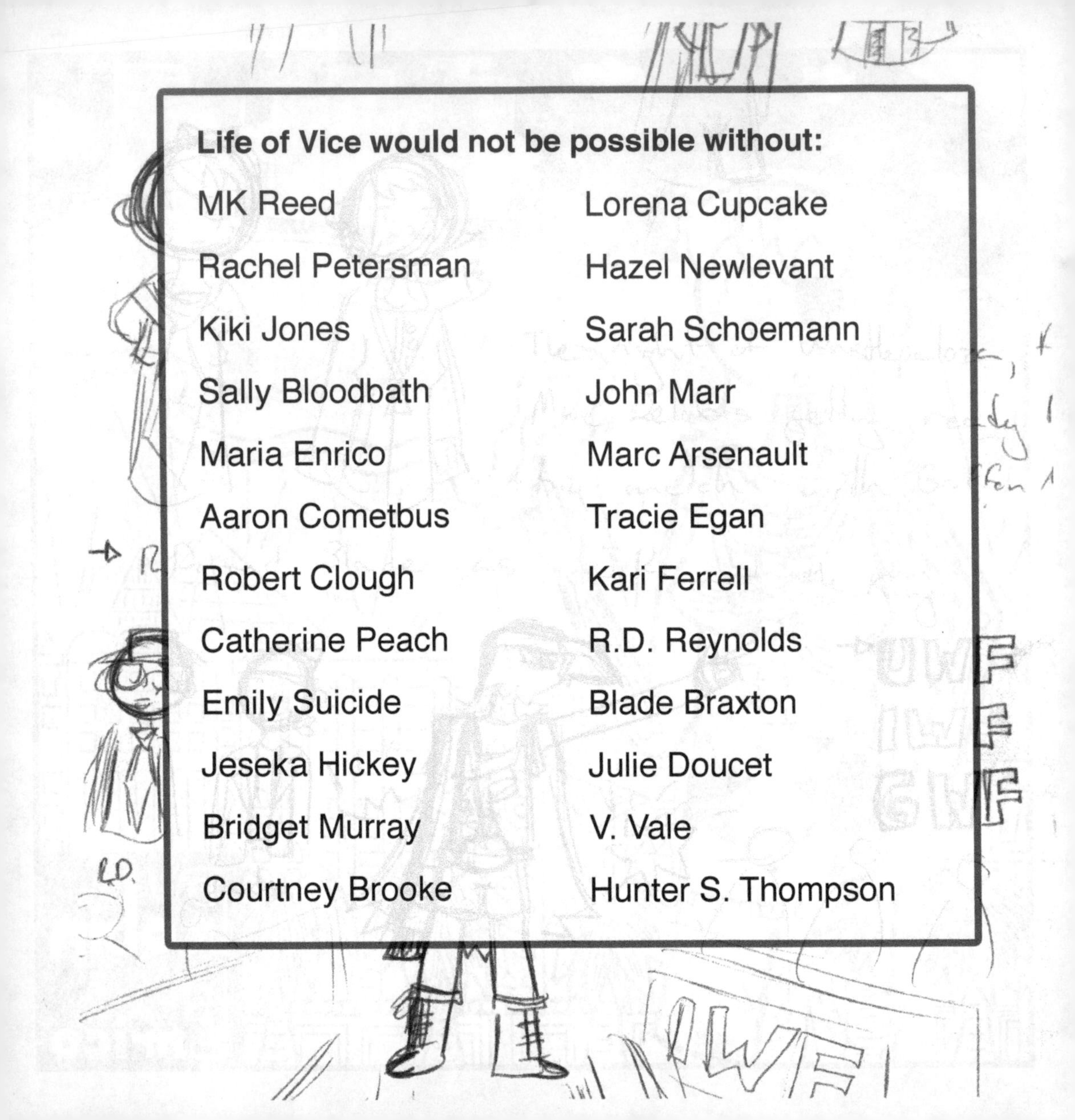

Life of Vice would not be possible without:

MK Reed
Rachel Petersman
Kiki Jones
Sally Bloodbath
Maria Enrico
Aaron Cometbus
Robert Clough
Catherine Peach
Emily Suicide
Jeseka Hickey
Bridget Murray
Courtney Brooke

Lorena Cupcake
Hazel Newlevant
Sarah Schoemann
John Marr
Marc Arsenault
Tracie Egan
Kari Ferrell
R.D. Reynolds
Blade Braxton
Julie Doucet
V. Vale
Hunter S. Thompson

CPSIA information can be obtained
at www.ICGtesting.com
Printed in the USA
JSHW010828060819
1049JS00001B/1